Hispanic/Latino Identity

A Philosophical Perspective

Jorge J. E. Gracia

BLACKWELL
Publishers

First published 2000

2 4 6 8 10 9 7 5 3 1

Blackwell Publishers Inc.
350 Main Street
Malden, Massachusetts 02148
USA

Blackwell Publishers Ltd
108 Cowley Road
Oxford OX4 1JF
UK

Library of Congress Cataloging-in-Publication Data
Gracia, Jorge J. E.
 Hispanic/Latino identity: a philosophical perspective / Jorge
J. E. Gracia.
  p. cm.
 Includes bibliographical references and indexes.
 ISBN 0–631–21763–0 (acid-free paper). — ISBN 0–631–21764–9 (pbk.: acid-free paper)
 1. Hispanic Americans — Ethnic identity. I. Title.
E184.S75G67 1999
305.868—dc21   99–30908
                     CIP

British Library Cataloguing in Publication Data

A CIP catalogue record for this book is available from the British Library.

Typeset in 10 on 13 pt Meridien
by SetSystems Ltd, Saffron Walden, Essex
Printed in Great Britain by MPG Books, Victoria Square, Bodmin, Cornwall

This book is printed on acid-free paper.

Contents

Preface

Why a book on Hispanic/Latino identity now? The answer to this question is not difficult; it has to do with demographics. There are obvious pragmatic reasons why everyone in the United States in particular, and in the world at large, should be paying attention to Hispanics/Latinos and asking who we are. It is common knowledge that the Hispanic/Latino population is growing at an unusual pace. In fact, we are already the largest minority group in the United States, and we certainly constitute one of the largest groups in the global population.[1] The only disagreement concerns actual numbers. If things keep going the way they have been going in the past few years, it could turn out that eventually there will be more Americans of Hispanic/Latino descent than of any other background in the country. In short, the United States will no longer be predominantly Anglo-Saxon and, one would expect, Anglo-Saxon culture will no longer set the pace. The sheer number of Hispanics/Latinos will force the nation to change ingrained patterns of behavior, and new ways of doing and living – *our* ways of doing and living – will become commonplace.

In a global context, too, the presence of Hispanics/Latinos is being felt with an increasingly greater force. It is not just that South America is almost exclusively Hispanic/Latina, or that North America is almost a third Hispanic/Latina, or that we are represented in Europe; it is also that our numbers worldwide are growing and Hispanics/Latinos are acquiring economic power and political clout everywhere.

What a prospect! For some it is frightening, but for us it is exhilarating. Hispanics/Latinos might constitute the largest social group in the most powerful and influential nation on earth. If to this we add the twenty-odd Hispanic/Latino countries elsewhere, it looks as if we will be one of the dominant groups of people in the world, and if not in the world, certainly in the Americas.

Who could have guessed this 600 years ago, when Europe was unaware of the continents to its west, and Iberia was an insignificant and divided land with some of its territory dominated by a Middle-Eastern culture? Who could have guessed it even 50 years ago, when attention was concentrated on Europe and Anglo America, and Latin America was regarded as a backwater, a source of raw materials for the industrialized world? But let us leave aside the future of Hispanics/Latinos worldwide and go back to the first question raised at the outset: Why a book on Hispanic/Latino identity now?

The answer should be quite clear. We, Hispanics/Latinos, need to begin the process of reflection about who we are, not just for our own sake, but for the sake of the whole world. And the reflection on, and discussion of, our identity should not be restricted to ourselves. Everyone needs to get involved in it, for the outcome of this reflection will affect all of us and could determine the future of humanity.

In the United States in particular, a change of the magnitude that we envision, a change that will result in a new ethnic and cultural composition of American society, could be catastrophic if it occurred suddenly. Such changes have happened in the world before. The great migration of Gothic tribes that overran the Roman Empire resulted in the virtual destruction of Roman culture and the onset of the Dark Ages. It took Europe hundreds of years to recover. Even smaller changes of this sort, where the influx of populations from other cultures and different ethnic origins has occurred, have often been traumatic to say the least.

Fortunately, we have time. We are dealing with a slow process in which a steady stream of Hispanic/Latino immigrants, added to a high rate of reproduction among some of those already here, has the potential of producing an absolute majority in the country, but that is a relatively long way off and not necessarily a certain outcome. No one has yet predicted, for example, that it will happen within the next 50 years.

There is no reason for other Americans to panic, but the facts cannot be ignored. We are here to stay, and our numbers are growing. It therefore makes sense to begin to reflect on how the changes in the composition of the population of this country and the growth of a Hispanic/Latino community – with its presumed differences in outlook and culture – will affect the future of the United States.

In spite of what I have said, some no doubt will read these words and think about the demographics of the Hispanic/Latino population with alarm. "They are going to overrun us! What shall we do? What *can* we do? What will happen to our way of life, to our language, to our values, to our morals?" The responses to these questions are already obvious in certain quarters. The call has already been made for the establishment of English as the official language of the nation. The demand for stricter immigration laws to limit the influx of Hispanics/Latinos into the United States is another response. A good part of the opposition to bilingual education is still another. These reactions are to some extent motivated by fear, of course – fear of the unknown, fear of the alien – and trepidation at the prospect of losing long-held privileges. Consider a report by the Council for Inter-American Security, in which Hispanics are portrayed as a dangerous, subversive force bent on taking over US political institutions and on imposing Spanish as the official language of the country.[2] Can anyone seriously believe that Hispanics/Latinos are engaged in a plot to take over the political institutions of the United States? And does it make sense to say that we also intend to impose Spanish as the official language of the country when many Hispanics/Latinos do not speak Spanish? Only fear can cause someone to entertain – let alone publicly articulate – such absurdities. Fear is no solution to anything, and measures adopted in fear usually backfire because they are irrational. Irrationality is always a poor foundation for stability, eventually promoting rather than preventing conflict.

This is why we must begin to reflect on the changes to come, and prepare the way for a smooth and profitable journey into the future. Hispanics/Latinos are here to stay. The United States in particular might as well begin to take us into account. Indeed, it is extraordinary that so little has been done so far to understand us. There are books on the subject, but they often deal with rather limited perspectives. And there is occasional lip service paid to affirmative action and to the value of immigration and Hispanic/Latino values. But the truth of the matter is that Hispanics/Latinos are a force not yet reckoned with by

American society at large; in many ways, we are still invisible. The most critical issues facing the United States are framed in terms of black and white, and African vs. European. Matters that pertain to Hispanics/Latinos fall through the cracks.

The situation is no better outside the United States. Obviously in Latin America, Spain, and Portugal considerable attention has been paid to our past, present, and future, and questions of identity have been discussed in painstaking detail. But the rest of the world has hardly taken notice of us. As far as most of Europe, Asia, and Africa are concerned, we hardly exist.

The first step toward remedying this situation is for us Hispanics/ Latinos to know more about ourselves. Because we need to know about our own individual identities, we need to know something about our collective identity. Indeed, the questions Who am I? Who are you? Who is he? Who are we? are fundamental and interconnected. The answer to any one of these questions requires answers to the others, as Buero Vallejo illustrated so well in his provocative tragedy *El tragaluz*. Non-Hispanics/Latinos also need to know more about us: for curiosity's sake, for the sake of the future of American society, and for the sake of humanity.

This is not all, for the way our identity is conceived and the terms used to refer to us have serious implications for the way in which we are viewed and treated. There are social, racial, ethnic, and class implications which can emphasize prejudice and result in discrimination. Indeed, even if we are not convinced of the pressing need to reflect on the question of Hispanic/Latino identity for the reasons already indicated, there are other concerns that should rid us of our skepticism. Consider affirmative action for Hispanic/Latinos in the United States.[3] The United States government, plus a large proportion of Americans, are committed to a policy of affirmative action for Hispanics/Latinos, and any meaningful implementation of this policy requires a clear notion of Hispanic/Latino identity. Yet it is not at all certain that the government, the American people, or even Hispanics/ Latinos ourselves know who we are. Indeed, some question whether we have an identity at all; others accept that we have, but nonetheless are at a loss to determine what it is; and still others frame our identity in exclusivist, essentialist terms that fail even under the most superficial inspection.

The confusion is deep and widespread. I can vouch for it in my own limited experience. For example, a few years back, one of my oldest daughter's high-school classmates, who came from a well-to-do family, was allowed to apply to, and was subsequently accepted into, an elite college on the basis of being Hispanic/Latino. In fact, his only connection to anything Hispanic/Latino was a great-grandmother from the south-west, whose Hispanic/Latino culture and values had been long forgotten by her descendants. At the same time, Puerto-Rican Americans living in Puerto Rico do not qualify for minority status as Hispanics/Latinos for medical-school applications.

These and many other examples reveal not just an abuse of affirmative action with respect to Hispanics/Latinos, but also great uncertainty about who is Hispanic/Latino and the bases on which one may be classified as such. If we are going to prevent such abuses of affirmative action we need to have a much clearer understanding of who we are. In short, we need to settle the question of Hispanic/Latino identity.

Still, one may wonder why we need a book about Hispanics/Latinos in general, written in English by someone who has spent a great part of his life in the United States, and a book which pays disproportionate attention to the Hispanic/Latino community in the United States. Is not Spanish the lingua franca of Hispanics/Latinos? Should not the book be written by someone who is more properly Hispanic/Latino, someone who has not yet been "contaminated" by Anglo-American culture and ways of thought? Is not the Hispanic/Latino community in the United States a small fraction, and a marginal and marginalized one at that, of the total Hispanic/Latino population in the world? How could what I write be considered representative of, and relevant to, the experience of Hispanics/Latinos outside the United States?

The answer to this question is political. The United States is the new Rome, with the rest of the world as its provinces. There are important differences between ancient Rome and the United States, no doubt. Rome had a political, economic, and military empire which extended throughout the Mediterranean basin, whereas the empire of the United States is mainly economic and cultural, and extends worldwide. The United States is both more and less than Rome: more in extension, less in power. Still, the position of the United States in the world today is very important, especially culturally. If you travel anywhere in the world, even to its remotest parts, you will soon understand that the world is trying very hard to copy everything that goes on in this country. This goes for practically every form of cultural expression, from the way news is reported to the kind of music people enjoy; from the most popular dimensions of culture to the highest reaches of so-called "high culture." To make it in the world today, one must make it in New York.

This reality has the extraordinary consequence that even small voices in the United States resonate throughout the world; a small voice here sounds much louder than a large voice elsewhere. This country, for better or worse, has become the model for the world, and its language is the lingua franca of humanity. To speak and write in another language condemns one to obscurity, unless Americans take an interest in what one says and translate it into English; to speak and write in English opens up the possibility of universal attention. This fact is recognized by those who live outside the US, especially intellectuals who wish to be heard. The "prophets" of Latin-American thought, for example, fight tooth and nail to have their work translated into English and published here, and they do all they can to come and be heard in this country. Those who seek power usually have a keen sense of where to find it, and watching them reveals, perhaps more than anything else, where it is.

Paradoxically, one must address Hispanic/Latino issues in English and in this country, for that is the way to ensure that they will be addressed elsewhere. Speaking in the United States is like speaking through a powerful microphone to the whole world. However, this does not fully explain the prominence given to the American Hispanic/Latino community in this book, which can be further justified for two reasons. The first reason – like the reasons already provided – is political. The power of the United States is such that any segment of its population has a disproportionate influence on the world at large. Although the Hispanic/Latino community in the United States is small, compared with other Hispanic/Latino communities its influence is disproportionately larger than its numbers would seem to warrant. In many ways, this community will have much more to say about the future of Hispanics/Latinos than other, larger, communities outside the United States. Note that this conclusion is not to be taken prescriptively, but descriptively. I am not arguing that this is the way things should be; I am merely reporting how things are.

The second reason is more a matter of rhetoric. American society tends to be parochial and concerned primarily with its own internal problems. It views the world through American spectacles, and the importance it attaches to a problem depends on how far that problem affects American society. Some people argue that this is typical of American society and that it is different in other societies. I do not believe so. I think every society is essentially parochial in this sense, for reasons of survival and self-preservation. Recall how the Greeks thought about the rest of the world; they regarded all non-Greeks as barbarians. There are only differences of degree between different societies in terms of parochialism. In any case, whether or not this is a unique phenomenon characteristic of American society is largely irrelevant here; the important fact for us is that there is such parochialism among Americans and if we wish to entice the American community to look at an issue we must show how it relates to American society. Any book on Hispanics/Latinos that seeks to attract the attention of the American public and consequently the rest of the world, must address the situation of Hispanics/Latinos in the United States.

There are dangers in this disproportionate emphasis on the American Hispanic/Latino community, however, for this community is not representative of all Hispanic/Latino communities outside the United States. It is different from other communities in that it is a minority community, composed largely of disadvantaged and marginalized peoples. Moreover, certain subgroups of Hispanics/Latinos are disproportionately represented. Mexican Americans and Puerto Ricans constitute its largest components, yet these are by no means the largest components of the Hispanic/Latino community in the world. Puerto Ricans constitute a very small minority within Hispanics/Latinos worldwide, and even the larger group of Mexican Americans constitutes only a minority in the whole Hispanic/Latino population. The danger we face, then, is that conclusions drawn from analyses based on the Hispanic/Latino community in the United States will be applied to other communities to which they really do not apply. We must keep this in mind and be wary of hasty generalizations. For this reason, this book makes an effort to take into account Hispanics/Latinos outside the United States.

The views I present here represent a rather particular perspective on the issues involved in Hispanic/Latino identity. This is not a scientific treatise. Rather, it is an attempt to grasp, from my own perspective, a reality with which all Hispanics/Latinos, and indeed all Americans, need to grapple at some point. The positions I take are frequently based on first-hand experiences, taking into account only a very limited slice of the experience of Hispanics/Latinos in this country.

Each of us, then, whether Hispanic/Latino or not, will have something to contribute by way of expanding, modifying, and developing the perspective offered here. No one will ever be able to see the complete picture or obtain the "God's-eye view" of which some philosophers dream, for no such view is possible for mere mortals. We see the world only partially and – to paraphrase St Paul – darkly. Yet that does not mean that all views are necessarily inaccurate or distorted.

A view can be inaccurate and distorted in two ways: (1) if it is a lie; that is, if we deliberately change something to make it appear different than it is; (2) if we present it as the only accurate view, as the God's-eye view. The first is dishonest, the second dogmatic. I am aware of both possibilities and have therefore tried to be as faithful as possible to my experience. For the view I present, I claim only the validity and accuracy of a reflection on my life. This is intended as an honest and non-dogmatic book. Those who try to read it differently distort my intention.

I do not want my views to be taken for more than they are. They are *my* views, based on *my* experiences and beliefs, on many years of reflection and reading, but still founded on just a particular slice of consciousness. I cannot lay claim to validity for all. There is also the fact that my experiences are very particular indeed. I am a *transterrado* (a person moved to a land other than his or her own), although that is nothing very foreign to Hispanics/Latinos, since many of us, particularly intellectuals, have had to live outside our native lands as a result of political oppression or economic necessity. I am a transplanted Cuban who has lived most of his life outside of Cuba: in the United States, Canada, Spain, Puerto Rico, and elsewhere. Consequently I am a kind of cultural platypus, an odd mixture of different elements which shape my perspective and beliefs. For this reason I cannot be taken as typical (if there is anyone who can): I am an oddity and so perhaps are my views.

I want, then, to distance myself from the many self-appointed representatives and spokespersons of the Hispanic/Latino community, whether in this country, in Latin America, or elsewhere. I represent no one but myself, and I speak for myself alone. I have not been given any illumination, divine or otherwise, and I have no privileged knowledge. If anything I say strikes a chord with someone else, it is because we have similar experiences. I do not want to be taken for one of the new breed of prophets for Hispanics/Latinos. Nor do I have a mission.

Those who do, frequently speak about others, but act as if their mission were their own welfare – their careers, stature, immortality. I want to dispel, right from the start, any impression that this book is the manifesto of a missionary enterprise, the revelation of a new social religion, or the credo of an ethnic faith.

Although the experiences on which I base my reflections are particular, and even perhaps idiosyncratic, they are not narrowly parochial. The point of view I present, then, need not be unique; it can be shared by those with similar experiences. The first nineteen years of my life were spent in Cuba, but I have lived more than thirty years in the United States, five years in Canada, one year in Spain, and one year in Puerto Rico. I have visited almost every country in Latin America, and have spent considerable time in some of them. My wife is originally from Argentina, and we have traveled extensively both in Canada and this country. Moreover, I have held many offices in which I have come in contact with the problems and issues that concern Americans, and particularly Hispanic/Latino Americans. I have studied the philosophical thought of Hispanics/Latinos from all over the world, and was the founding chair of the Committee for Hispanics of the American Philosophical Association. This does not mean that I speak with authority – there is no authority in the matters addressed by this book – but it does mean that what I say is the result of broad exposure. For that reason, I trust that this book will be helpful to others, whether Hispanics/Latinos or not. Indeed, perhaps precisely because I am the oddity, the unusual, what I say will have something to contribute, for sometimes the odd and unusual reveal more clearly some aspects of the whole.

The reader should be relieved to know that, although I am by profession a philosopher – and the book presents a philosophical perspective – there is not much technical philosophy in this book, and the thoughts it contains are generally expressed in ordinary language. There is philosophy in it, but I have tried to couch it in language understandable to anyone with a moderate education. Philosophers bring to everything they discuss a general point of view often missing in the more specialized studies of anthropologists, sociologists, social psychologists, and cultural historians. We can fill in the gaps left by others, and thus present an overall picture where others have only knowledge of details. This should work well in the present context.

There are two more points that need to be made clear. First, it is common to refer to the United States as America and its citizens as Americans. This ignores the fact that America is the name for North America, Central America, South America, and the Caribbean and that, strictly speaking, the inhabitants of all these places deserve to be called Americans. I know of no place, however, where "American" is generally used for any person other than a citizen of the United States. Indeed, even Latin Americans speak this way. So I will follow general custom and use "American" to refer only to citizens of the United States, although I will sometimes include non-citizen residents of the United States as well. "America," on the other hand, is not exclusively used to refer to the United States everywhere. In Latin America the United States is known as North America (an inaccurate term since both Mexico and Canada are part of North America) or the United States. For this reason I will not refer to the United States as America but rather will reserve the term for the whole, composed of North America, Central America, South America, and the Caribbean.

This book is divided into seven chapters and a conclusion. Although these chapters are meant to present a single point of view and, therefore, are closely related, most of them can be read independently. They are intended as provocative essays on the topics they discuss, whose aim is more to stimulate further reflection than answer questions. Chapter 1 presents the controversy surrounding the naming of Hispanics/Latinos. It begins with a discussion of the origins of the terms "Hispanic" and "Latino" and then proceeds to explore the arguments in favor and the objections against their use, as well as the use of no name at all.

Chapter 2 formulates the problem of identity and its relation to the names we use to identify, particularly ethnic names. It introduces distinctions between different types of identity, as well as between epistemic and metaphysical approaches to it. This chapter is an exercise in conceptual analysis necessary to prevent confusions in the subsequent discussion, and because of this it is the most abstract and technical part of the book. Those who have no patience for conceptual technicalities might wish to skip it.

Chapter 3 explains the way I propose to understand Hispanic/Latino identity, namely, in historical familial terms. I reject any essentialistic view according to which Hispanics/Latinos have common properties which constitute their essence and which may serve to distinguish them absolutely from others. Instead, I propose that Hispanics/Latinos constitute a family tied by changing historical relations which in turn generate particular properties which can serve to distinguish Hispanics/ Latinos from others in particular contexts. This inclusive and relational conception, moreover, justifies the use of "Hispanics" to refer to ourselves.

Chapter 4 illustrates the unity of the Hispanic historical family by examining the origin and character of Hispanic philosophy in the sixteenth century. Chapter 5 discusses the historical origins of this identity in *mestizaje*. It examines the peoples that make up the Hispanic family before we came together, at the moment when we first met, and in subsequent history. Its main thesis is that the encounters of Iberia, America, and Africa changed Iberia and America, and forged a new reality.

Chapter 6 aims to reveal some of the elements present in any search for group identity, through the examination of the conscious search for a Latin American philosophical identity both in Latin America and the United States. Chapter 7 illustrates our situation in the United States through a discussion of our situation in the American philosophical community. It argues that, in contrast with African-American philosophers, for example, Hispanic-American philosophers are perceived as foreigners. This, joined to the Eurocentric and Anglocentric spirit of American philosophy and its emphasis on lineage, tends to exclude Hispanics from the American Philosophical Establishment and to banish Hispanic philosophy from the philosophy curriculum. Finally, the Conclusion briefly recapitulates the main theses of the book and makes some remarks concerning the future.

In writing this book I have used some previously published material, although everything I have used has been modified substantially and integrated into my argument. It includes the following: "Hispanics, Philosophy, and the Curriculum," *Teaching Philosophy* 22, 3 (1999), 241–8; "The Nature of Ethnicity with Special Reference to Hispanic/ Latino Identity," *Public Affairs Quarterly* 13, 1 (1999), 25–42; chapters 1 and 2 of *Filosofía Hispánica: Concepto, origen y foco historiográfico* (Pamplona: University of Navarra, 1998); "Hispanic Philosophy: Its Beginning and Golden Age," *Review of Metaphysics* 46, 3 (1993), 475–502; and (with Iván Jaksić) "The Problem of Philosophical Identity in Latin America: History and Approaches," *Inter-American Review of Bibliography* 34 (1984), 53–71. Parts of chapter 7 were read at the University of San

Francisco's conference in 1998, "Hispanics in the US: Cultural Locations" and several broadcasts of the presentation were made in C-SPAN. I thank the editors of these journals and collections, and the co-author of the mentioned article, for their permission to use these materials.

Let me add in closing that I am grateful to several persons who read and commented on various drafts of the whole or parts of the manuscript. They brought to my attention inconsistencies and gaps which would surely have escaped me. I am particularly grateful to Linda Martín Alcoff, Pablo De Greiff, J. Angelo Corlett, Rodolfo Rondón, Gregory Pappas, and Vicente Medina, who read early versions of the manuscript and offered many useful suggestions. Oscar Martí, Elizabeth Millán, Leonardo Zaibert, Peter H. Hare, James Marsh, Judy Green, Eduardo Mendieta, and Jorge García offered helpful comments on parts of the manuscript. I am also grateful for the cooperation of the National Office of the American Philosophical Association, and particularly its Director Eric Hoffman, and for the help of my research assistants, David Kaspar and William Fedirko, from Buffalo, and Sarah Borden, from Fordham, who not only read the manuscript with care but also checked the endnotes and the bibliography.

There is a normal type of character, for example, in which impulses seem to discharge so promptly into movements that inhibitions get no time to arise. These are the 'dare-devil' and 'mercurial' temperaments, overflowing with animation, and fizzling with talk, which are so common in the Latin and Celtic races, and with which the cold-blooded and long-headed English character forms so marked a contrast. Monkeys these people seem to us, whilst we seem to them reptilian.

William James, *The Principles of Psychology*

The will of Anglo-Saxons tends to be calculating, and in that sense to be governed by reason; while the more improvising will of Hispanic people is directed by feeling.

Jorge Mañach, *Frontiers in the Americas*

1

What Should We Call Ourselves?

Should we call ourselves Hispanics? Should we call ourselves Latinos/ Latinas (henceforth, Latinos/as)?[1] Or should we reject any name? These are the only realistic alternatives we have, for there is no other term in wide use to refer to us. "Ibero Americans" and "Latin Americans" exclude important components of the worldwide Hispanic/Latino population, and they are not generally accepted. Indeed, both terms exclude United States citizens and Iberians, so they are of no use if we want to be more inclusive.[2] *Raza* and *Chicano* have been proposed by some sociologists and activists to refer to those of us who live in the United States, but they are objectionable for many obvious reasons, and have also failed to establish themselves.[3] *Chicano* is simply too narrow, comprising only members of the Mexican-American community; it is a term completely foreign to anyone who is not a member of that community, in this country or elsewhere.[4] And *raza*, which means "race" in Spanish, is too racial a term to be of any use and, again, is narrowly associated with the American south-west.[5] Moreover, some of the objections that will be raised here against "Hispanics" and "Latinos/as" apply even more clearly to *raza* and *Chicano*.

This issue has to do with the following questions: What does the use of names like "Hispanic" and "Latino/a" entail? Should we use one and not the other? Should we reject any name? And if we are going to make decisions of this sort, on what basis should we make them? These questions are important because names *identify*; they tell us both about what they name and about what we know concerning what they name. Is there, then, as philosophers would say, a set of necessary and sufficient conditions associated with either of these two names that defines who we – Hispanics or Latinos/as – are? Moreover, if these conditions exist, do they apply to us regardless of time, at a particular time, or at more than one, but less than all, times? In this chapter I examine arguments against the use of "Hispanic," "Latino/a," and any other name. Let me begin by pointing out some facts about the origin and grammar of "Hispanic" and "Latino/a" which are seldom acknowledged and which explain some of the controversy and confusion concerning their use.

1 Hispanics vs. Latinos/as

"Hispanics" and "Latinos/as" are used as nouns and adjectives. Their adjectival forms clearly indicate that they were originally intended to be descriptive. This or that was called Hispanic or Latino/a, and to this day we speak of Hispanic or Latino/a foods, countries, and so on. But we also use "Hispanic" and "Latino/a" as nouns, in which case we speak of individual persons or groups of persons. We speak of a Hispanic or Latino/a, and of Hispanics or Latinos/as.

"Hispanic" in English is a transliteration from the Spanish *hispánico/a*, which is always an adjective. The corresponding noun is *hispano/a*, which is also used as an adjective.[6] In Spanish one refers to *un hispano* or *una hispana*, but not to *un hispánico* or *una hispánica*. All these terms come from a common root: the Latin term *Hispania*, which was used by Romans to refer to the Iberian peninsula. The origin of the term *Hispania* is itself clouded in mystery. A common view is that it is of pre-Roman origin and originally meant "land of rabbits." In time, linguistic evolution turned the Latin *Hispania* into the Castilian *España* (Spain), which, because of the military successes of Castilians in the Iberian peninsula, came to be appropriated by them for the kingdom they established and the country which to this day they largely control.

Castilian hegemony was slow in establishing itself. The process that led to it began with the *Reconquista*, the 700-year campaign waged against the Moors by Christian kingdoms in the Iberian peninsula. There were several fronts along which this campaign took place, but three were particularly significant and gave rise to three important political units: the one in the west gave rise to Portugal; the one in the east, to the Principality of Barcelona; and the one in the center, to Castile. There were also other kingdoms which were eventually integrated into these three, such as Navarre, Aragon, the Balearic Islands, and Valencia.

Of the three most important kingdoms, Castile was particularly aggressive and successful in conquering territory. Ferdinand of Aragon (at the time, Aragon was already unified with the Principality of Barcelona, the Kingdom of Valencia, and the Balearic Islands) and Isabella of Castile were married in the fifteenth century, so after the death of Isabella in 1504 and some squabbles among the throne's heirs, modern Spain first came under the rule of a single monarch, Ferdinand himself. From this time on, *España* has been reserved for this political union, although there was a relatively brief period of time in the sixteenth and seventeenth centuries in which Portugal was part of it, insofar as the King of Spain ruled over Portugal also.

One of the consequences of these historical events is that the term *español* came to be used not only for the citizens of Spain, but also for the Castilian language. Today in Spain and Latin America, when referring to language, *español* means the language of the Castilians, although *castellano* is also used to refer to it. In the United States, the English translation of the term ("Spanish") is used likewise. Interestingly, however, *hispano* is used not only in connection with the inhabitants of Spain, regardless of their ethnic origin, but also for the inhabitants of Spanish-speaking Latin American countries and for persons of Spanish or Latin American descent who live in the United States. Sometimes, however, the term is reserved for Latin Americans of presumably pure Spanish ancestry.

"Hispanic," the English counterpart of *hispano/a*, is used essentially in the same way in the United States, except that sometimes Spaniards are excluded from the class of people it denotes. "Hispanic" frequently carries the sense of not being European.[7] It has the connotation of being derivatively Spanish and therefore not truly Spanish. If one is called Spanish, this means that either one is a Spaniard or is a descendant of Spaniards, and this in turn means that one may be Spanish, or sometimes, but not always, derivatively Spanish, namely, Hispanic. On the other hand, the official position taken by the United States Bureau of the Census in 1988 treats "Spanish" and "Hispanic" in the same way.[8] This reflects a usage that goes back quite a bit. Indeed, contrary to claims sometimes voiced in the US, "Hispanic" was not created by the American Census bureaucracy in the 1970s, although it is true that the Census did not officially adopt it until that time.[9]

The situation is different with the use of *hispano/a* in Latin America and Spain, for this term is used for Latin Americans, Spaniards, and descendants of Latin Americans and Spaniards in the United States. Note also that the Portuguese and the Brazilians are not generally included under the category of *hispano/a*.[10] *Hispanoamérica* usually includes countries which were former colonies of Spain, not Portugal. But the English "Hispanic" frequently includes both descendants of Spaniards and Portuguese, and of course of Latin Americans.

Clearly, this is a confusing picture; there is no consistent reason why the terms *hispano/a* and "Hispanic" are used in the way they are.[11] If these terms are to be used we must clarify some of these confusions and establish some parameters. Interestingly, very little has been done in this regard in Spain or Latin America in spite of the fact that *hispanismo* has been much discussed by both Spaniards and Latin Americans. Since the so-called Generation of '98 to this day, there has been a steady stream of literature surrounding this theme.[12] Indeed, during Francisco Franco's dictatorship in Spain there was a concerted effort to establish *hispánico/a* as the term of choice to describe Spanish and Latin American cultural phenomena in an effort to bring Latin America back into the Spanish fold. This effort was not restricted to the government. One of the Spanish intellectuals who left Spain because of the aftermath of the Civil War, Eduardo Nicol, proposed the term *hispánica* to refer to Spanish and Latin American philosophy.[13]

Unfortunately, the situation is not much better with "Latino/a." This term was created by the French to distinguish non-Anglo America from Anglo America. They needed a term that could integrate French America, Spanish America, and Portuguese America into a single unit in order to contrast it with Anglo America, and they successfully introduced *Amérique Latine*. "Latin," of course, means of Latin origin, as opposed to Anglo-Saxon. Like many things the French have done, this one stuck; although generally the French living in North America and the West Indies have come to be excluded from the category. The world generally refers to Spanish and Portuguese America as Latin America, and the inhabitants of Latin America refer to themselves as *latinoamericanos* and to their part of the world as *Latinoamérica* or *América Latina*. Few include Quebec and the French Antilles in Latin

America. *Latinoamérica* and *América Latina* are direct translations from English and French respectively.

This linguistic background gave rise to the term "Latino/a," which has become an English word and, following English conventions, is capitalized. The term is widely used to refer to persons of Latin American descent, regardless of their ancestry. Thus the children of persons of Polish–Jewish descent born in Latin America, who emigrate to this country, and their children, are considered Latinos/as. African Cubans and their children who live here are also considered Latinos/as. All descendants of pre-Columbian populations from Latin America and most of those from parts of the United States who were part of the Spanish colonial empire are considered Latinos/as. However, Native Americans, i.e. United States citizens who are of pre-Columbian origin, but whose ancestors lived in areas outside what constitutes United States territory today, are not so considered. Moreover, children of Spaniards born in Latin America again are considered Latinos/as, although Spaniards themselves are not, and the children of Spaniards who emigrated directly to the United States are sometimes considered Latinos/as and sometimes not.

So here we are, with two names to choose from to refer to ourselves. Of course, it should be one of the dearest principles of decent human conduct that every person should be allowed to choose how he or she is called, even though this is seldom in fact the case. Everyone should be allowed to choose his or her name, because names have serious consequences. Some names disempower those who have them in ways that have serious repercussions throughout their lives.[14] And every group should, in principle, be allowed to choose its own name as well, as long as the members of the group are permitted to object and call themselves by whatever other name they choose. I say "in principle" because ignorance and prejudice should not be allowed to go unchallenged. It is not good to allow a view based on misinformation to go unchallenged, particularly when that view affects other people. It is for this reason that I have decided to speak, although what I am going to say here should not be taken as an attempt to thwart creativity and the rights of individuals and groups with respect to this issue.

These remarks should be enough warning that we are quite divided when it comes to the name we want to be called, to such an extent that some of us become very agitated and even angry when someone calls us what we do not wish to be called. Some of us want to be called

Hispanics and object to "Latinos/as," whereas others want to be called Latinos/as and will not tolerate "Hispanics."[15] Indeed, some go so far as to forgo association with other Hispanics/Latinos because of the use of one of these terms. A few years ago, when the Committee for Hispanics in Philosophy of the American Philosophical Association sent out a survey to determine how many of us there were in the philosophical community, faculty and graduate students in general responded and voiced no serious objections. But at least one large group of undergraduate philosophy majors in a California school chose not to answer the survey because of the term "Hispanic" in the Committee's title.

Apart from those opposed to "Hispanic" or "Latino," there are others who reject any name which unites them with other groups of Hispanics/Latinos. Matters have been aggravated because of bureaucratic efforts on the part of US government agencies since the 1970s to impose the term "Hispanics" without proper acknowledgment and respect for the legitimate differences of various groups lumped together under the term. The use of the term "Latino/a" has been in part a grassroots effort to oppose this artificial bureaucratic homogenization.[16] So, what is the issue? Why the fuss?

2 The Case Against "Hispanics"

Of the many objections that could be mustered against the use of "Hispanics" to refer to us, five stand out.[17] They are quite different arguments, and their logical and persuasive force is also quite different. The first and second could be described as empirical, for they argue that there is no empirical justification for the use of the term. The third is more difficult to characterize. I am tempted to call it moral but, when we examine it, it will become clear that this is not quite right. And the fourth and fifth objections are pragmatic in the sense that they point to the undesirable consequences of the use of "Hispanic." Let me run through these objections.

The first objection argues that "Hispanic" is at least useless and at most confusing because it has no clear connotation; that is, a clear set of properties shared by the things it names. In this sense, the use of "American," for example, is both useful and fairly clear, for at least Americans have in common that they are citizens of the United States.

There is, then, something common to all persons called American, and this makes effective the term's denotation (i.e. the things it names). Some will want to argue that there are other features common to Americans but if so, this is icing on the cake; for a single property is sufficient to justify the use of the term.

Something similar can be said about some more general terms such as "human," for example. The claim is that every human being has something in common with every other human being. Although there is some dispute as to what that is, many accept the view that it is at least the capacity to reason, or the capacity to use language, and so on. Likewise, red things have in common that when we look at them under certain conditions, they appear to us in a certain way that allows us to distinguish them from other things we do not call red.

Now, the argument against the use of "Hispanics" is precisely that there is no property or set of properties connoted by the term and, therefore, that "Hispanics" cannot be effectively used to denote anything. In short, because we cannot point to any definite, precise connotation for the term, it cannot be used to pick out anything.[18]

One of the premises on which this objection is based is that, in order for a term to be used effectively, it must connote some property, or set of properties, which is common to all the things of which the term is predicated. This is what philosophers usually refer to as an essence: a set of properties which always, and only, characterizes the things called by the same name. This is a widespread view for which much support has been offered in the history of human thought.

The objection is substantiated by pointing out that "Hispanic" may be understood in a variety of ways – among others, territorially, politically, linguistically, culturally, racially, genetically, and pertaining to a class – yet none of these ways of understanding the meaning of "Hispanic" is effective in carving out an essence, that is, a property, or set of properties, which can be easily identified as essential to Hispanics.

Consider a *territorial* understanding of Hispanic. The justification of this use would consist in pointing out a territory on the basis of which the term could be effectively applied. But this makes very little sense if taken by itself, for on what basis can one establish boundaries to a territory? One can talk about mountains and rivers, but that can hardly explain how to use a term like "Hispanic." Suppose that someone were to insist that Hispanic has to do with everything which involves the Iberian peninsula, for example. This approach has the advantage that the limits or boundaries of this peninsula appear to be quite clear. There is water all around it except for the north-east, where the mighty Pyrenees rise, separating it from the rest of Europe. So in principle it appears to make sense to have a term to describe the people who live on this piece of land. Yet problems of demarcation arise, for where exactly is the place where the boundary between the peninsula and the rest of Europe is to be drawn? Perhaps at the highest level of the mountains. This could be done, but does it make sense? Suppose there is a little town whose inhabitants are the descendants of six families who settled in an area of the Pyrenees and have now become thoroughly mixed together, although three families came from one side of the Pyrenees and three families came from the other. And suppose the town is located on a plateau through which the highest point crosses and that this point divides the town into two. In accordance with our criterion, we would have to call one of the two sides Hispanic and the other Gallic, or whatever. Surely, this makes no sense in a town which is one town, with people related to each other in various ways.

The attempt to draw territorial boundaries between Hispanic America and Anglo America would encounter similar difficulties. Let us suppose that we accept the Río Grande as the dividing line between them. What do we make of the people of Mexican ancestry on this side of the river and of the people of Anglo-Saxon ancestry on the other? And what do we make of cultural similarities and differences? No matter how one looks at territorial justifications for the use of terms like "Hispanic," they fail, for there is nothing in a territory that can justify many current legitimate uses of the terms.

Consider, then, a *political* understanding of "Hispanic."[19] Here we have several possibilities, all equally unacceptable. One is to consider Hispanic as the political unit we know as Spain. In this sense, Hispanic refers to people who are part of the country, Spain. But there are at least two objections to this understanding of the term. First, the term seems to duplicate another term already in use: "Spanish." Why do we need "Hispanic" when we already have "Spanish" to refer to persons who are part of the Spanish state? Second, the political unit we know as Spain has not always had the same boundaries and, therefore, it has not always included the same groups of people. Indeed, this political unit came into being only after the deaths of Isabella and her successors, Joan the Mad and Philip the Fair, leaving Ferdinand of Aragon as sole ruler of Castile and Aragon. Prior to this time, there was no Spain. The unification of Spain is supposed to have become complete when Ferdinand annexed the Iberian part of the Kingdom of Navarre in 1512, but this political unit has not always had the same boundaries. During the reign of Philip II in the sixteenth century, for example, Portugal became part of it, although only for a relatively short time. Gibraltar was part of Spain for a couple of centuries before it became British over 200 years ago. And something similar can be said about Perpignan.

Another possibility would be to think in terms of all the political units of the Iberian peninsula taken together: Spain, Portugal, Catalonia, Navarre, and so on. But this is not very helpful, for why should these units be included and others excluded? Why leave out the French Basque region? Why not include Perpignan? What about the Azores and the Canary Islands? And, of course, this leaves out all of Latin America. On what basis can we draw such distinctions to justify the use of "Hispanic?"

Another way to try to justify the use of "Hispanic" is in terms of people who speak Spanish.[20] But, strictly speaking, "Spanish" is not the correct name for the *language*, for the language that goes by that name is in fact Castilian. Castilians have appropriated "Spanish" by a process similar to that by which the United States has appropriated "America." It is a matter of prominence and power. Moreover, this language is spoken by many people who are not native speakers of it and have learned it as a second language. Some of these live in the Iberian peninsula, like the Catalans, the Galicians, and the Basques. Some of them live in Latin America, like the Maya and the Tarahumara. But some of them live in the United States, in Australia, and in Germany. Are all these peoples Hispanics? No one would think so, which means the linguistic criterion is not effective.

Besides, there are people considered Hispanics who do not have Castilian as their native tongue. Consider the case of some Bolivians whose native tongue is Aymara. According to this criterion they could not be considered Hispanic, and yet those who favor the use of "Hispanic" would want to so consider them. Moreover, if the Bolivians were brought to the United States, they would be classified as Hispanics. There is also the case of people who do not speak Castilian at all but are nonetheless regarded as Hispanics. Consider the case of children of Puerto Ricans and Cubans in this country who have never learned Castilian and yet not only are thought of as Hispanic by many, but also often think of themselves in this way. Clearly, "Hispanic" and "Castilian-speaking" are not synonymous. Besides, there is also the matter of proficiency. How proficient in the language does one need to be in order to qualify as Hispanic? If a level of proficiency is set too high, it would disqualify children and some mentally handicapped persons. And if it is set too low, then it would qualify many students of the language whom no one regards as Hispanic.

Assume for a moment that none of what has been said against making language the criterion of "Hispanic" has merit. Even under these conditions, the linguistic criterion could be questioned insofar as it involves too little for identity. The argument would be that Castilian, or Spanish if you will, is very little more than the elements of a grammar and this would not explain the group's identity. Indeed, how much do some African Cubans, some native Bolivians, and some Asturians have in common linguistically? The accent would be very different, and so would be the vocabulary and even much of the syntax. Would they understand each other? To some extent yes, but one cannot assume so. Under these conditions, then, can language really be taken as the source of Hispanic identity?

To expand the understanding of Hispanic to include other Iberian languages and perhaps even Amerindian languages would not help, for the criterion would be both too narrow and too broad.[21] It would be too narrow because it would not solve the problem of French Basques, for example, or again, of people from other cultures who learn these languages. And it would be too broad because it would have an even greater lack of cohesiveness than Castilian. The linguistic criterion, then, is of no use.

The *cultural* criterion is more promising, although upon careful scrutiny it also fails.[22] At first it looks as if culture could function as an effective demarcating criterion of what is Hispanic and what is not.[23] After all, certain cultural practices and traits appear to separate Hispanics from other cultures. Hispanics seem to share all sorts of cultural characteristics which are idiosyncratic to them and are not found in other cultures. These could include language or families of languages, values, religion, social customs, and so on. Culture could solve the problems that territorial and political demarcations pose; it would provide borders for a territory and it would cross artificial political lines. But even culture fails under scrutiny.

Consider the way in which we speak of Hispanics as referring to persons who share the Spanish culture. This certainly raises questions, for what is Spanish culture? The culture of the political unit we know as Spain? Does it include Catalan and Basque cultures? Why do we separate it from Portuguese culture and not from these? But perhaps it is separable from all these, in which case we may be speaking of, say, Castilian culture. But Castilian culture then reduces to the culture of those people who speak Castilian. Should we then say Castilian as a native tongue or Castilian as an acquired language? Or does it have to do with territory after all? Or with political boundaries? And why exclude Latin America? The problem with including Latin America is that we have here a variety of cultures which are well integrated in some cases, and in some cases not, but which cannot under any circumstances be regarded as Spanish. A brief walk through Mexico City's Zócalo and Madrid's Plaza del Sol is sufficient to get the point. Which boundaries should we use and who, then, should we call Hispanic? Clearly the cultural criterion is too vague to be of help, and when we try to pin it down we end up reducing it to the other criteria which we have already found to be inadequate.

Race would prima facie appear to be a better choice. It certainly sounds more scientific. Race does not seem to depend on culture, and those who belong to a race are supposed to share certain clearly identifiable physical characteristics. There would seem to be nothing difficult in separating people according to race. Yet this criterion also runs into trouble: its problems are twofold. First, race is hardly a clear criterion of separation insofar as it appears after all to include cultural and sociological elements.[24] We see frequently that people who look different are classified as members of the same race, and people who look similar are classified as members of different races. In some cases, racial classification has to do with recent lineage rather than with anything else. Certainly, the situation of South Africa and the United States is quite ambiguous when it comes to race. In South Africa, race classification has often been changed through legal procedures, and it is generally accepted that in the United States a good proportion of people of color become white every year.[25]

But this is not all, for even if race were an incontestable criterion of distinction among people, there does not seem to be any race that can properly be called Hispanic. Many of the people who are called Hispanic belong to different races. What would be the characteristics of a Hispanic race? Even in the Iberian peninsula itself, or even within what we know today as Spain, there is no uniformity of looks or physical make-up. There are even physiological differences between some Iberian groups (for example, the blood profile of Basques is different from that of other Iberians in some important respects). The inhabitants of the Iberian peninsula are perhaps one of the most mixed people in Europe. Apart from the Celts, Iberians, Basques, Greeks, Phoenicians, Carthaginians, Berbers, Romans, Vandals, Suebi, and Visigoths, the peninsula had a large infusion of Moors beginning in the eighth century and of Jews at various points in its history, and descendants of Amerindians have often moved to it and lived and mixed with other members of the population. Indeed, there are even Africans, Indians (from India), and Asians who have settled (voluntarily or by force) in Iberia at various times, and who have mixed with the population in Spain and Portugal. It would be completely impossible to speak of a Spanish race, or an Iberian race, if one were trying to refer to the people of the Iberian peninsula. And the situation becomes even more complicated when we include Latin America in the picture, for the African and Amerindian elements in Latin America are substantial and they are themselves variegated and intermixed. Moreover, there is the more recent immigration from non-Iberian Europe and Asia. Alberto Fujimori – elected President of Peru in 1990 – is of Japanese ancestry, and there are significant numbers of Asians in Paraguay, Italians and Welsh in Argentina, Germans in Chile, French in Cuba, and so on. What is the Hispanic race, then?

At the beginning of this century, when philosophers were greatly impressed with biology and the evolutionary theory of Darwin, José Vasconcelos, a Mexican philosopher, proposed the idea that in Latin America there were the makings of a fifth race which, instead of being exclusionary, like the other four, would be a true mixture of all the others. It is a race, he speculated, guided by love rather than interest.[26] Vasconcelos's theory was inspiring, but it was flawed from the beginning, for it relied on the unclear notion of race. There is one point in it, however, that is important and of which we should take note: there is no single discernible race in Latin America but, rather, a veritable melange of races and racial mixtures. This point can be extended to cover Iberians and Hispanic Americans. If there is to be a Hispanic race, which I very much doubt, it is still in the making and would necessarily be an extraordinary mixture.

Some argue that it is not race but *genetic lineage* that serves to give unity to Hispanics: genetic lineage is both a necessary and sufficient condition for the proper use of the term and of the identity of those to whom it is applied.[27] Prima facie this seems to make considerable sense. It certainly solves many of the problems raised earlier with respect to territory, political boundaries, language, culture, and race. Hispanics can move about, join different nations, speak different languages, have different cultures, and belong to different races and racial mixtures.

Still, there are at least three serious problems with this view.[28] The first is that it involves either circularity or a reduction to some other factor, for genetic lineage must always have an origin. Membership in a genetic line presupposes the genetic line. The problem arises because the identity of the genetic line has to be assumed (thus the circularity) or analyzed in terms of non-genetic factors, such as territory, political unit, language, culture, and so on (thus the reduction). If I am Hispanic because I can trace my lineage to my grandparents, what makes them Hispanics?

The second problem is that genetic lineage is both too narrow and too broad as a criterion of identity. It is too narrow because there are Hispanics who have no genetic link to other Hispanics; for instance, some children of Welsh immigrants to Argentina and of Jewish immigrants to various Hispanic nations. It is too broad because it would have to include tenth-generation descendants of Hispanics, who have not lived in a Hispanic country, have not associated with other Hispanics, and do not share with them any cultural traits.

This brings me to the third difficulty: genetic lineage is too imprecise a criterion insofar as it is not clear what it involves. What constitutes genetic lineage? A completely unmixed genealogy or a partially mixed genealogy? If the first, I doubt many of us would qualify; if the second, then the existence of a single Hispanic ancestor, ten generations removed, would be sufficient to qualify. But this does not make much sense.

Finally, "Hispanic" could be used to denote a certain *class* of people. The problem is that it becomes very difficult to speak of any such class. In order to speak meaningfully in this way, we would have to begin by separating out a larger group of people, from among whom we could distinguish some as belonging to the class of Hispanics. But which is that larger group of people? Those who speak Castilian? Those who live in Spain? Those who live in Latin America? Those of a certain race or ancestry? We already saw the difficulties posed by the attempt to demarcate any of these categories. All the same, suppose we were able to do this. We would still have to separate the Hispanic subgroup from the larger group and do it in terms of class, for example. But which subgroup or class should we refer to as Hispanic? Some think that Hispanics should be those with Spanish ancestry. But surely that would bring back the problems associated with the use of "Spanish" and, moreover, this is not how most people use "Hispanic." And other criteria, such as education, social status, and so on, also fail, for they would obviously tie the group to non-Hispanic groups which have the same level of education, social status, and so on. It does not seem to be possible effectively to distinguish Hispanics from other groups of people on the basis of education or any of the criteria mentioned.[29]

In short, the empirical objection is that there is in fact no identifiable property, or set of properties, that one can identify which is shared by those people one would want to call Hispanics, and that therefore we lack a proper criterion for distinguishing them from others. Using philosophical jargon, we could say that the use of "Hispanic" is unjustified insofar as there are no identifiable necessary or sufficient conditions either for its proper use or for the identity of those to whom it is applied. None of the conditions mentioned – territory, political unit, language, culture, race, genetic lineage, or class – functions either as a necessary or a sufficient condition. We must, then, abandon the project of trying to identify Hispanics based on any kind of empirically discernible property.

Note that this objection can be used not only against the use of "Hispanic" but also, more radically, against any attempt to lump Iberians, Latin Americans, and some Americans into a group. I shall return to this when we speak of the no-name alternative, but now let me turn to the second objection against the use of "Hispanics."

The second objection is also empirical insofar as it argues that there are no empirically discernible grounds which justify the use of "Hispanic." It argues thus not because it finds the term has *no* connotation, as the first objection did, but because the connotation of the term (1) is too narrow, excluding some necessary elements, and (2) is skewed, privileging some elements over others. The point is made that the use of "Hispanic" to describe members of the Latin American community in Latin America, or the Latino community in the United States unfairly privileges the Spanish, Iberian, and European component, cultural or racial, of these communities, leaving out, sometimes altogether, essential elements. "Hispanic" means somehow derivatively Spanish or Iberian, and therefore European, privileging this element in contrast to the Amerindian and African elements which are integral parts of our community. Sometimes this argument is made in terms of nationalities. It is claimed that the use of "Hispanics" is not sensitive to national differences which must be respected. This version of the argument is weaker, for these so-called national differences are often no more than artificial constructs superimposed on widely different peoples by certain powerful elites.

Understood in its cultural or racial sense, however, this is a powerful objection. Labels and names establish priorities and send messages, and if "Hispanic" does indeed privilege the Spanish, Iberian, or European elements to the detriment or exclusion of Amerindian and African elements in our community, then it is certainly unacceptable. If the term can only be understood in this way, then it should be dropped in favor of some other more inclusive and less biased term.

The third objection against the use of "Hispanics" argues that, although the term may be perfectly appropriate when applied to Spaniards in particular or Iberians in general, and even when applied to descendants of Spaniards or Iberians in Latin America and the United States, it is unconscionable to use it to refer to Latin Americans or to Latinos/as in the United States who have no Spanish or Iberian ancestry. The reason is that the ancestors of these people suffered enormous atrocities and egregious abuses at the hands of the Iberian conquistadors and, in many cases, the consequences of those atrocities and abuses are still quite evident. "Hispanics" is primarily descriptive of the people responsible for those atrocities and abuses; to apply the same term to those who suffered at their hands is not only indelicate but morally repugnant.

It should be clear why earlier I characterized this objection as a moral objection. Its force is largely a moral one: it is morally wrong to call Latin Americans and Latinos/as "Hispanics." Nonetheless, it is not clear that there is any justifiable moral principle from which this conclusion could be derived. Perhaps one could argue that it is derived from the principle "It is wrong to use a name for the oppressed that belongs to the oppressor." But this is not helpful, for it is not clear in turn why this principle has any moral force. That is, although the form of the principle is prescriptive, it is not at all obvious why it should be adopted. Indeed, there are situations in which it is certainly beneficial to use a name that belongs to an oppressor for the oppressed, since identification with the oppressor might help the oppressed avoid some oppressive measures. And if life, death, and the just apportionment of goods to the oppressed depends on the use of the oppressor's name, someone who is defending the oppressed would seem to be morally compelled to use the name. It is not clear, then, that the principle in question is morally justifiable in all circumstances. Nonetheless, the fact that both the principle and the objection are presented as moral judgments could warrant characterizing the objection as moral even if its moral justification is missing, unclear, or impossible.

There is a version of this objection that is particularly significant for the use of "Hispanics" to describe those of us who live in the United States, and especially Hispanics/Latinos from the south-west who are *mestizos* or consider themselves Mexican American. The objection is that "Hispanic" has been appropriated in the south-west by a small group of people who consider themselves to be of pure Spanish ancestry, in order to distinguish themselves from "Mexicans," whom they consider *mestizos* and, in their racist eyes, a lower class of human being. Under these conditions, does it make sense to use "Hispanics" to refer precisely to *mestizos*, or to Mexican Americans?[30] Two points merit reflection. First, if this term has been used to differentiate and discriminate, it cannot now be used to unite. Second, if the use of the term implies pure Spanish, non-*mestizo*, and non-Mexican, then how can it be used to include *mestizos* and Mexicans?

The fourth objection against the use of "Hispanics" is pragmatic. It argues that the use of this term has unacceptable consequences. These result from the fact that, no matter what one says, "Hispanics" first and foremost applies to Spaniards, and thus can be used to refer to Latin Americans and Latinos/as only secondarily or derivatively. This makes the latter two second-class citizens as it were, and perpetuates a relation of dominator–dominated between Spaniards in particular and Iberians in general, on the one hand, and Latin Americans and Latinos/as on the other. It would not be practically beneficial for the latter two, then, to allow themselves to be called Hispanics. This is not to claim that there would be effects of the sort that took place during colonial times. Latin American countries are now completely independent from Spain and some are even more powerful and richer than Spain.

Moreover, Latinos/as in the United States are completely out of reach of any kind of power, political or otherwise, that Spain could exercise over them. Still, there would be a kind of psychological dependency and a sense of cultural subservience which would not be salutary for Latin Americans and Latinos/as.

The fifth and final objection is also pragmatic. It points out that the use of "Hispanics" has negative associations. Not only does "Hispanic" imply "derivatively Spanish," but it is associated in many places with negative qualities: laziness, shiftiness, lax morals, low class, lack of education, drug use, and so on. It also suggests mixed race, which in racist societies can have negative consequences. The use of "Hispanics," then, can create a hostile atmosphere for us, may lead to discrimination, and obstructs our proper integration in societies where we constitute a minority, such as American society.[31]

3 The Case Against "Latinos/as"

The case against the use of "Latinos/as" begins with an empirical objection similar to the first objection given against the use of "Hispanics.'[32] I say "similar" rather than "the same" because those who propose the use of "Latinos/as" do not include Iberian countries in the designation. Indeed, one of the reasons why they favor "Latinos/as" rather than "Hispanics" is that they associate the latter with Spain. They are impressed in particular with the second, third, and fourth objections presented earlier against the use of "Hispanics." They will have nothing to do with a term which they believe primarily designates a former oppressor and whose cloud still hangs over those whose ancestors it once dominated. But even if one restricts the use of "Latinos/as" to Latin America and certain members of the population in the United States, the empirical issues raised in connection with the use of "Hispanics" can still be applied, *mutatis mutandis*, because the population of Latin America and the presumed Latin American population in the United States appear to have as little in common as the presumed referents of "Hispanics" have. There is no need, however, to go over the ground we have already covered. Instead, I shall turn to five other objections which apply in particular to the use of "Latinos/as."

The first of these argues that if the designation "Latinos/as" is held not to apply to the Iberian countries, then it is too narrow to be of use.

If the argument in favor of "Latinos/as" and the rejection of "Hispanics" is that "Hispanics" is not acceptable because of the abuse Iberians bestowed on the native population of America, then what do we make of descendants of Iberians who live in America and whose ancestors first settled here several hundred years ago? Certainly they could not be Latinos/as. But if they are not so, what are they? In short, what do we make of the *criollo*?

Criollo was used during the colonial period to designate persons of Spanish ancestry who were born in America.[33] Obviously, *criollos* and their descendants are descendants of Spaniards; they have some elements of Spanish culture, including the language; and they never suffered the atrocities that the conquistadors inflicted on Africans brought to America as slaves and on Amerindians. Indeed, some of them, or their ancestors, may have been responsible for some of those atrocities. This means that if the use of "Latinos/as" is precisely intended to leave out everything Spanish or peninsular, then *criollos* and their descendants must also be left out. What are these people going to be called? How are we to regard them? I imagine some would want to undo history by sending them back to Iberia, but wants will not change anything in this case. Descendants of *criollos* are in Latin America to stay.

A comparison with Africans brought over to Latin America makes clear further problems. Africans are as foreign to America as *criollos*.[34] Indeed, there are *criollos* whose families have been in America longer than any African family living in America. So if *criollos* are to be excluded from the extension of "Latino/a" because they are of non-Amerindian descent, then Africans should also be excluded. Moreover, the same reasoning will force us, if we are interested in unbiased consistency, to exclude mulattos (the mix of European and African) and to raise the question of what to do with the population resulting from the mix of Amerindian with non-Amerindian. Should we also ship Africans back to Africa and drown anyone of mixed lineage? And what do we do with mixed culture? Do we reject anything Iberian? This would include the language, of course. But what do we put in its place? English, the language of other oppressors?

Even a short perusal of the history of most of Latin America will show that much that is valued and constitutive of Latin America today is the result of the efforts of *criollos*, mulattos, and *mestizos*. It makes no sense to use a designation which necessarily excludes any of them.

But this is not all. There is another important fact that must be taken into account in this matter, and this is that Latin America is eminently mixed. There are some Latin Americans who can claim pure Iberian ancestry. And there are also some Latin Americans who can claim pure African or Amerindian descent. But the overwhelming majority of the inhabitants of Latin America and the majority of Latinos/as in the United States are mixed. For them to reject "Hispanics" is to reject part of who they are genetically. But not only that, it is also to reject part of who they are historically and culturally. Latin America today is not pre-Columbian America, nor is Iberia what it was before its encounter with America. The current culture of Latin America and Iberia is a mixture of elements from America, Africa, and Iberia which came together in its history.

A second reason against the use of "Latinos/as" is that Latin Americans or American Latinos/as should not be allowed to monopolize the term. If "Latinos/as" is taken to mean "of Latin origin," as opposed to Anglo-Saxon, then Iberians have as much right to the name as do Latin Americans and American Latinos/as. Indeed, their right to the name is certainly greater than that of Amerindians, for there is nothing that these have genetically, culturally (except through Iberia), or historically (again except through Iberia) in common with the Romans. Furthermore, who is going to tell the French, who first coined the term precisely in order to separate themselves and other "Latins" from Anglo-Saxons, that they and their descendants in America do not have a right to the term? On what basis can the argument be made?

This brings us to the third objection, namely, that "Latinos/as" is too broad a designation. "Latinos/as" means Latin or of Latin origin, and the Latins were the ancient Romans – in fact, only a small group of people from Latium, the land around Rome. The term "Latin," however, is also used as an adjective to refer to certain parts of Europe in the Middle Ages in which the Latin language was used or to peoples who used the Latin language. In this sense, the Latins are contrasted with the Muslims or the Jews, for example. According to this criterion, not just residents of what later came to be Italy and Spain were called Latin, but also residents of Germany and Britain. Moreover, eventually the term has come to be applied to peoples whose languages are derived from Latin, speakers of so-called Romance languages. Thus speakers of Spanish, Italian, Catalan, French, Romanian, and so on are called Latins, but speakers of English, German, or Russian are not.

Recall that the reason for the introduction of the term "Latin America" was precisely to encompass all Latins from America, so that they could be contrasted with Anglo-Saxons, speakers of non-Latin derived languages. Indeed, if we go back to the nineteenth century, when the term was placed in use, we see that those who advocated it emphasized precisely the Roman and French connection: Latin America is Latin because of its legal (Roman law) and religious (Roman Catholic) traditions.[35]

In short, the exclusive appropriation of "Latin" by Latin Americans and "Latinos/as" in the United States is unwarranted. Moreover, the use of the Spanish version of the term, namely "Latinos/as," is even more paradoxical. Why in God's name use a Spanish translation of "Latin" to refer to oneself when one wants to avoid any Spanish connotation? And if what is desired is to get away from any Eurocentric terminology, why use anything that has to do with what is quintessentially European: Rome? Have we forgotten that Rome has been the symbol and icon for all European imperialism, expansion, militarism, conquest, and colonization for the past 2,000 years? Have we forgotten Charlemagne, Charles V, Napoleon, and Hitler? Rome has been the inspiration, the fuel that has kindled the ambition of every tyrant who has wanted to set himself up as the king of the world, and of every nation that has had aspirations of establishing preeminence above all others. Never mind the argument that Roman imperialism, military expansion, conquest, and colonization also resulted in the spread of learning and the advancement of those conquered. Such advantages were unintended and accidental byproducts of a process initiated for very different reasons, and they could have been achieved by other, more peaceful and beneficent means. Rome stands for the dark side of this process. Thus, to use "Latin" or "Latino/a" as an act of rebellion against Iberian and European expansionism is not just paradoxical; it is ridiculous. Those who argue strenuously for this term either have a very short memory or a very selective one. Good foundations, however, require both a good and an integral memory. This is a lesson that those peoples who suffered at the hands of Hitler have learned well, and we should learn from their experience. We must be faithful to the facts, and we must be careful with what we establish as our symbols.

There is one last objection against the use of "Latinos/as" that needs to be voiced. If it is objectionable to adopt any name imposed by a foreign group of people, why should we adopt the name the French gave us? The adoption of the French name seems to be another example of the servile attitude some of us have with respect to certain European countries, and particularly the French and the English. To bow to the French or the English is as bad as bowing to the Spanish or the Portuguese; in fact, it may be worse, for most of us have some Iberian blood and certainly much of the Iberian cultures, but how much have we taken from the French or the English in comparison? If the point is to liberate ourselves, then we must certainly not follow the French initiative; we should be the ones to find a name for ourselves.

4 The Case Against Any Name

The picture I have painted does not bode well for the enterprise that seeks to find a name for the group of people some call Hispanics and others call Latinos/as. Indeed, perhaps the best thing would be to abandon the whole enterprise: there should be no name for us. And here in some ways the arguments mirror those already rehearsed. I should like to refer to four in particular, which may be characterized as empirical, political, logical, and pragmatic.[36]

We have seen versions of the empirical argument already; it points out that there is nothing that so-called Hispanics/Latinos have in common. There is no unity, no reality which stands behind the name, for there are no common properties to all Hispanics/Latinos. Any name, then, would be an artificial creation by a few who have aims of their own in mind: political dominance, wealth, or whatever. A search for elements of unity, as we have already seen, leads nowhere. Indeed, as some scholars have pointed out, even denominations like "Latin America" are problematic.[37] There is no Latin America. There is only a group of countries and very different societies which, as wholes, have nothing in common. The denomination "Latin America," just like the denomination "Hispanic" or "Latino/a," has been imposed by persons or groups of persons for whom it is convenient to lump together the countries or peoples from this part of the world. The purpose behind this is usually domination and exploitation.

Consider the following four countries, all of which are regarded as Latin American: Argentina, Brazil, Ecuador, and Mexico. Spanish is the lingua franca in three of these countries (Argentina, Ecuador, and

Mexico), while the other (Brazil) has Portuguese. In Argentina the population is primarily Caucasian and of European descent; in Ecuador the population is predominantly Amerindian, composed of descendants of various tribes which were under Inca domination before the encounter; in Brazil, most of the population is of African origin or it is a mixture of African and Portuguese; and in Mexico the population is primarily of Amerindian origin and includes such different Amerindian peoples as the Maya and the Aztecs. The geography and economies of these four countries are different, and so are many elements of their cultures. On what basis, then, can they all be lumped together under the term "Latin America?"

Now let us turn to Hispanics/Latinos in the United States. Do we really form a community? What do Chicanos, Cubans, Dominicans, Puerto Ricans, Colombians, and so on have in common? What does a wealthy Cuban, who claims to have pure European ancestry, and who came to the United States in 1960 as a political exile, have in common with a poor *bracero* of Meso-American ancestry, who crossed the United States border with Mexico illegally in search of manual labor? Some say: not race; not social status; not economic means; not values. It is even questionable that they speak the same language or have the same religion. Perhaps their languages follow the same grammar, but when it comes to vocabulary, accent, and pronunciation, the differences between them are as large as one would expect of peoples who speak languages as different from each other as Portuguese and Castilian. And something similar can be said about religion. A case could be made that the version of Catholicism in which most Cubans believe is a different religion from the Catholicism permeated with elements of the Amerindian religions in which many *braceros* believe.[38]

This same comparison could be repeated over and over again. The point is obvious: the Hispanic/Latino community in the United States does not share anything in common. But this should not be surprising, since we already saw that the Hispanic/Latino community outside the United States does not share anything in common either. If we are going to talk about communities, we must talk about smaller groups, perhaps national groups: Cubans, Chicanos, Dominicans, and so on. Perhaps we should in fact divide these groups: Cubans from Cuba and American Cubans; Puerto Ricans from Puerto Rico and Puerto Ricans in the United States. Or perhaps we should subdivide them even further: Cubans from Cuba, Cubans from Miami, Cubans from New

York, and so on. Indeed, Puerto Ricans themselves have found a name for Puerto Ricans from New York: Neo-Ricans. And then we must also think in terms of gender differences. Perhaps the units should be reduced even further, to female Neo-Rican, and so on. It is these smaller units that share something, and it is to these smaller units that individual persons feel attached. Their sense of belonging is first to them and only later, if at all, to this artificially created category of Hispanic or Latino/a.[39] And I say "if at all" because there is considerable evidence that points to deep-rooted rivalries and resentment between some of these communities. I remember, for example, that the first thing I heard on the radio in 1972, when I went to Puerto Rico as visiting professor, was an ultimatum from the "Comando Anticubano" to all Cubans living in the island: "Leave Puerto Rico within a week or your personal safety will be in jeopardy."

The use of any single name for these diverse groups involves a forced homogenization of what is not homogeneous, and thus a distortion of the reality in which we live. There is no Hispanic or Latino natural kind; rather, this kind is an artificial one created by bureaucrats, government agencies, foreign nations, or particular groups who want to exert their power over others or establish hegemony over them. Homogeny leads to hegemony.

The political argument against the use of a single term to refer to Hispanics/Latinos goes something like this. The reason that there are no properties that can be associated with the peoples for whom we are seeking a name is that they are not a cohesive group of people, free to develop as a community and a society. The only thing that these diverse peoples have in common is their marginalization and the domination imposed on them by others. But even here the marginalization is different and the domination comes from different sources, failing to justify a common name. Latin America in particular has been pushed to the margins of both Anglo-Saxon America and Europe and has suffered domination from a variety of colonial powers and industrialized nations. The countries of Latin America have suffered political domination from Spain, Portugal, and other powers that ventured into America. And all these countries have endured the economic exploitation of the United States, and some of them have experienced economic exploitation from France and Britain as well. The exploitation and domination that this part of the world has suffered has divided it into classes whose interests are diametrically opposed and who share only a patina of culture. Deep down, there is no cohesive society, no people, for their authenticity has been stolen and their only unity lies in their being the object of exploitation of one sort or another. Until the forces of oppression are defeated, there will not be a people, a society, a group of persons that will share characteristics that make them one. Therefore, any attempt at naming us should be resisted.[40]

The sociological objection argues that there is no evidence that all members of the group to which others refer as Hispanics/Latinos use a single name to refer to themselves, or have any consciousness of being a unified group. Yet, so the argument goes, self-naming, or at least consciousness of identity, is a necessary condition for ethnicity.[41] It makes no sense, then, artificially to impose a name on people who do not accept it, and who do not think of themselves as one people.

The logical argument can be formulated as follows. Human beings all have the same nature, and cultural and ethnic differences are merely superficial and accidental.[42] To think otherwise is to confuse what is essential with what is accidental, and thus to make a kind of type mistake.[43] There is no point in trying to find something that characterizes Hispanics/Latinos and that separates them from other societies and groups. Logically, the search for the essential characteristics of a culture or ethnic group is futile. Cultures and ethnic groups are in a constant process of change, and are merely superficial. The essential elements of human society are not different from one group to another, but are rather the same for all human beings. We should stop the effort to find common characteristics of groups that separate them from other human beings and, likewise, we should stop trying to find names that are appropriate to identify them. Humanity is one, and any attempt to break it apart is bound to fail.

The last argument is pragmatic. We should stop any attempts to give a name to all so-called Hispanics/Latinos, not just because there is no evidence that we share anything that other human beings do not also share, but more importantly because to do so facilitates our oppression, marginalization from the mainstream, and alienation. Giving us a name provides a handle for our manipulation. Identification and naming always have a practical aspect, even when it is not the only aspect of naming. When a group identifies and names itself, it is usually to separate itself from others with whom it does not wish to be identified, and often such an act is preparatory to hostile action against those others. When a group is given a name by some other group, the

24

aim is also similar: separation and hostility. Hence, when it comes to groups of people, identification and naming are seldom benign, carrying with them dangers to those identified and named, or to others who become contrasted with them.

There are other problems with identification and naming as well, for identifying and naming always involve an emphasis on similarities and the neglect of differences. This in turn may generate false generalizations about the members of the group which is identified or named. They are all regarded as the same or as largely the same, and their individual differences are ignored in order to make them fit the general mold which justifies their name. This gives rise to stereotypes, caricatures, and distortions which in turn are used to justify prejudice and bias.

From this it is a short step to the obliteration of individuality. Individual persons become indistinguishable members of a set whose members are essential replicas of each other. The individual person ceases to be who he or she is and becomes merely one unit of a kind.[44] Why take the risk, then? It is better to be without a group name and to have only individual names. In this way we are who we are, as individuals, and can be treated as such. We do not have to suffer by association. Nor will we be tempted, as individuals, to regard ourselves as higher, greater, or superior to others. The twentieth century has had enough superior and inferior nations, races, cultures, and societies. Let us abandon any attempt to reestablish them by giving up the effort to find a common name for any group of people, including those some like to call Hispanics and others Latinos/as. We are better off as Jorge, María, and Cuauhtémoc.

One version of this objection argues against all existing ethnic names, and particularly "Hispanics" or "Latinos/as," because these labels have bad connotations among the general population. They create a negative perception of those named and tend to perpetuate their disadvantageous situation in society. To call someone Hispanic or Latino/a, like calling someone negro or colored, carries with it all sorts of negative baggage, demeaning the person and harming him or her in diverse ways.

Finally, there is the question of distribution of resources. In a country like the United States, where many resources are administered by a vast bureaucracy, the distribution of resources depends on the understanding by the bureaucracy of the groups among which they are to be distributed, and this in turn depends on the classificatory categories and names used by the bureaucracy. The lumping together of all Hispanics/Latinos into a group which ignores the different features and conditions of different groups of Hispanics/Latinos has serious and adverse consequences for the well-being of some members of these groups.[45] Faulty science leads to faulty public policy and faulty social justice. Resources are given to those who do not need them simply because they are classified in a certain way. This strains available resources, depriving those who really need them. I can vouch for this personally, for I have seen college scholarships go to children of well-to-do families merely because they are classified as Hispanic/Latino, whereas really needy students have had to do without assistance.[46]

5 Conclusion

There is no reason why anyone should doubt the good faith with which the reasons presented against the use of "Hispanic," "Latino/a," or any other name used to identify us are proposed. Indeed, the honesty and frankness with which these reasons are stated vouches for their authenticity and gives them credibility. But there is more to it than this. Opposition to naming in general, and especially to the particular names we have discussed, is rooted in the deep-seated need to feel worthwhile, to validate what and who we are. There is nothing so destabilizing to one's self, as an individual person or as a group, than being treated and regarded as something other than what one thinks of oneself. It implies a splitting of one's identity, the undermining of one's credibility, and the destruction of one's dignity. Names have the power to do this. To find out that one is regarded as what one thinks one is not, is shattering. No wonder many of us resist naming in general, or are opposed to some particular name which we think does this. Nevertheless, this is not the whole story. Names are important because they reveal our identity. This is the topic of the next chapter and a useful propaedeutic to the presentation of my thesis in chapter 3, where I argue not only that a name is useful for us, but it is also necessary in order to understand ourselves.

2

What's in a Name?

The Relation of Names to Identity and Ethnicity

In the Preface I said that this book is not strictly speaking philosophical. Nonetheless, in order to carry out the task before us effectively, it is advisable that we use some philosophy. Its purpose is to clarify the pertinent issues and terminology, so that we do not miss important points simply because the language used is imprecise, or because the conceptual apparatus is inadequate or unclear. The topic of this chapter in particular requires a more technical approach. I begin, then, with a brief philosophical analysis of the problem of identity and at least three different forms it can take. Next, I turn to the relation between names and identity, for names are generally used to identify. Finally, I briefly take up the peculiarities of ethnic names. My overall thesis is that names serve to establish identity and, in particular, ethnic identity. This means that their use has important implications for ethnic identity and how ethnic groups are regarded and treated in society. Those readers who find this chapter hard going, or who are not especially interested in philosophical technicalities, should move directly to chapter 3; they will find the rest of the book more accessible.

1 The Problem of Identity

In spite of widespread use in common parlance, the term "identity" is erudite in origin. It is a transliteration of the Latin *identitas* (in turn a derivative of *idem*). The corresponding term of English (Old Norse) origin is "sameness" (in turn a derivative of "same"). For all intents and purposes, these terms are equivalent in meaning. To say that something is identical to something else and to say that something is the same as something else generally makes no difference.

The notion of identity is one of the most versatile in our everyday conceptual framework. We apply it to all sorts of things, such as colors, persons, times, spaces, relations, essences, experiences, events, and concepts. We speak of persons or their lives as being identical or as being of an identical type; we say that a daughter is identical to her father with respect to this or that characteristic; we refer to the use of identical concepts in thought; we agree that sometimes we have identical experiences; and we talk about being in identical places at the same time, being essentially identical, and witnessing identical events. Indeed, a very large number of examples could be given here to illustrate the usefulness and pervasiveness of this notion in everyday discourse, but for our purposes the examples provided should suffice.

The notion of identity is obviously related to the notion of similarity. Indeed, it is not unusual to find authors who use "identical" (or its rough synonym, "same") and "similar" interchangeably. This is so because in ordinary language we do use these terms interchangeably on some occasions. For example, we sometimes say that two red-colored objects have identical color, even though the shades of red in question might be different. In this sense, there is no difference between identity and similarity. But it is likewise true that we often entertain and use notions of identity and similarity which are different. Indeed, in the very example just used, we also say that the two red-colored objects are similar in color precisely because the particular shades of red they have are different.

Important distinctions can be made between the notions of identity and similarity. Perhaps the key distinction is that similarity occurs always in the context of difference. For two things to be similar, they must also be different in some respect, although the difference in question must refer to aspects other than those on which the similarity is based. Thus one may speak of two persons as being similar provided that they differ in some way. If they do not differ in any way, then they are regarded as identical, i.e. as the same person. The conditions of similarity of two things, say X and Y, may be expressed in the following way:

X is similar to Y, if and only if X and Y: (1) have at least one feature that is identical in both and (2) also have at least one feature that is not identical in both.

Features are understood very broadly in this formulation. They may include anything that may be said of a thing and thus not only qualities, but also relations, position, temporal location, states, actions, and so on. Now, in contrast with similarity, identity does not require – indeed it precludes – difference. This does not mean that two things could not be regarded as identical with respect to some feature or other and different with respect to something else. A daughter, for example, may be identical to her father with respect to hair color while being different with respect to personality. The point is, however, that for the daughter and the father to be identical with respect to hair color, their hair color must not involve any difference whatsoever. If there were some difference, so that one were, say, lighter than the other, one would more properly speak instead of a "similarity of hair color." We might express this understanding of the identity of two things, say X and Y, and the identity of their features in the following two propositions:

X is identical with Y, if and only if there is nothing that pertains to X that does not pertain to Y, and vice versa.

X is identical to Y, with respect to a particular feature, if and only if there is nothing that pertains to that particular feature in X that does not pertain to that particular feature in Y, and vice versa.

The first formula expresses what might be called *absolute identity*, because it applies to the whole entity in question; the second, what might be called *relative identity*, because it applies only to some feature(s) or aspect(s) of an entity.[1]

Part of the reason for the frequent blurring of the distinction between identity and similarity in English discourse is that a single term, "difference," is often used as the opposite of both, even though there exists another term that more properly expresses the opposite of similarity: "dissimilarity." Similar–different and identical–different are generally regarded as pairs of opposites in English. This usage does not necessarily extend to other languages, however. In the Middle Ages, for example, a concerted effort was made to keep the notions of similarity and identity separate, and this was supported by the use of two opposite terms for each. "Difference" (*differentia*) was used, at least in technical philosophical discourse, as the opposite of "similarity" (*similaritas*), whereas "diversity" (*diversitas*) was used as the opposite of "identity" (*identitas*).[2]

Now, of course, for identity to be significant it must presuppose non-identity. One presupposes the other, just as the other presupposes the one. The identity of something implies its non-identity with something else. These notions are interdependent in the same way that the notion of cat and the notion of non-cat are. Cat is significant as long as non-cat is, and vice versa. If in fact there were nothing that were not a cat, the very notion of cat would lack relevance. Identity is necessary to non-identity and the identity of something implies its non-identity with something else.

Not all identity about which we speak is of the same sort, however. There are at least three fundamental but distinct kinds of identity, which I shall respectively call *achronic, synchronic,* and *diachronic.* Achronic identity is identity irrespective of time, whereas synchronic identity and diachronic identity have to do with time. *Achronic identity* has no reference to time; *synchronic identity* applies at a particular time; and *diachronic identity* applies at two (or more) different times.

These three sorts of identity generate three different problems for those who wish to account for them. In the case of achronic identity, one needs to determine the necessary and sufficient conditions that make a thing identical irrespective of time. This is another way of saying that one needs to establish what makes a thing be the thing it is. For the achronic identity of President Clinton we need to establish the set of conditions, such as properties, relations, and so on, that make him to be President Clinton. I call this issue *the problem of identity* properly speaking.

Because time is not relevant to this inquiry, atemporal entities, such as numbers and matter, could be included in it, although the achronic identity of temporal entities may also be investigated. Indeed, this sort of investigation can be applied to anything that may become the subject of discourse. We may ask about the necessary and sufficient conditions of an individual person or a group of persons, but also of concepts, propositions, events, and so on.

Note that the conditions of achronic identity may include temporal conditions. This may be the case when the entities whose identity is being established are temporal in such a way that their identity is tied to their temporality. For example, one may want to argue that being born at a certain time is part of the identity conditions of an individual historical figure such as President Clinton. To say, however, that the identity conditions of President Clinton include temporal conditions does not entail that the question of his identity has to be framed in temporal terms. It is one thing to ask what makes President Clinton to be President Clinton, another to ask what makes President Clinton to be President Clinton at a particular time, and still another to ask what makes President Clinton to be President Clinton at two (or more) different times, even if the answers to these questions turn out to be the same. The conditions of X being X may include temporal conditions, but the question is not temporal. We can inquire into the conditions of the identity of President Clinton without referring to those conditions at any particular time. This is the difference between achronic identity, on the one hand, and synchronic and diachronic identity, on the other.

The case of synchronic identity is different from that of achronic identity insofar as what is sought in the former is to account for the necessary and sufficient conditions that make a thing be the thing it is at a particular time. What is it that makes President Clinton to be who he is on January 1, 1998? This difference is significant because it restricts the relevant kinds of things to temporal ones. It would make no sense to ask for an account of the identity of atemporal entities at a particular time. For example, questions concerning synchronic identity could not apply to mathematical entities, or even to God if God is conceived as being outside of time, as Augustine and many Christian theologians do. Apart from this significant difference, achronic and synchronic identity are similar because their analyses abstract from the *passage* of time; this abstraction is what distinguishes them both from diachronic identity.

In diachronic identity, what is at stake is the determination of the necessary and sufficient conditions that make a thing be identical at two (or more) different times. What is it that makes President Clinton the same on the day of his inauguration and today? Indeed, it is usual for philosophers to speak of the problem of accounting for diachronic identity as the problem of accounting for "identity through time" or as the problem of "temporal continuity."[3] Diachronic identity applies only to those entities to which temporal passage applies. It makes no sense to talk about the diachronic identity of instantaneous entities or atemporal ones.

In the present context we are dealing with a group of people: Hispanics/Latinos. This group is temporal not only insofar as it is located in time, or its individual members are located in time, but also insofar as the group and its members are subject to the passage of time. In general, the question that pertains to us concerns the necessary and sufficient conditions whereby the group is the group it is. Achronically, the question concerns what makes Hispanics/Latinos to be who we are irrespective of time, although this does not entail that temporal conditions, such as certain events which happened at particular times, or even temporality itself, that is, being subject to time or its passage, could not be used to answer this question. Just as, for example, being born on a certain date is part of the conditions of the achronic identity of President Clinton, so a certain temporal origin or event could in principle be part of the conditions of the achronic identity of Hispanics/Latinos.

Synchronically, on the other hand, the question concerns what makes Hispanics/Latinos to be who we are at a particular time, say today, or last January 1. And diachronically, the conditions that need to be identified are those that make Hispanics/Latinos to be identical at two (or more) different times. For example, what makes Hispanics/Latinos the same in 1550 and 1750, or in 1673 and 1842, or throughout history.

In principle, then, we could have three different questions with respect to Hispanic/Latino identity. One is atemporal: What makes us who we are? A second is temporal, but abstracts from the passage of time: What makes us who we are at time t (where t is replaced by any particular time one wants: now, last year, 200 years ago, etc.)? And a third both is temporal and takes into account the passage of time: What makes us who we are at time t^n and t^n+1? In all three cases what is sought are sets of conditions: necessary conditions without which we are not who we are; and sufficient conditions which distinguish us from all others. In principle the sets of conditions for achronic, synchronic, or diachronic identity could be different, and whether they are or not is part of the debate. Furthermore, from what was said earlier it follows that, if there is Hispanic/Latino identity, this very fact implies the identity of something other than Hispanics/Latinos and the non-identity of Hispanics/Latinos with it. What constitutes our identity is also presumably what sets us apart from others. Identity, then, is bound up with difference.

Another matter that should be mentioned at the outset concerns the distinction between the problem involved in accounting for identity and the problem involved in accounting for the discernibility of identity. The problem of identity, whether achronic, synchronic, or diachronic, is an ontological problem, a problem that has to do with what a thing is (whence the term "ontological," which means discourse about being) apart from the way we may think of it. Its solution, if such can be had, consists in the determination of the necessary and sufficient conditions of the identity of the thing in question. The problem of discernibility is an epistemological issue that involves the determination of the necessary and sufficient conditions of our knowledge (whence the term "epistemological," which means discourse about knowledge) of identity, whether achronic, synchronic, or diachronic.

The ontological question, then, involves an inquiry into the necessary and sufficient conditions of the identity of Hispanics/Latinos. The epistemological question involves an inquiry into the necessary and sufficient conditions for the identification of Hispanics/Latinos, that is, the conditions that enable a knower to identify Hispanics/Latinos. To keep these two questions separate and avoid unnecessary complications when answering them, I prefer to refer to the second issue as *the problem of identification*, rather than *the problem of identity*. Moreover, when the identification in question involves different times, that is, diachronic identity, then I refer to the search for its necessary and sufficient conditions as *the problem of reidentification*. For our present purposes, however, to adhere to these philosophical delicacies is not necessary, although it is always reassuring to preserve a certain background awareness of them.

2 Names and Identity

In ordinary discourse, we approach issues of identity and identification with questions like "Who am I?", "Who are you?", "Who is Perón?" When I am asked "Who are you?" the most frequent answer I give is: "Jorge Gracia." I answer by stating my proper name. But I could also say something like: "The son of Ignacio Gracia" or "the oldest member of the Department of Philosophy at the University at Buffalo who is a native speaker of Spanish." In the last two cases I give what philosophers call a definite description, that is, the kind of description that begins with the definite article and is supposed to apply only to the referent of the question. Likewise, when someone asks "Who is he?" or "Who is Perón?" the answers are usually given in terms of proper names or definite descriptions. Now, sometimes we also ask this kind of question of groups, and again the answer can take the form of some sort of name or definite description. "Who are they?" They are English, Papists, the people of the Book, or what have you. Or we might ask, "What are they?" And we answer: French people, the people of God, or the damned.

The case of reidentification is slightly different. In this case we usually ask something more concrete: "Is he Jorge Gracia?" "Are they the people of the Book?" That the question in this case contains the proper name or the definite description for what is wanted is a confirmation that someone at a particular time is the same at some other time, and this assumes identification or identity in the first place.

These questions and answers have to do with identity because they concern the conditions that make something whatever it is. What is it that makes me who I am? But they also have to do with identification because they involve the conditions that make us know what something is. What is it that makes me, or others, know who I am? These conditions are specified through the names and descriptions we use in answering these questions. Names and descriptions, therefore, are rather important; they appear to tell us something fundamental about the things we name with them; they make explicit what make us who we are. It is in fact unfortunate that our individual proper names are given to us at birth and that we have no choice in the matter, for certain proper names can be heavy burdens to their bearers. Consider the case of one of my grand aunts. Our family name, Gracia, means grace. This person was given the name of Soila Pura, so that her full name was Soila Pura Gracia. Any one who knows Spanish gets the pun. When pronounced, "Soila Pura Gracia" sounds like "Soy la pura gracia," which means "I am pure grace." I remember my father telling me when I was small and I was vexed because something went against my wishes: "Keep in mind that things could be a lot worse. You could have a name like that of your grand aunt!" At first I did not quite get his meaning, but later it dawned on me that this lady must have suffered a lot during her lifetime because of the whims of my great grandparents. Obviously, one of the most serious consequences of her name was that she was never taken very seriously. Imagine her being introduced to an audience she was supposed to address. The audience would break into giggles at the mention of her name, and that would be the end of the matter.

A popular view among our contemporaries concerning names, however, holds just the opposite of what I have been illustrating: names do not tell us anything about the things that we name with them. Names do not convey information; they are mere indicators. A name is like the pointing of a finger. When I point, I call attention to something, but I am not saying anything about the thing to which I point.

Names are of two basic sorts: common and proper. Common names are names that apply to more than one thing and they are supposed to indicate common properties or relations of the things to which they apply. Some of these properties or relations are instantiated only by individuals which can exist by themselves. "Cat," "tree," "human," and "woman" are of this sort because cats, trees, humans, and women exist by themselves. Other properties or relations can be instantiated by individuals which do not exist by themselves. "Strong," "red," and "virtuous" indicate properties which are not instantiated by individuals which can exist by themselves, because this or that red, or this or that strength, do not exist by themselves, but rather in this or that thing which is red or strong.

Proper names, on the contrary, are supposed to apply only to one thing and the thing in question is usually a person, an animal, or a likeness of these; these names are called proper because they belong to someone. "Jehova," "Rigoberta Menchú," "Hernán Cortés," and "Chichi" are all proper names. The first applies to the Judeo-Christian God, the second and third to individual persons, and the fourth to my late cat. Of course, some proper names, like "Mary" or "Patrick," apply to more than one person, but this is just a coincidence, in part the result of the lack of linguistic imagination we have. In any case, proper names, unlike common ones, do not indicate anything common between things.

Those who have developed the view that names tell us nothing about the things they name take their cue from proper names. They express their theory in terms of the notions of denotation (or reference) and connotation (or sense). Connotation is the set of properties a named thing has. Denotation, on the other hand, is the thing or things named. Their view is that a proper name, like "Perón" for example, does not connote, but only denotes.[4] If the proper name "Perón" had connotation, the connotation would consist of the properties that characterize Perón, such as, for example, that he was Argentinian and the husband of Evita, had an aquiline nose, was president of Argentina, etc. The denotation of "Perón," by contrast, is the individual we call Perón. A proper name like "Perón," according to this view, does not really tell us anything about Perón; it merely singles Perón out.

There are some very good reasons why this theory is proposed, but perhaps the most convincing of them has to do with identity through time, that is, diachronic identity. The individuals to whom we give proper names do not have fixed properties throughout their existence and, yet, the names we give them continue to single them out effectively through time. I was baptized Jorge and I continue to use this name even though, fortunately for my friends and for myself, I have since that time learned to control certain biological urges which I did not know how to control at the time the name was given to me. This is all very well, but it does suggest a difficulty. If names do not have connotation and there are no properties in the things they name throughout their existence, how is it that we identify those things as being the same throughout their existence? There are ways of doing this, namely by arguing that proper names have both denotation and connotation, but it is not easy.[5] This is the reason why many have given up on the attempt.

For our present purposes, it is important that what has been said concerning proper names has also been applied to common names, like "cat" or "dog." In this case, the theory holds that common names function like proper names and, therefore, have no connotation because the properties that the named things have can and often do change. Indeed, those who favor this view argue that there is no way to fix the properties of anything, for there are no such things as essences, that is, sets of properties which always belong to certain kinds of things. Things change, and yet we can still refer to them with the names we have given them, which means that the names in question are not necessarily related to any particular set of properties. Tigers do not have to have stripes – we could always find one that does not – and dogs do not necessarily have the capacity to bark – aren't there in fact some dogs that cannot bark?[6]

All this sounds quite reasonable, and yet we do learn names through descriptions of some kind and, when we use them, we do think about certain properties of the objects we name with them. Moreover, in answering questions of identity, we frequently and effectively exchange names and descriptions. When I ask "Who is he?" the answer can be either "Perón" or "The husband of Evita." So it appears as if the proper name is equivalent to the description. Indeed, when someone mentions Perón to me, I immediately think of Evita's husband, because that is the person I associate with the name, and I also think of some properties I have been told Perón had, such as being Argentinian, president of Argentina, and aquiline-nosed. Of course, it may turn out that the person who mentioned Perón to me was a disgruntled Peronist and was thinking of her dog. But, in that case, it eventually becomes clear in the conversation that the individuals about whom we are speaking are different, that is, that they do not fit the same description. True, at first this might not be so obvious. I might say that I have a great admiration for the wisdom of Perón and the fact he generally got what he wanted, which my interlocutor, knowing my *modus operandi*, might take as an ironic reference to her dog. But eventually she will come to see I am talking about a different individual altogether. When I remark that I particularly admire the way Perón managed to return to Argentina as president after having stolen millions from the treasury, the point will get across.

Moreover, if I want to let my students know the person to whom I refer when I use the name "Socrates" in class, I have to use some kind of description. It would not do to keep repeating the name, and since I cannot use my index finger to point him out, because he is dead and gone, I can only describe the properties that make possible for us to distinguish him from other things. These properties, some argue, make up the connotation of the name.[7]

When we come to common names, this matter seems more obvious. These names are always translatable into other common names with which we appear to describe the properties that characterize the things about which we are speaking. Take any common name we use, such as "cruelty." The use of this term is associated with certain types of behavior and not with others. Torture is described as a kind of cruelty, but the act of helping a blind person cross the street is certainly not.

This is why we have dictionaries, where words are defined and their proper uses are outlined. Dictionaries tell us about the properties associated with the things in connection with which we use the names in question.

What I have said so far does not necessarily go against the theory that names, whether proper or common, are never associated with necessary sets of properties that are found in the things that we name through them. One can hold that names function effectively even when there is no such necessary set of properties. This is possible because there is always a set of properties, even if composed of different ones, to which those who use the name can appeal in order to communicate. Users of the name learn to use it based on a set of properties, although not all those who learn to use the name have the same properties in mind when they learn to use it.[8] As long as there is always something in common between what the speakers who use a name think at a particular time, and something common between what they think and what other speakers think, there is no problem about the use.

Consider the following case. Say that Isabelita thought of Perón both as the husband of Evita and as the president of Argentina; that Evita thought of Perón both as her husband and a general in the Argentinian army; and that I think of Perón both as the husband of Evita and the husband of Isabelita. It is quite obvious that the properties that Isabelita and I attribute to Perón are different. Yet Isabelita and Evita can claim that they are talking about the same individual, and Evita and I can claim that we are also talking about the same individual; and even Isabelita, Evita, and I can claim that we are talking about the same individual. And this, although when I think of Perón, I think of nothing Isabelita thinks about. The key is Evita, for she functions as a bridge between Isabelita and me.

In short, a name tells us something, and because of it a name can be a dangerous thing. A name is a message to others; it is what we want the world to think. A name is a tag we put on things; it can be a badge of honor or a mark of shame. Think about a medal; consider the scarlet letter. Both have a function: to identify and to tell. As Harold Isaacs points out, "Names seem to be the simplest, most literal, and most obvious of all symbols of identity."[9] Names are about telling and, even more, they are about thinking. For every time we try to catch ourselves thinking, we find ourselves using names. No wonder the Bible attributes the task of naming to the first human being. One might think it is quite surprising that it does not attribute this task to God, for there appears to be something truly divine in this business of naming.

Names serve to carve out the world because they are accompanied by concepts, that is, the ways we think about things and the properties we attribute to them. Concepts are windows to the world. Picture the world as a field in which we find ourselves. The field is so vast that in order to grasp it we must ignore this and that aspect, otherwise we cannot take in the whole of it. We must ignore details in order to see the entire composition. If we look at this vast field through a window, however, we see both more and less. Here, all of a sudden, there is a manageable area that we can examine; we can concentrate on the details without the almost infinite distractions of an encompassing view. We see the bird singing on a branch of a tree we had missed before, when we were in the field, overcome by the immensity of the view. There was so much else to see there that we had to concentrate on larger items to the detriment of smaller ones. A large view requires broad principles; a small view can be organized in terms of more limited parameters.

Concepts are windows that allow us to view particular aspects of a large panorama. And, because a name is the tag for a concept, it allows us to handle the world. Names are powerful instruments and some philosophers have gone so far as to hold that they are all there is.[10] There is much in a name and, therefore, it is important to choose the names we use carefully. It is even more important when we are talking about naming ourselves or when the name applies to a group of persons. Indeed, sociologists and social psychologists have found that different group labels make a difference when it comes to the attitudes and responses of those who use them.[11]

3 Ethnic Names

Many kinds of names are used to talk about groups of persons. Indeed, every common name applied to persons can in principle serve to name a group, namely, the set of persons of whom the name is predicated. "Strong" can be used to talk about the group of all strong persons; "just" for the group of all just persons; "Roman Catholic" for the group of all those who belong to the Roman Catholic Church; "philosopher" for the group of all philosophers; and so on. For our purposes, however, only ethnic names are of interest.

Ethnic names are sometimes confused, as we shall see later, with racial, national, and regional names, but they should not be. Racial names, such as "Caucasian" (or the more common "White") and "Negroid" (or the more common "Black") indicate community in racial characteristics and these characteristics are most often conceived in physical terms. National names, like "British" and "Ecuadorean," indicate common political provenance. The British are citizens of Britain, a political unity, and Ecuadoreans are citizens of Ecuador, another political unity. And regional names, like "African," "Asian," and "European," are supposed to indicate geographical origin: Africans are from Africa, Asians from Asia, and Europeans from Europe. Ethnic names, on the other hand, do not refer to racial characteristics, political provenance, or regional origin. Terms like "Polish" or "Italian," when used to designate United States citizens, do not refer to a race, the political unity of which these persons are citizens, or the region in which they live. Of course, as these two examples indicate, often the same name is used both nationally and ethnically. "Polish" can be used to designate a citizen of Poland, in which case it is being used nationally, or it can be used to designate an American citizen, in which case it is being used ethnically. And sometimes the same name is used racially and ethnically. This is the case with "African" and "Hispanic."

Ethnic names, or ethnically used names, are very often believed to refer to common cultural traits, but this is incorrect. Something that seems quite clear, however, is that these names serve to identify, both in the epistemological sense of revealing and in the ontological sense of establishing, ethnic group identity.[12]

An interesting feature of ethnic names, or labels, as sociologists refer to them, is that they function as common and proper names. They function as common names because they apply to several individuals and are generally treated as if they referred to some common property or relation among the individuals. And they function as proper names because they apply to groups which are often treated as individuals, and the name is frequently given in a way similar to that in which a proper name is given. This means that much of what one can say about both common and proper names applies also to ethnic names.

A common view of ethnicity among sociologists in the United States is that it refers to certain traits associated with social groups of alien origin within a country.[13] Thus, for example, we can speak of ethnic Poles in Germany, ethnic Russians in Estonia, and ethnic Hispanics/ Latinos in the United States because they form identifiable social groups which have social features derived from countries and societies foreign to the countries where they live. The conditions of ethnicity, then, appear to include at least the following:

1 There must be a social group (individual persons by themselves are not ethnic unless they belong to an ethnic group).
2 The group must have distinct and identifiable cultural or social traits.
3 The cultural and social traits that distinguish the group must come from outside the country where the group resides.
4 Those traits must be considered alien to those accepted as mainstream in the country of residence.

Poles living in Germany are ethnic because they constitute a group with identifiable cultural and social traits distinct from those of German society, traceable to Poland, and thought by Germans to be foreign. Likewise, Hispanics/Latinos are ethnic in the United States because they form a group with identifiable cultural and social traits that are alien, and considered to be such by other Americans, to Anglo-American society and which arise from their ancestral homelands.

Of course, at least two of the four conditions of ethnicity mentioned, namely (2) and (4), can be easily challenged in the case of Hispanics/ Latinos in the United States. For many Hispanics/Latinos, their ancestral homeland is the territory where they actually reside, namely the American south-west, and it is questionable whether all Hispanics/ Latinos share common cultural or social traits. I will have more to say about this in the next chapter, but for the moment I only want to point out that the connection to a foreign ancestral homeland poses a serious problem. It does so not just for the reason given, but also because in a country like the United States, largely composed of immigrants, mainstream cultural traits also come from outside the country. Anglo-Saxon cultural traits are not native to the territory which constitutes the United States today.

These problems indicate that ethnicity must be understood differently. There is no reason one could not speak of an ethnicity that transcends political lines.[14] Why should Poles in Germany constitute an ethnic unity and Poles in Poland not? Why can't Poles in Germany and Poles in Poland be part of the same ethnic group? There is no reason to think of ethnicity solely within the context of a particular political unit. Indeed, there are problems of demarcation that arise and make such a restricted view of ethnicity unacceptable. What happens, for example, when an ethnic group becomes larger than the dominant group? Could not a situation like this turn the tables in such a way that the dominant group becomes ethnic and the large group non-ethnic? Or does ethnicity have to do with dominance and political and social power? There is also the question of what makes an ethnic group ethnic. If it is culture, which is the view of most of those who accept the conception of ethnicity under discussion, then how can one distinguish an ethnic group within a country from an ethnic group outside the country?

There are other difficulties that can be raised, but let me dispense with them and propose instead to distinguish between ethnic groups in national, regional, or global terms. Nationally we could speak of Poles in Germany as ethnic, but regionally (say in Europe) and globally (in the world) we may speak of Poles as forming also an ethnic unity. Likewise, we may speak of Hispanics/Latinos as forming an ethnic unity in the United States and also as forming an ethnic unity in the world, or in America. There is no particular reason why one must restrict the notion of ethnicity to the context of a nation, a region, or the world. Of course, sometimes it is convenient to distinguish Poles in Germany from Poles in Poland. And one way of doing it is to speak of ethnic Poles (in Germany) and just Poles (in Poland). But this is confusing because it unduly restricts the notion of ethnicity. It is much better to speak rather of Poles in Germany and Poles in Poland. In all cases, it is important to be clear about the context. For present purposes, I shall use the more globally encompassing context.

4 Conclusion

In this chapter I have distinguished, first, between identity – which precludes difference – and similarity – which requires difference. Second, I have distinguished between three kinds of identity: achronic (apart from time), synchronic (at a particular time), and diachronic (at two or more times). These distinctions will help us formulate more precisely the question of Hispanic/Latino identity.

I have also claimed that names matter because they tell us something about the identity of those they name; they stand for concepts which shape the way we think about the world. The use of ethnic names in particular has important implications for ethnic identity and how ethnic groups are regarded and treated in society. Finally, I argue that ethnicity does not have to be restricted to national boundaries; we can also speak of regional and global ethnic groups. This does not tell us, however, how ethnicity is to be conceived and particularly, how Hispanic/Latino ethnicity is to be understood. This is the task of the next chapter.

3

What Makes Us Who We Are?

The Key to Our Unity in Diversity

After all that was said in chapter 1, it would appear impossible to argue in favor of a name, let alone a common identity for us. Yet this is precisely what I am going to do in this chapter. First, I am going to propose the use of one of the two names we found objectionable, namely, "Hispanics." Second, I am going to argue that, in spite of the many differences that separate Hispanics, we have a common identity of a familial, historical sort, although this identity is not based on common properties.

1 Identity and the Need for Ethnic Names

In chapter 1 we examined what appeared to be very powerful objections not only against the use of "Hispanic" and "Latino/a," but also against the use of any ethnic name. The arguments in question were not against the use of any name, for certainly we cannot do away with all common and proper names. We cannot dispense with all common names because we can utter no meaningful sentence which does not have in it at least one common name in the form of a noun, an adjective, or a verb. And we cannot do away with all proper names because they are one of the means whereby we anchor our discourse in the world.[1] If all our thoughts were expressed in sentences which contained nothing but common names, we could not tie what we say to anything in concrete experience. The arguments given earlier, then, concerned only ethnic names.

Four different types of objections were raised against the use of ethnic names for Hispanics/Latinos, but their general thrust was the same: ethnic names are inaccurate and dangerous. One way to answer these objections, then, albeit indirectly, is to show that at least one of these names is neither inaccurate nor dangerous. This seems to be an effective and economical way to proceed, and I have adopted it in the body of this chapter. The features which make the use of ethnic names inaccurate and dangerous are that they supposedly homogenize what is not homogeneous and imply common characteristics when there are none. The view I present here avoids both homogenization and the false identification of common characteristics. This in turn should help avoid the dangers of oppression, domination, discrimination, marginalization, and the inequitable distribution of resources.

This way of proceeding is quite specific insofar as it deals with particular objections and proposes a way to understand the notion of Hispanic. There are also general considerations which argue in favor of the adoption of ethnic names by those named by them. Insofar as they tell us something about those they name, ethnic names both identify them and have the power to mold attitudes toward them. Epistemologically, they convey information about those they name; ontologically, they help establish their identity. These can be harmful to the degree that ethnic names are used to stereotype, objectify, and disempower. But they can also be beneficial when ethnic names are the source of knowledge and empowerment.

Whether the use of ethnic names is harmful or beneficial depends to a large extent on at least three factors: (1) those who do the naming and set the concomitantly required conditions; (2) the positive or negative character of those conditions; and (3) the breadth and rigidity with which the conditions are understood. Let us look at these in more detail.

The first factor is important because it is one thing to adopt a name to identify ourselves, and quite another to be named and have our identity defined by someone else. Note that I say "define" rather than "establish" or "discover." I do this because, for present purposes, I want to stay away from the controversy between social constructivists and nonconstructivists. The first argue that identities are the result of social construction; the latter, that they are the result of events outside the power of societies and, therefore, discovered rather than constructed. By using "define" I intend to separate myself from either one of these extreme positions. Indeed, my view is that group and ethnic identities are the result of both social construction and factors outside the power of societies.[2] Now, leaving aside this issue, the point that needs to be emphasized is that to adopt a name and define one's identity is both a sign of power and an act of empowerment. It is a sign of power because those without power do not even have the prerogative of doing it; others establish how they are to be called and who they are. In this, those without power are at the mercy of those who establish what is important or pertinent in them. This has serious consequences, for social perceptions change social realities. How one is perceived determines how one is treated, and this in turn eventually affects who one is. Social perception is a factor in social change. Our individual or group identity depends on others.

To adopt a name and define one's identity is, moreover, an act of empowerment because it limits the power of others to name and identify us. It tells others: Look, I am who I am, and not who you think or want me to be. I tell you who I am, and you have to honor this; you have no power to tell me who I am, only I have such power. Indeed, it is not surprising that Yahweh ("I am who I am") is the name God chose for himself in the Bible.

The second important factor in the adoption of ethnic names is the positive or negative character of the name and the conditions associated with the identity it defines. Obviously, a name whose connotations are negative can do much harm, whereas one with positive connotations can do much good. But keep in mind that the adoption or reassertion of names with bad connotations by groups who have suffered discrimination can be a sign of defiance and an act of empowerment when accompanied with an appropriate understanding of the name. This is, for example, what has happened with "Jew." Thirty years ago, this term carried with it all sorts of bad connotations among non-Jews, and for these reasons it was avoided by those opposed to anti-semitism, whether Jewish or not. Today, however, the use of the term has become a sign of power and pride.

The third important factor in the adoption of ethnic names is the rigidity and breadth with which the identity conditions they define are understood. Part of the reason that the adoption of an ethnic name is empowering is that it liberates those who adopt it from a relation of dependence with those who do, or may, impose other names on them.[3] Naming ourselves and defining our identity may also imply liberation insofar as it makes explicit prejudices that may hinder us from acting in various ways, opening the way to discard those prejudices and change the way we act. Knowing who we are can change not only the way others think about us, and even how we think about ourselves, but also the course of our actions in the future. But there is also a danger: A name and the identity conditions it implies can function as limiting factors and as sources of conflict if they are conceived too narrowly and restrictively. To be something may be taken as making it impossible to be something else. Recall the ancient Parmenidean conundrum: What is is, and what is not is not. If a group is conceived as having certain abilities and limitations, this may be used to close avenues of development and growth. For this reason, the value of an ethnic name and the conditions of identity it implies will depend on the breadth of those conditions and the rigidity with which they are understood.

In short, then, the use of ethnic names and the definition of the conditions of group identity can in principle be beneficial for the groups in question. It is generally beneficial if three conditions are met: if the naming and defining is done by the group; if the conditions used in the definition are positive; and if the conditions are neither narrow nor rigid. To this extent, the use of ethnic names and the corresponding self-identification are important insofar as they help establish self-meaning and direction.[4] Otherwise, the use of ethnic names and the definition of the conditions of the group's identity can do more harm than good. It is my claim in this chapter that the name I propose for Hispanics/Latinos and the way I conceive our identity are beneficial if measured by the requirements noted.

2 The Argument for Hispanic Identity

In order to support my thesis, I need to go back to an assumption that was behind the discussion of the previous chapters. According to this assumption, the effective use of a common name requires the identification of an essence, that is, a property or set of properties which characterizes the things called by the name. If there is no essence that can be identified, the name is meaningless, merely a sound without substance, and therefore must be abandoned lest it should cause confusion.

Joined to this is another assumption frequently made by those who discuss identity. This is that a proper identity corresponding to a name should involve both consistency and purity.[5] To have an identity requires properties which constitute a coherent whole and are themselves unmixed.

The view that the effective use of names requires a property, or a set of properties, that can be identified has been effectively challenged in contemporary philosophy. This does not mean that there are no names whose use is justified by an essence. It means only that not all names are of the same sort and, therefore, their use need not be justified in this way. Some names are such that they can be effectively used even when there is no property, or set of properties, they connote. Wittgenstein gave the example of "game."[6] This term is effectively used in English and yet, when we try to identify even one common property to all games that also distinguishes them from other things, we can never find it. Some games use balls, some do not; some games give pleasure, some do not; some games take a long time, some do not; some games require concentration, some do not; some games involve physical effort, some do not; and so on.

We can grant, then, that there are no common properties to all those people whom we wish to call Hispanics, and yet that does not mean that the use of the term is unjustified or meaningless. In general, my point is that there is a way to understand the concept of Hispanic that allows us to speak meaningfully of, and refer effectively to, Hispanics, even when the people named by it do not share any property in common at all times and places. More particularly, my thesis is that the concept of Hispanic should be understood historically, that is, as a concept that involves historical relations. Hispanics are the group of people comprised by the inhabitants of the countries of the Iberian peninsula after 1492 and what were to become the colonies of those countries after the encounter between Iberia and America took place, and by descendants of these people who live in other countries (e.g. the United States) but preserve some link to those people. It excludes the population of other countries in the world and the inhabitants of Iberia and Latin America before 1492 because, beginning in the year of the encounter, the Iberian countries and their colonies in America developed a web of historical connections which continues to this day and which separates these people from others.[7]

This group of people must be understood as forming a unit which goes beyond political, territorial, linguistic, cultural, racial, or genetic frontiers. It is not even necessary that the members of the group name themselves in any particular way or have a consciousness of their identity. Some of them may in fact consider themselves Hispanic and even have a consciousness of their identity as a group, but it is not necessary that all of them do. Knowledge does not determine being. What ties them together, and separates them from others, is history and the particular events of that history rather than the consciousness of that history; a unique web of changing historical relations supplies their unity.[8]

Obviously, historical relations tend to generate common properties, but such properties might not go beyond certain periods, regions, or subgroups of people. There can be unity without community. A may follow B, and B may follow C, and C may follow D, implying a connection between A and D even when A has nothing in common with D. Let me explain this further. Consider the case of A, B, C, and D. A has a relation (aRb) with B; B has a relation (bRc) with C; and C has a relation (cRd) with D. But there are no direct relations between A and C or D, or between B and D. (In order to simplify matters I assume that the relation between A and B is the same as the relation between B and A, and so on with the others.) Now, the mentioned relations allow us to group A, B, C, and D even though there is no property common to all of them, not even a relation that unites them directly. There is, however, a relation between A and B, another between B and C, and another between C and D. At the same time, these relations allow us to separate the group ABCD from other groups, say MNOP, because none of the members of ABCD has relations with the members of MNOP, or because the relations between A, B, C, and D are different from the relations between M, N, O, and P. To group implies to unite and separate, and to unite and separate are made easy when it is done in terms of properties common to all the members of a group, but it is not necessary that it be done on the basis of such properties. It can be done on the basis of properties or relations that are not common to all the members of the group as long as there are relations or properties that tie each member of the group with at least one other member of the group.

This is the kind of unity that I submit justifies the notion of Hispanic. We are speaking here of a group of people who have no common elements considered as a whole. Their unity is not a unity of commonality; it is a historical unity founded on relations. King John II of Portugal has nothing in common with me, but both of us are tied by a series of events that relate us and separate us from Queen Elizabeth II and Martin Luther King. There is no need to find properties common to all Hispanics in order to classify them as Hispanics. What ties us is the same kind of thing that ties the members of a family, as Wittgenstein would say.[9] There may not be any common properties to all of us, but nonetheless we belong to the same group because we are historically related, as a father is to a daughter, an aunt to a nephew, and grandparents to grandchildren. Wittgenstein's metaphor of family resemblance is particularly appropriate in this case, for the history of Hispanics is a history of a group of people, a community united by historical events. But the metaphor of the family must be taken broadly to avoid any understanding of it as requiring genetic ties. One does not need to be tied genetically to the other members of a family to be a member of the family. Indeed, the very foundation of a family, marriage, takes place between people who are added to a family through contract, not genesis. And in-laws become members of families indirectly, again not through genesis. This means that the very notion of resemblance used by Wittgenstein is misleading insofar as it appears to require a genetic connection which in fact is not required at all. It also means that any requirements of coherence and purity do not apply. Families are not coherent wholes composed of pure elements. They include contradictory elements and involve mixing. Indeed, contradiction and mixing seem to be of the essence, for a living unity is impossible without contradiction and heterogeneity.[10] We are related clusters of persons with different, and sometimes incompatible, characteristics, and purity of any kind is not one of our necessary conditions. This is why families are in a constant process of change and adaptation. My claim is that this is how we should understand ourselves as Hispanics.

Now, families are formed by marriages. So we are entitled to ask: Is there a point in history where our Hispanic family came to be? Since our community includes not only the inhabitants of the Iberian peninsula, but also those of the parts of America appropriated by Iberian countries, we must find a point in history when we came together, and this, I propose, is the encounter of Iberia and America. It makes no sense to speak of Hispanics before the encounter in 1492. Our family first came into being precisely because of the events which the encounter unleashed.

In spite of all that has been said, one can still question the need or advantage of using the category "Hispanic." If there are no common properties to all Hispanics, what can we get out of an account of Hispanics that is not already present in accounts of the countries and the peoples that are gathered under this category? In short, by using this term can we get to know anything that we do not already know through the study of, say, the Spanish, Catalan, Mexican, Argentinian, and Hispanic-American peoples? My answer to this question is that in this way we understand better a historical reality which otherwise would escape us.

The study of people involves the study of their relations, how they influence each other. In particular, a historical account must pay careful attention to the events and figures that played important roles in history, avoiding artificial divisions in the account. Keeping this in mind, I submit that the notion of Hispanic represents, better than any other, the people of the Iberian nations and of Latin American countries that were former Iberian colonies, as well as the descendants of these people who live elsewhere but maintain close ties to them, because it emphasizes the fact that there is a historical reality that unites us. To divide Hispanics in terms of political, territorial, racial, linguistic, ethnic, genetic, or cultural criteria results in the loss of many dimensions of this historical reality.

The concept of Hispanic allows us to see aspects of our reality that would otherwise be missed. They would be missed to a great extent because the conceptual frameworks used would be either too broad or too narrow to allow us to see them. Earlier I pointed out that concepts are windows to reality. The concept of Hispanic is indeed a window to the history of a chapter in universal human history, our history. In the vast panorama of humankind, it introduces a frame that directs the attention of the observer toward something that, under different conditions, would be given little attention, or missed altogether, because of the vastness of the view. Thanks to it, we see more of less. "Hispanic" opens for us a window to ourselves which yields knowledge we would otherwise not have. At the same time, it allows us to notice things which we would miss if we used narrower concepts such as

Mexican, Argentinian, Spanish, and so on. These are also windows, but like any window, they reveal something by excluding something else. By using these narrower categories, we would be losing a larger view. The use of "Hispanics," then, reveals something unique by narrowing and widening our view at the same time.

This does not mean that the use of the term should be exclusionary. To speak and think about Hispanics should not prevent us from speaking and thinking in other ways as well, that is, from using other principles of organization, and therefore from including the consideration of other unities. For these other organizations and unities will surely explain, emphasize, and reveal other facts which, under different arrangements, would go unnoticed. We need not look out only through one window. My point is that the perspective based on the notion I have proposed explains, emphasizes, and reveals aspects of our reality which would otherwise be neglected. I do not mean to exclude other arrangements. Indeed, there are many other enlightening ways of thinking about the reality comprised under the term "Hispanic." We could think in regional terms, such as Latin American, Iberian, Central American, and South American; in linguistic terms, such as Quechua, Castilian, and Basque; in political terms, such as Brazilian or Mexican; and so on. And all these would, if the notions are historically warranted, reveal to us aspects of the Hispanic reality which, under different conceptions, would be overlooked.

In short, my proposal is to adopt "Hispanic" to refer to us: the people of Iberia, Latin America, and some segments of the population in the United States, after 1492, and to the descendants of these peoples anywhere in the world as long as they preserve close ties to them. Moreover, I have argued that the use of this term does not imply that there are any properties common to all of us throughout history. Its use is justified rather by a web of concrete historical relations that ties us together, and simultaneously separates us from other peoples.

Note, moreover, that the use of "Hispanic" is not intended to reflect just that some persons choose to call themselves Hispanics. Applying a contemporary name theory to ethnic names, it is sometimes argued that self-naming (or self-identification, as it is often put) is both a necessary and sufficient condition of the appropriate use of an ethnic name.[11] If I choose to call myself Hispanic, others should call me so. But, in fact, self-naming is neither necessary nor sufficient in this way. It is not sufficient because the use of a name calls for a rationale of its use. There must be a reason why I choose to call myself Hispanic. And it is not necessary because, even if I do not choose to call myself Hispanic, it may be appropriate to call me so. Indeed, there are names we reject even though we deserve them. Not many criminals, for example, would be willing to call themselves criminals even though the epithet may be appropriate. The theory I have proposed does not face these objections for, although it does not accept that there are common properties to all Hispanics at all times and in all places, it allows for common properties at certain times and places arising from particular historical relations. My view, then, does not suffer from emptiness or circularity.

Now we must go back to the question of identity and see the implications of what has been said concerning the use and understanding of "Hispanic" for this question. Recall that identity and identification had to do with sets of necessary and sufficient conditions which could be understood achronically, synchronically, or diachronically. Achronically, the set of conditions in question would make explicit why something is whatever it is irrespective of time; synchronically, the set of conditions would reveal why something is whatever it is at a particular time; and diachronically, the set of conditions would specify what makes something whatever it is at two or more different times. The achronic identity of Hispanics, then, involves the properties which make Hispanics who we are, apart from any consideration of time; synchronic identity involves such properties at a particular time; and diachronic identity has to do with such properties at two (or more) different times.

The question is: Are there such conditions? Does it make sense to talk about an achronic Hispanic identity, a synchronic Hispanic identity, or a diachronic Hispanic identity? It should be clear that, achronically and strictly, it makes no sense to speak of any set of necessary and sufficient conditions which apply to all Hispanics, for as I have argued, Hispanics do not share any properties in common which they must have and which distinguish them from others. Nonetheless, it does make sense to speak of an achronic Hispanic identity in the sense mentioned earlier, based on historical, familial relations, rather than on relations of commonality.

Synchronically, again, the issue is not simple. There is no reason why, in principle, all Hispanics could not have some properties in common which tie them together and distinguish them from others at some particular time. But the reality appears different. For Hispanic ties, even at a particular time, tend to be familial and historical rather than across the board. Every Hispanic group is tied to some other Hispanic group, but no Hispanic group is tied to all other Hispanic groups in the same way.

Finally, diachronically, a similar phenomenon occurs. There are easily discernible resemblances among those we count as Hispanics at different times, but those resemblances tend to be historical and familial, rather than based on common properties. Throughout our history, Hispanics display the kind of unity characteristic of families rather than the unity characteristic of sets or classes based on shared properties.

In this, Hispanics appear to be different from Asians and Asian Americans, Africans and African Americans, and Amerindians and Native Americans. Asians are, like Hispanics, divided into many sub-groups – Koreans, Chinese, Japanese, Malaysians, and so on – but unlike Hispanics, these groups do not easily form a historical family in the way Hispanics do. Indeed, rather than one family, they appear to be clusters of families only occasionally related to each other. And the same can be said about Africans and Amerindians. Apart from superficial and controversial unifying factors, such as territory and race, Africans and Amerindians seem to constitute clusters of largely independent groups.

The situation of Hispanics is also different from the situation of Asian Americans, African Americans, and Native Americans. Asian Americans generally reflect the diversity of their origins and cultures without a strong historical tie to unite them. In this case, then, a common name is particularly artificial. The situation with African Americans is just the reverse. The Africans who were brought into the United States were as diverse as the Asians; they came from different parts of Africa, from different nations, and from different cultures. But here they were forced to homogenize. Culturally, they were beaten into a pulp to such an extent that some of their most idiosyncratic characteristics were obliterated, or nearly obliterated: their language, values, religion, and so on. The case of Native Americans resembles that of Asians, for this group is composed of subgroups which have very little to do with each other except in a remote origin. What do Seminoles, Mohicans, Apaches, and Pueblos have to do with each other? The lumping together of all these under the label "Native Americans" is just as artificial as the lumping of Vietnamese, Chinese, Koreans, and other groups who live in the United States, under the label "Asian Americans."

In contrast with Asian Americans and Native Americans, Hispanics have a historical tie that unites them and, in contrast with African Americans, they lack the homogenization that characterizes them to a large extent. History ties Hispanics together in a way that is missing in the cases of Asians, Asian Americans, Africans, Amerindians, and Native Americans. There is a sense in which Hispanics all over the world belong together that does not apply to Asians, Africans, and Amerindians. There are perhaps stronger physical ties between all Africans, including African Americans, and between all Asians, including Asian Americans, and between all Amerindians, including Native Americans, than between Hispanics, including Hispanic Americans. But there is a historical and familial element which is absent in Asians, Africans, and Amerindians which is strongly evident among all Hispanics.

3 Two Initial Objections

There are at least two serious objections to the view I have proposed that I must take up. The first attacks my view by arguing that it does not do justice to the fact that Hispanics are, indeed, different from other groups, and that this difference cannot be explained merely in terms of historical connections. Hispanics are different from the Chinese, the French, and certainly Anglo-Saxon Americans, so the argument goes. We can tell who is and who is not Hispanic and we are quite aware of the differences that separate us from other groups. A good explanation of these differences must refer to deep ways of thinking and acting. It will not do to argue, as I have done, that there are actually no properties that Hispanics have in common, for if this were the case, then it would not be possible, as it in fact is, to tell us apart from others. Of course, uncovering such common properties might be difficult, or even factually impossible at times, but that does not entail that such properties do not exist. That those which have been suggested thus far do not work does not entail that the task is logically impossible.

The answer to this objection is that I do not claim that there are no common properties to Hispanics and, therefore, that we can never in fact tell Hispanics apart from other groups. Rather, I have argued that there are no properties common to all Hispanics at all times and in all places that are discernible. This view does not prevent one from holding that there are properties common to some Hispanics at all times and in all places, at all times and in some places, or at some times and in all places; or properties common to all Hispanics at all times and in some places, or at some times and in all places. Nor can my position be construed as implying even that there are no common properties to Hispanics at all times and places. My point is only that there are no properties which can be shown to be common to all Hispanics at all times and in all places. Indeed, I believe there are properties common to Hispanics at some times and in some places and it is precisely such properties that serve to identify us at those times and in those places. At every time and in every period, some Hispanics have properties that tie them among themselves and distinguish them from other groups, but these properties do not necessarily extend beyond those times and places and, indeed, they do not need to extend beyond them to account for our identity and distinction from other groups.

At any particular time and place, there are familial relations that Hispanics share and which both distinguish us from non-Hispanics and are the source of properties which also can be used to distinguish us from non-Hispanics. Particular physical characteristics, cultural traits, language, and so on, can serve to distinguish Hispanics in certain contexts, although they cannot function as criteria of distinction and identification everywhere and at all times. In a place where all and only Hispanics speak Spanish, for example, the language can function as a sufficient criterion of Hispanic identification even if, in other places, it does not. Likewise, in a society or region where all and only Hispanics have a certain skin color, or a certain religion, and so on, these properties can be used to pick out Hispanics, even if elsewhere there are Hispanics who do not share these properties. Even though Hispanics do not constitute a homogeneous group, then, particular properties can be used to determine who counts as Hispanic in particular contexts. Hispanic identity does not entail a set of common properties which constitutes an essence, but this does not stand in the way of identification. We can determine who counts as Hispanic in context. Just as we generally and easily can tell a game from something that is not a game, we can tell a Hispanic from a non-Hispanic in most instances. But there will be, as with games, borderline cases and cases which overlap.

In the case of Hispanics in the United States in particular, there are added reasons that facilitate an answer to the question, Who counts as Hispanic? Two of these may be considered. First, we are treated as a homogeneous group by European Americans and African Americans; and second, even though Hispanics do not constitute a homogeneous group, we are easily contrasted with European and African Americans because we do not share many of the features commonly associated with these groups. Our identification in the United States, then, is not just possible, but relatively unproblematic.

This clarification of my position serves also to answer the second objection mentioned earlier. This objection argues that the criterion for Hispanic identity I have proposed is too weak because it could describe a situation in which only a single property is shared by any two individuals, and that would not be enough to set the group apart from other groups. Consider two groups of, say, six individuals each which we wish to distinguish from each other: Group 1 is composed of members A, B, C, D, E, and F. And group 2 is composed of members G, H, I, J, K, and L. Now, according to the view I have proposed, there would be nothing wrong with a situation in which each of the members of each group had only two properties. For the first group the properties would be as follows (in parentheses): A(*a, b*), B(*b, c*), C(*c, d*), D(*d, e*), E(*e, f*), and F(*f, g*). For the second group the properties would be as follows: G(*g, h*), H(*h, i*), I(*i, j*), J(*j, k*), K(*k, l*), and L(*l, m*). Now, the point to note is that the last member of the first group has one property in common with the first member of the second group. The significance of this fact is that this makes the break between the two groups arbitrary. That is, there is no more reason to end the first group with F and to begin the second group with G than to end the first group with B and begin the second group with C. True, the set of properties of the first group (*a, b, c, d, e, f,* and *g*) is different from the set of properties (*g, h, i, j, k,* and *l*) of the second. But the fact that there is at least one common property (*g*) between the first and the second group makes the break into the two groups arbitrary, for we could say that the first group, rather than being composed of A, B, C, D, E, and F, is composed of A, B, C, D, and E; and the second group, rather than being composed of G, H, I, J, K, and L, is composed of F,

G, H, I, J, K, and L. And, of course, other combinations and break-downs would also be possible.

The situation is even more serious when one considers that in reality the members of any group, and certainly the members of a group such as Hispanics, share not one, but more than one property with members of other groups that presumably we want to distinguish, as groups, from the group of Hispanics. In short, the view I have presented, so the objection goes, is too weak.

One way to answer this second objection is to modify the view I have proposed as follows. Instead of speaking of members of a group, each of which shares at least one property with at least one other member of the group, propose a set of properties several of which are shared by each member of the group. We could call this position the Common-Bundle View. Say that we identify a group with six members: A, B, C, D, E, and F. And let us propose a set of six properties also: a, b, c, d, e, and f. According to this view each member of the group would have several of these properties as, for instance: A (a, b), B(a, b, e, f), C(c, d, f), D(b, c, d, e, f), E(a, e), and F(b, e, f). The advantages of this answer should be obvious. Here we have a stronger position and one that can solve the weaknesses pointed out earlier. Clearly, now we have a tighter bond between the members of the group we want to distinguish, and we can also easily set the group apart from other groups by simply showing how individuals who are not members of the group do not have any, or a sufficient number, of the set of properties used to define the group.

Now let us apply the Common-Bundle View to Hispanics and say that there is a set of 12 properties several of which all Hispanics have (the selection presented here is purely arbitrary and should be given no significance): speaker of Iberian language, Iberian descent, born in Iberia, born in Latin America, Amerindian descent, African descent, citizen of Iberian country, citizen of Latin American country, resident in Iberian country, resident in Latin American country, Iberian sur-name, lover of Latin American music. Using this criterion, Juan de los Palostes qualifies as Hispanic because he is of Iberian descent, was born in Latin America, and speaks Spanish. His daughters also qualify because they speak Spanish, are of Iberian descent, have Spanish surnames, and love Latin music, although they were not born and do not reside in an Iberian or a Latin American country. And some children from Anglo-American fathers and Latin American mothers who do not speak Spanish and were born in the United States can also be considered Hispanic because of their partial Latin American descent and their love of Latin American music. At the same time we can distinguish this group from those who might have one of these properties, say that they speak an Iberian language or were born in Latin America, but do not have any other. Moreover, it would exclude, for example, children of Anglo-Saxon missionaries in Latin America and African Americans who have learned Portuguese in school.

Clearly, adopting the Common-Bundle View is a promising way of answering the objection against my original position, the Historical-Family View. And there is in fact no reason why it cannot be integrated into my view, except that, upon further reflection, there are problems with it. I see three difficulties in particular that make me hesitate. First, there is the problem of determining the particular set of properties we should identify as pertinent. How and on what bases do we decide on the set of properties which Hispanics share? Indeed, even in the rather innocuous list I provided as an illustration, there are some properties that are bound to create difficulties. For example, why should the child of Anglo-Saxon American missionaries who was born in Colombia, holds Colombian citizenship, and speaks some Spanish, not be considered Hispanic? And we might keep in mind the problems raised earlier concerning political, territorial, cultural, racial, and other such properties.

A second problem with this way of answering the objection that should also be obvious from the example is that, even if we were able to settle on a satisfactory list of properties some of which all Hispanics share, we have no easy way of determining the number of these properties required for someone to qualify as Hispanic. Two? Three? Four? Twenty? And does it make a difference which properties are involved? In the earlier example, does it make a difference whether we include love of Latin American music and Amerindian descent or not? Indeed, are two of some kinds of properties sufficient (e.g. lover of Latin American music and Amerindian descent), whereas of other kinds three or four are needed? Obviously, this complicates matters tremendously, and it is not clear on what basis a decision can be reached.

The third problem is still more vexing. It has to do with the fact that, even if we were able to settle on a set of properties and on the number that need to be shared, this could turn out to be of use only for the past and the present and not the future. We do not know what properties will be pertinent for Hispanic identity in the future. The set of properties which Hispanics share could change, and so could the proportion of properties necessary for qualification. After all, we are speaking of a historical reality, and historical realities are in a constant process of change. Our identity is flexible and subject to evolution and transformation.[12] We can easily illustrate this point with a reference to language. Suffice it to say that the English spoken in the Middle Ages would be unintelligible to an American today, and yet we still consider it to be English. So, whatever we think pertinent for Hispanic identity in the past and present could in time change. If tigers can be bred to lose their stripes, there is no reason why Hispanics could not become quite different than they are today or were in the past.

In short, the view we have been discussing as an answer to the second objection is simply too unhistorical and inflexible. There cannot be a fixed list of properties in which Hispanics share. There can be, of course, a list at any time, but the list must always remain open-ended. This is why it is still better to think in terms of history and family ties rather than in terms of a list of properties. Hispanics are part of a historical reality and, therefore, the criteria to identify them must take cognizance of that fact. Note that I began by allowing the possibility that in principle there could be such a list of properties even if we cannot identify it. Now, however, it should be clear that I am not willing to allow the possibility of such a list even in principle. This does not mean, however, that Hispanics cannot be identified as such in particular contexts. Even though there are no essential properties, there can be criteria in context. Consider, for example, that knowing how to swim is not an indication of being human. But in a place where only humans know how to swim and all humans know how to swim, knowing how to swim can function effectively as a criterion of being human.

4 Answers to the Objections Raised in Chapter 1

The view I have presented here takes care, I believe, of some of the objections against the use of "Hispanic" voiced in chapter 1, but it does not answer all the objections raised there. Indeed, it does not deal with the most serious objections that were presented against it: "Hispanic" is repugnant because of what Iberians, and particularly Spaniards, did to Amerindian populations, and it is particularly repugnant to Hispanic Americans from the south-west of the United States because it is the term used by an ethnocentric and racist group to distinguish itself from *mestizos* and Mexican Americans; "Hispanic" unfairly privileges Spanish, Iberian, and European elements to the detriment of Amerindian and African ones; "Hispanic" perpetuates or tends to perpetuate the submission of America to Europe, and particularly of Latin America to Spain; and, finally, "Hispanic" is a deprecatory term whose use serves only to degrade us in the eyes of others and to put obstacles in the way of our social acceptance and development.

These objections, although appearing very powerful prima facie, when examined more carefully reveal that they are based in part on misinformation, prejudice, and ignorance. Moreover, they result in the same sort of bias and discrimination they are aimed to prevent, although those who suffer such bias and discrimination are not the same people. Indeed, these objections presuppose the same totalizing and exclusionary principles against which they are formulated.

Consider, for example, that these objections reject "Hispanic" because they identify everything that is Hispanic with racial purity, Eurocentrism, exploitation, and oppression. But Hispania has been from the very beginning a place where Europe and other parts of the world meet. The Iberian peninsula is eminently *mestiza*, both racially and culturally. From its earliest history this piece of European land has been the place where Africa, Europe, and the Middle East have met and mingled in every possible way. Indeed, some have gone so far as to say that Spain is a part of Africa rather than Europe. It is a misconception to think of anything Hispanic as exclusively European or exclusively Caucasian, even if "Hispanic" is restricted to what is Iberian. A short trip through certain parts of Spain and Portugal should quickly disabuse anyone, who has eyes to see, from this prejudice. So much then for the connotation of racial purity or Eurocentrism. After 1492, it makes little sense to speak of Iberian purity, a culture separate and distinct from that of Latin America.

As far as the identification of "Hispanic" with oppression and exploitation, again this charge is partly based on both ignorance and prejudice. Mind you, I do not agree with the fallacious argument that we should not blame the conquistadors for the atrocities they committed because others did it too. This kind of reasoning is not only fallacious, but pernicious, even though it seems to carry quite a bit of weight in some quarters. My argument is rather that to blame all Iberians for the crimes of a few is as unjustified as saying that all Mexicans are lazy because a few are, that all Colombians are drug traffickers because a few are, or that no Cuban is serious because there are some who are not. These generalizations are false, and not only that, they are malicious and nefarious. But just as malicious and nefarious is the one that lumps all Iberians together into one group of monsters. Atrocities were committed in the encounter, but many of these atrocities were denounced from the very beginning by Iberians themselves. Indeed, the great names of Bartolomé de Las Casas, Juan de Zumárraga, and Vasco de Quiroga should be sufficient to show that not all Iberians were monsters and that many prominent ones took up the cause of the natives and the oppressed. Nor can it be said with impunity that even the Iberian governments were completely biased and generally silenced dissenters. The famous disputation between Las Casas and Sepúlveda shows that there was concern among some members of the Spanish government to do the right thing, or at least to provide a forum for dissenters.[13] Indeed, at a time when the world in general had little awareness of the rights of conquered and oppressed peoples, some laws were enacted in Spain and Portugal for the protection of Amerindians and of African slaves, indicating that at least some Iberians were concerned about their welfare.[14] Moreover, philosophers like Vitoria and Suárez openly and unambiguously tried to think through all the issues that the encounter with America brought up without considerations of profit or power.

So, no, not all Iberians are to be blamed and regarded as evil. Therefore, "Hispanics" need not denote only bad guys and connote only what was evil about some Iberians. Indeed, the selfless sacrifices of many who tried to mitigate the effects of what was, without a doubt, a tragic catastrophe of epic proportions, cannot, because of that, be ignored or disregarded. Most identities have been forged in blood, but it is not the blood alone that counts. Besides, there are countless cases, both in Latin America and the United States, where Iberians have been key players in the advancement of non-Iberian Hispanics. It makes no sense to demonize all Iberians because of the sins of some of them.

But this is not all, for what are we going to do with the many residents of the Iberian peninsula who had nothing to do with the conquest of America? What about the farmers, the members of the small bourgeoisie, the maids and servants? What about the Catalans, who, because of an agreement between Isabella and Ferdinand, were largely kept out of America? And what about the descendants of those people who now live in Spain or Portugal and never had anything to do with the conquest and colonization of America? Are they also to be rejected, repelled, and blamed? They are as Hispanic as the conquistadors and yet they have nothing to do with the atrocities committed by them. So why should "Hispanic" be rejected simply because of what some Iberians did between 1500 and 1900? We certainly do not change our last name every time a member of our family does something reprehensible. And few, if any, Americans today would reject the term "American" merely because some Americans committed atrocities against some segments of the American population at some point in the history of the United States.[15] There is something drastically wrong with judgments based on faulty logic, and the faulty logic in this case is the understanding of the connotation of a term based on properties which apply only to some of the members of the set the term names.

Moreover, why should "Hispanic" be associated only with Iberia, or even more narrowly, Spain or Castile? That Castilians appropriated the name for themselves because of their aggressive and imperialistic behavior, should not force others to surrender their rights to bear the name. I refuse to give up what is mine by right, even if others can be easily convinced to do so. I am Hispanic, but not Castilian or Spanish. I speak Castilian, not Spanish, but with a Cuban accent. And in being Hispanic I share with Catalans, Basques, Galicians, Portuguese, Andalucians, Mayans, Aztecs, Argentinians, Brazilians, and some Africans, among many others, a history which ties us together in a plurality of ways.

That certain ethnocentric and racist groups in the south-west of the United States appropriated the term "Hispanics" and used it to distance themselves from *mestizos* and Mexican Americans, out of racist concerns, and that other groups elsewhere also do so for similar reasons, should not be sufficient reason for us to acquiesce. First of all, ethnic and racial purity is a myth when it comes to Hispanics of any kind. We are not pure in any meaningful sense of the word. So it makes very little sense to use "Hispanic," or any other term for that matter, to indicate the purity of any of our groups. Second, if not absolute purity, but merely Spanish purity is involved, namely, pure unmixed Spanish ancestry, then "Hispanic" is the wrong term to use. The right term is "Spanish" or "of Spanish descent." "Hispanic" connotes mixture and derivation, as we saw in one of the other objections voiced earlier. "Hispanic" in this sense is like "Hellenistic," not like "Greek." Third, although there is considerable racism among Latin Americans, Iberians, and Hispanic Americans, this has never reached the levels it reached among Anglo-Saxons in the United States.[16] After all, it was after and because of the annexation of the Mexican south-west by the United States, and the immigration of Anglo Americans into the newly acquired territories, that an attempt was made by certain groups to distinguish themselves from *mestizos* and Mexicans, precisely because Anglo Americans made Mexican Americans feel inferior.[17]

As I said, there is considerable racism in Latin America. Generally, the darker one is, the worse one is. But there is not a great deal of favoritism towards Iberians either. Spaniards in particular are often regarded as uncouth, ignorant, provincial, and inflexible by Latin Americans. To be Spanish or Iberian is not a status symbol, but quite the contrary. Whiteness that comes from English, German, and French origins is more coveted, however. So we find the common custom of tacking some English, German, or French name from a distant ancestor to the Spanish last name in order to emphasize the non-Iberian, European connection. To have English, German, or French blood really counts.

Even more significant is that there is no distinction between Hispanics and *mestizos* in Latin America. Latin Americans have made distinctions between whites, blacks, indians, *mestizos*, *castizos*, mulattos, *criollos*, and various other labels at various times in history, but some of these terms are more cultural than racial, and to my knowledge the term *hispano* has never been used to distinguish upper-class pure descendants of Spaniards from *mestizos*, indians, blacks, or mulattos.[18] This phenomenon is American, and a result of Anglo-American racism.[19]

My thesis can also be used to answer the third objection, namely, that the use of "Hispanic" should help perpetuate a sense of cultural subservience in America toward Europe in general and Spain in particular. If the notion of Hispanic does not connote a particular set of properties, it cannot be argued that it necessarily connotes anything European or Spanish. True, some may understand it so, but this is inaccurate, and should not deter us from using a name which can otherwise be useful and whose justification is rooted in history. African

Americans should not cease to call themselves so because some, or even many, think "African" means racially or culturally inferior; Jews should not cease to call themselves so because some, or even many, associate that term with negative qualities; and we should not surrender "Hispanic" because some, or even many, mistakenly think it means Spanish.

This leads me to the last objection, that the use of "Hispanics" is counterproductive because it is associated with negative traits. Again, that some people put the wrong spin on certain terms should not make us avoid them if those terms reflect something historically important about us. Indeed, I am not sure that name changes are a good thing. Are we going to change our name every time someone decides to use it negatively? And is not something important lost every time a name is changed? Doesn't a name change often create unnecessary division and dissension in the community whose name is being changed?[20] Should we not rather concentrate on defending the historical bases of the term? A term like "Hispanics," which makes historical sense, should be kept even if some people choose to interpret it negatively. Rather than dropping it, we should wear it with a certain defiance and assertion; this will eventually do more for our image than a change of name. We need to change people's attitudes toward us rather than acquiesce to the rules of a game they impose on us; and a name can be an effective tool in this task.

This does not mean that the community to which I refer as Hispanics is here to stay forever, or that it is a closed community which allows no one to leave or enter it. We cannot deny the past. If we have been part of that community, we will always have been part of it – this should not need to be stated – but to be part of it, or to have been part of it, does not entail continuing being part of it in the future. And not to have been part of it in the past does not preclude the possibility of joining it in the future. Communities are fluid, open, forever changing; members come and go, enter and leave, as they forge new relations with others. I am no historicist. We are not trapped in our history, albeit history cannot be denied. Nor am I proposing a kind of neo-essentialism. There is no essence here; there is only a complex historical reality. Only a misguided sense of identity, based on notions of coherence and purity, leads to essentialistic conceptions of ethnicity.

5 Conclusion

In conclusion, the category "Hispanic" is useful to describe and understand ourselves. It also serves to describe much of what we produce and do, for this product and these actions are precisely the results of who we are, and we are in turn the result of our history. "Hispanic" is a term that serves a purpose today, and will continue to serve a purpose in the study of our past. It is possible, however, that at some future time it could cease to be useful for the description of a reality current at the time. The term is justified now because of a historical reality, that is, the relations among us; if those relations should diminish considerably or cease altogether, then the term could become obsolete. The extension of the term should not be understood to be hard and fast, for human relations are anything but that. There is constant regrouping, and our understanding of these relations requires the constant realignment of our conceptual framework. For the moment, however, there is use for "Hispanic."

The strength of the position I have presented here lies precisely in that it allows us to speak of a common identity to all Hispanic/Latinos without imposing a homogeneous conception of who or what we are. It is an open-ended, historically based conception of our identity which permits multiplicity and development. It recognizes our diversity; it respects our differences; it acknowledges our past; and it prevents totalizing, homogenizing attitudes that could be used to oppress and dominate all or some of us. It is meant to provide understanding in the recognition of both the strength and weakness of our ties.

Part of my task has been to do a bit of conceptual analysis to clear the way for a more precise understanding of a notion that I think can be used to refer to all of us. Moreover, I have tried to show how there are historical grounds for accepting my conclusions. My argument has been in fact, contrary to what some believe, that the use of "Hispanic," as I have understood it here, does not strip us of our historical identity, reduce us to imputed common traits, or imply our false homogenization. Indeed, I have argued just the reverse, for it is my position that the use of "Hispanic," rightly understood, helps us respect diversity, is faithful to our historical reality, and leaves the doors open to development in many directions. Moreover, the lack of a homogeneous conception should be sufficient to preclude oppressive and discriminatory uses of "Hispanic." My most powerful answer to the objection in chapter 1 against the use of "Hispanic," or any other ethnic name, to refer to us, is that "Hispanic" works by helping us understand the bases for the identity of our ethnic family.

Note also that I have stayed away from the political argument some use in support of a single name for all Hispanics in the American context. According to this argument, Hispanic Americans need a common name to strengthen our political clout. A large group has more muscle than a small one. The overarching notion of Hispanic (or Latino, for that matter) should make the rest of the United States take us seriously.

This is, indeed, a strong argument that has been routinely voiced by those who favor a single name for Hispanic Americans.[21] The problem with it is that it does not properly take into account the diverse character and needs of the various groups which are covered by the name. Politically, the name does not produce the right results and may in fact be counterproductive. Puerto Ricans do not have the same needs as Chicanos, or Argentinians as Venezuelans, for example. Whether we speak of international or national politics, the use of one name need not be a good thing if the proper emphasis on the diversity among Hispanic groups is not maintained. The justification for one name should not be based on politics, but on historical fact, and should recognize that a common name for all Hispanics does not arise from common properties or political needs, but from a historical reality which is founded on diversity and *mestizaje*. This leads us directly to the consideration of the origins of our identity explored in chapter 5.

Note that the objections raised against the use of "Hispanic" work also against some labels proposed by those who oppose it. Terms such as "Latin American" and "Latin America" are very problematic, and if this is the case, so is "Latino/a." Indeed, even more restrictive terms based on national origins, favored by some groups opposed to "Hispanic," are questionable. For the countries of Latin America, like other countries of the world, are to a large extent artificially created.[22] Even a brief trip through the territories of various Latin American countries should convince anyone who is not ideologically blind that in terms of identity other than political identity, these nations do not have much to do with many of the peoples who are considered part of them. This means that the use of terms based on national origins for Hispanic groups in the US is even more artificial, for most of these Americans are not politically related to these countries today. The case of recent immigrants is different, of course, but that does not change the situation for others. Keep in mind also that, historically, the territorial integrity of many of these countries has more to do with how Spain and Portugal divided and governed their empires in America than with the identity of the current or past inhabitants of those countries. This makes the use of terms of national origin for Hispanic Americans, by those who want to avoid anything Spanish or Iberian, particularly paradoxical.

Of course, the reason why some Hispanic Americans want to emphasize their ties to particular countries of Latin America is quite understandable. After all, repeated attempts have been made to strip them of their values, dignity, culture, language, political power, and social status. Naturally, they need to fight these attempts, and the idea of a country of origin, with a great past and potential for the future, appears to be just the right tool to counteract ethnic discrimination and racism. Just as African Americans find a source of strength in Africa, so Hispanics find it in Mexico, Brazil, or Peru. All this is very well, as long as it is based on a realistic understanding of the situation and is not used to encourage misguided nationalism, ethnic strife, and unrealistic expectations.

Considering that I do not favor the use of "Latino/a" to refer to Hispanics in general or to Hispanic Americans in particular, consistency would seem to require that I choose a term other than "Latin American" to refer to Hispanics who live in America but outside the United States. And, indeed, many of those who have written about this issue have pointed out that "Latin American" is inappropriate. The most appropriate term, if a term is necessary or desirable, would be "Ibero American."[23] The extension of this term encompasses the parts of America in which an Iberian element has played a role while excluding those in which France, Holland, and Britain have played roles. Still, the fact is that, in the English-speaking world, "Latin American" is generally used and "Ibero American" is practically unknown. For this reason, and in spite of the voiced objections against it, I have kept the term throughout this book.

Finally, let me point out two major positive advantages of the use of "Hispanic" and the conception of Hispanic identity I have proposed. First, they allow us to participate fully in the cultural diversity of Hispanics without losing our more particular identities. The diversity, variety, and mixture which characterize Hispanics are enormous. It is probably not an overstatement to say that Hispanics are more diverse and varied than any other group in the world. Think of African Hispanics, Catalans, Tarahumaras, and so many others who are part of our historical family. Indeed, think of Sephardic Jews, who, after centuries living outside Hispanic territories, are still closely tied in many ways to the rest of us. Conceiving our identity in the terms I have outlined helps us understand this phenomenon, and allows us to share in each other's cultural riches: Paraca cloth, Maya architecture, African rhythms, Spanish literature, and Portuguese pottery, to name a few examples.

The second major advantage of the conception of Hispanic identity I have proposed is that it is not hegemonic; it does not rule out other identities, for it does not conceive Hispanics as sharing a set of properties which actually conflict, or can potentially conflict, with other properties shared by members of Hispanic subgroups. This conception of who we are is open and pluralistic, allowing the coexistence of other, multiple, and variegated identities.[24] Its social and political implications are substantial then, for this way of conceiving Hispanic identity undermines intolerance and any totalizing and hegemonic attempts at imposing on others narrow conceptions of who we are.

4

An Illustration: Hispanic Philosophy

The use of the term "Hispanics" is advantageous across the board. It makes sense when we speak about culture as well as history. The histories of Iberians, Latin Americans, and Hispanic Americans are tied in significant ways since 1492, but our peoples are also tied in other ways, in art, traditions, attitudes, values, and so on. In literature, of course, it makes sense to speak about a Hispanic literature, for the linguistic, stylistic, and thematic ties between Iberians, Latin Americans, and Hispanic Americans are very strong. It is the history of our thought, however, that can perhaps serve as the best illustration of the use and justification of "Hispanics." Thought is, in some ways, the most self-conscious expression of who we are and how we perceive ourselves and our reality. So an argument in favor of Hispanic philosophy is a powerful argument in favor of the more general use of the category "Hispanic" for all of us. Moreover, an explanation of the notion of Hispanic philosophy should serve further to clarify the notion of Hispanic in general, and to illustrate the thesis presented in the previous chapter.

1 Hispanic Philosophy

Studies of the philosophy of Spain, Portugal, Mexico, and other Latin American countries and their relation to world philosophy present large gaps. These gaps are, to a great extent, consequences of an attempt to view the history of philosophy in these countries as separate and largely unconnected developments. This is evident in the standard categorizations according to which the philosophical thought of these areas is divided and studied: Spanish philosophy, Portuguese philosophy, Catalan philosophy, Latin American philosophy, Spanish-American philosophy, Ibero-American philosophy, Argentinian philosophy, Mexican philosophy, Peruvian philosophy, and so on.

The category "Spanish philosophy" usually includes only the philosophy that has taken place in the territory occupied by the modern Spanish state, whether before or after the state was constituted in the sixteenth century. Most histories of Spanish philosophy discuss the thought of Roman, Islamic, and Jewish philosophers who worked in that territory, as well as of medieval and subsequent thinkers who did likewise. In some cases, these accounts concentrate on Castilian-speaking philosophers, and at other times they include those that spoke or wrote Catalan and Portuguese. They generally ignore, however, the work of Latin American authors and seldom explore the close ties of those authors to philosophers working in the Iberian peninsula.[1]

General histories of philosophy seldom, if ever, do justice to the historical relations between Iberian and Latin American philosophers, not to mention the philosophy of Latin America itself.[2] Indeed, it is particularly rare to find any reference to Latin American contributions to philosophy in histories other than histories of Latin American philosophy.[3] This becomes quite evident when one turns to particular periods of the history of philosophy, such as the sixteenth and seventeenth centuries. This period is studied under such labels as Renaissance Philosophy, Counter-Reformation Philosophy, Late Scholasticism, Late-Medieval Philosophy, Second Scholastic, and Silver-Age Scholasticism, to mention just the most frequently used labels. Some historians may want to argue that there is justification for this oversight in some cases. Indeed, one could argue that the impact of the Renaissance in Latin America came too late to be incorporated into a general history of the Renaissance, and also that the vector of influence went only one way, from Europe to Latin America, and not vice versa.[4] It is not true, however, that the impact of European Renaissance thought on Latin America came too late to be considered in histories of Renaissance thought; humanism influenced Latin American thought via Iberian thought beginning in the first half of the sixteenth century. Moreover, although it is true that Latin American humanism did not influence

European humanism, it does nonetheless present some interesting characteristics which should not be ignored in an overall history of Renaissance philosophy.[5] Moreover, just like histories and studies of Renaissance thought, histories of the Counter-Reformation, late Scholastic philosophy, and so on generally neglect Latin America, even though they do make reference to Iberian contributions to philosophy.[6]

The general neglect of Latin American thought outside Latin American countries makes no historical sense. It is particularly distressing to see the failure to take into account the close relations of the philosophy of Latin America and the countries of the Iberian peninsula even within studies produced in Latin America and the Iberian peninsula. Texts dislodged from the tradition which produced them are silent, and many of the texts produced by Latin American and Iberian philosophers are the product of close relations between Latin America and the Iberian peninsula. This is especially clear in the case of Latin American Scholastics, because their link to the thirteenth- and fourteenth-century authors they emulated was mediated by Iberian Scholastics. Alonso de la Vera Cruz (1504?–84) and Alfonso Briceño (1587?–1669?) cannot properly be understood when one does not take into account the work of Iberian Thomists and Scotists on whom they partly relied or through whom they approached the work of Thomas Aquinas (1225?–74) and Duns Scotus (1265?–1308).[7] Neither is the problem restricted to this period. The work of some Latin Americans in the twentieth century who looked to Nicolai Hartmann and Max Scheler as their intellectual mentors, for example, is incomprehensible unless one keeps in mind that they first learned about them through José Ortega y Gasset (1883–1955). Indeed, there is an Orteguean "color" to the Germanism of Samuel Ramos (1897–1959) and others who relied on Hartmann and Scheler for many of their ideas.[8] Although this color fades somewhat as Latin Americans learn German and become directly acquainted with German texts, it never quite disappears, for the patterns of interpretation and emphasis established at the beginning left discernible traces.[9]

The same can be said about studying Iberian philosophy apart from Latin American philosophy, for even in cases in which the *philosophy* of Latin America did not explicitly influence Iberian philosophers, the Latin American *reality* did. Consider the case of Iberian philosophers from the sixteenth century, like Francisco de Vitoria (1492/3–1546) Can we ignore the fact that much of what they thought about philo.

sophically was prompted by the new reality they confronted as a result of the encounter?[10] Did they not see that new reality through the eyes of those who lived in and traveled to the colonies? It was Latin Americans, whether adopted or native, who provided Iberian philosophers of the sixteenth century with many of the issues and themes they were to explore. Again, this need not be restricted to that age. The most distinguished group of Spanish philosophers in the twentieth century, the *transterrados* (fugitives from the Spanish Civil War), moved to Latin America. There, they not only exerted extraordinary influence on several generations of Latin American philosophers, but they themselves were influenced by Latin American thinkers and by the circumstances in which they lived.[11]

The use of the category "Hispanic philosophy" is helpful in focusing attention on historical relations and phenomena which are generally ignored in histories which use other categories and divisions. It should be made clear, however, that the use of this category does not imply that there is something peculiar, some idiosyncratic feature or features, which characterize such philosophy throughout its history.[12] As we shall see in chapter 5, much Spanish and Latin American thought of the last 100 years has devoted itself to the search for the unique features which characterize Spanish, Latin American, and national philosophies, distinguishing them from each other and from the philosophies of other countries and cultures. This effort, however, has been to a great extent fruitless, for it has been difficult to identify even one feature that can serve to characterize any of these philosophies, let alone what I refer to here as Hispanic philosophy. There are no doubt certain concerns, certain approaches, and certain methods in philosophy that characterize one or more periods of the history of Hispanic philosophy, a fact which is well established in numerous studies.[13] But there is no definitive evidence that indicates this may be true for all the philosophy that may be included under the epithet "Hispanic."

The category of Hispanic philosophy needs to be understood differently. Following the thesis I defended earlier, I propose to understand it as the philosophy produced by a group of philosophers who span diverse political, territorial, linguistic, ethnic, and racial boundaries, but who are closely tied historically. It is not language that unites these philosophers, for some of them write in Latin, whereas others write in Catalan, Spanish, or Portuguese. Nor do they come from the same country or geographical area. Some of them were born in Spain or Catalonia, but others were born in Portugal and the various Spanish and Portuguese colonies and countries of Latin America. Indeed, in many cases they taught and wrote in lands other than their native countries. Finally, they cannot be regarded as having the same ethnic or racial background, since their origins differ, some being European, others being descendants of Africans or Native Americans, and still others representing a mixture of various races and ethnic groups. What these philosophers have in common is not language, country, location, race, or ethnic background, but rather a history. It is the events of that history, the historical reality they share, that provides the unity which brings them together.

This is the kind of unity that Hispanic philosophy has. It is not a unity of common elements. Francisco Suárez (1548–1617) may not have anything in common with Francisco Romero (1891–1962) except for their given name, but both Suárez and Romero are tied by a series of events which places them together and separates them from Descartes, Hume, and Kant. It is not necessary, then, to find common characteristics for all Hispanic philosophers in order for them to be justifiably categorized as Hispanic. What unites them is the same sort of thing that unites a family. There may not be common features among all of them, but they belong together because they are all historically related in various ways. The notion of family is particularly useful here, for a history of philosophy is always the history of the philosophical thought of a community. Beginning in the sixteenth century, the Hispanic community comprises both the inhabitants of the Iberian peninsula and also those of Latin America.

Still, one may question the need for or benefit of using the category of Hispanic philosophy. One may object, first, that if there are no characteristics common to all Hispanic philosophers, what can an account of Hispanic philosophy add to accounts of periods or countries which more clearly have characteristics in common? What is to be gained from the study of Hispanic philosophy that we do not already get from the study of Spanish, Catalan, Portuguese, Mexican, Argentinian, and Latin American philosophy?

My answer to this objection is that we gain a greater understanding of the historical reality of a particular area of the history of philosophy, one which is otherwise missed. A history of philosophy is an account of how ideas developed and thus involves an account of how philosophers influenced each other. For an account to be historical, it must pay careful attention to the events and people which played roles in history, and avoid the introduction of artificial divisions between them. My claim is that the notion of a Hispanic philosophy more than any other notion reflects the historical reality of the philosophy produced in the Iberian countries and Latin America, for it recognizes that there are no fast boundaries among the philosophers of these countries. Consider Francisco Suárez, who was born in Spain but taught in Portugal for many years, and consider Antonio Rubio (1548–1615), who worked in Mexico but whose *Logic* became a textbook in Spain.[14] More recently, the example of Ortega y Gasset stands out, for his influence in Latin America was perhaps greater than in Spain.[15] These are just a few of the many examples that reveal the historical unity of Hispanic philosophy. To parcel out Hispanic philosophy into various compartments according to political, territorial, racial, or linguistic groups is to miss many of the historical ties making up the philosophy of the Iberian countries and Latin America.

A second objection against the use of "Hispanic philosophy" points out that it is misleading because it suggests that Latin American philosophy depended throughout its history on the thought of the Iberian peninsula, whereas in fact this is not so. Indeed, so the argument goes, after the colonial period Latin America turned toward France, Britain, and Germany for philosophical inspiration, ignoring what went on in the peninsula; so, it makes very little sense to use an epithet which emphasizes the ties between Latin American philosophy and Iberian thought.

In response, I must agree that, at least since around 1750, Latin America has been heavily influenced first by the thought of philosophers from France and Britain, and later by philosophers from Germany. But this does not militate against the notion of a Hispanic philosophy for two reasons. First, because the term "Hispanic philosophy" used here is not meant to convey a sense of philosophical dependence of Latin America on the peninsula. My point in using the term does not concern philosophical dependence, but historical relations in general. Indeed, the history of Hispanic thought shows that the vector of influence did not always go from Iberia to America, but often the other way around as well. We shall see later that there was a vector that went from Latin America to Iberia in the sixteenth century. But this did not stop in subsequent centuries. There are significant examples of this phenomenon in every age. Even in the second half of the nineteenth century we find a Cuban, José del Perojo (1852–1908), introducing neo-Kantianism in Spain and founding *Revista Contemporánea*. This journal contributed substantially to the modernization of Spanish philosophy at the time.

Second, it is not only in Latin America that the influence of France, Britain, and Germany has been felt, but also in the Iberian peninsula itself.[16] In this sense, there is much that looks the same in Latin America and in the Iberian peninsula. Much of the influence of the thought of French, British, and German authors, whether we Latin Americans like it or not, did come through Iberia. Ortega's introduction of German thought to Argentina and elsewhere and the influence of the *transterrados* in Mexico and other countries should suffice as illustrations.[17]

In short, the category of Hispanic philosophy is a useful one for the description and understanding of the past history of the philosophical thought of Latin America and the countries of the Iberian peninsula since 1492. Whether it will continue to be so is, of course, a matter to be determined by the future. For the present it serves well the purpose of those who wish to understand the thought of the world created by the European encounter with America.

2 The Beginning of Hispanic Philosophy

It is only after 1492 that it makes sense to speak of Hispanic philosophy, for two reasons. First, this was the first time that a new intellectual unity distinguishable from European philosophy was formed by the Iberian peninsula and its Latin American colonies. For the first time in history there was a political unity of the kingdoms of the Iberian peninsula and thus of the colonies of those kingdoms. There was also religious unity after the expulsion of the Muslims and the Jews. In addition, there was a strong sense of mission which permeates the activities and thinking at the time. This was the period in which the international medieval intellectual union, which had characterized Europe for over a thousand years, broke up under the stresses of humanism, the Reformation, and the political pressures exerted by modern European states. Moreover, Iberia, in spite of its strong political and ideological interests in Europe, gradually directed its attention toward the colonies of America, with both the extraordinary opportunities they made available, and the enormous demands those colonies exerted on the peninsula. Iberia, then, not only became unified in various ways, but at the same time became increasingly separated from the rest of Europe and closer to America. Indeed, we must keep in mind that, historically, the political unification of Spain was posterior to the encounter with America and, in many ways, may have been influenced and strengthened by it. And something similar could be said about Portugal. This new reality was reflected in the intellectual life of both the peninsula and the colonized territories and thus justified for the first time the category "Hispanic."

It makes no sense to employ this category in historical accounts of periods prior to 1492. The Roman philosophers of Iberian origin, such as Seneca, belonged culturally and intellectually to a unit that was centered elsewhere and extended well beyond Iberia. Likewise, Islamic philosophers of Iberian origin, such as Averroës, belonged to a world which gravitated toward a different axis. Something similar can be said of Maimonides and other Jewish philosopher–theologians of the medieval period, for their history grouped them in ways which had little to do with the Iberian peninsula. Likewise, medieval Scholastics from the peninsula were part of the greater unit represented by European Scholasticism. They were at home in that philosophy and their historical and intellectual relations were not so much with each other as with the common heritage of the age. Indeed, the agenda that moved them was centered primarily elsewhere, in Paris, Oxford, Cambridge, and Rome.

All this changed in the sixteenth century. Although the Iberian and Latin American philosophers of the time continued to address issues of general concern to Europeans and to be influenced by sources which originated outside the peninsula and Latin America, there was a strong surge of interest in problems and issues which arose from the historically unique situation posed by the encounter with and colonization and evangelization of America. Moreover, as a result of common interests among other factors, there was a tightening of the relations among philosophers of these various lands, who exchanged ideas and disputed among themselves in ways which were not common before. Indeed, recent studies show a strong predilection in some of the Hispanic authors of this period for their Hispanic contemporaries.[18]

This leads me to the second reason why this is the first historical period for which the description "Hispanic philosophy" is justified. The philosophy produced in the Iberian countries and their colonies after 1492, and before the colonies' independence, sprung forth to a great extent as a response of a well-established Iberian Scholastic tradition to the issues that confronted Iberian and Latin American intellectuals at the time, and that resulted from the encounter with and colonization of America. It was a philosophy, then, grounded in an Iberian tradition and in the consideration of issues and problems of which Iberian and Latin American philosophers had first-hand experience in most cases. This lends their philosophy an autochthonous character which is missing in most subsequent Iberian and Latin American thought. Indeed, many Iberian and Latin American philosophers have complained repeatedly about the derivative nature of more recent Iberian and Latin American philosophical thought. They charge, often with reason, that philosophical thought in these areas has resulted from uncritical borrowing from non-Hispanic, European, and Anglo-American sources, and thus lacks originality and authenticity.[19] The reasons for this lack of originality and authenticity are to be found precisely in the fact that Iberian and Latin American philosophers have forgotten their roots and that philosophy must begin in human experience. It does not pay to talk about what others say if we have no first-hand experience of what gave rise to what they say. This is, of course, what makes the sixteenth and early seventeenth centuries different. For the thinkers of that period were not only well-grounded historically in their intellectual traditions, but concerned themselves with what they knew best. That is why they can be accurately regarded as Hispanic philosophers and why they were able to excel to the degree they did.

The development of the kind of intellectual unity in the sixteenth century which I have used to justify the category of Hispanic philosophy can be understood if one considers the four challenges faced by the period in question: the encounter with America, the rise of Renaissance humanism, the spread of the Reformation, and the growth of skepticism. The encounter with America had a profound and lasting impact on the thinking of Europeans. For Iberians in particular, it posed a set of problems which were new and which required immediate solution. They were confronted with hitherto unknown peoples, with different cultures and religious beliefs, who nonetheless possessed enormous riches and who quickly became subject to them. What were the rights of these people? Should Christianity be imposed on them?

Should they be treated as slaves? Who was the rightful owner of the riches which hitherto had belonged to them? What should the conquerors make of the natives' laws and traditions? Questions such as these were raised and had to be answered. Issues ranged from international mercantile laws to the validity of pre-Columbian marriages.

Obviously, the encounter of America and Iberia represented an enormous challenge to intellectuals in the Iberian peninsula, forcing them to raise and deal with issues that they had not confronted before. This oriented their thinking toward new issues, away from traditionally traveled European topics. The impact of the encounter on philosophy was an awakening to the need to deal with legal and ethical issues which were new to the times and which tended both (1) to form a core of concerns which tied Iberian and Latin American thinkers together and, at the same time, (2) to distance them from their European counterparts who had other concerns and agendas.[20]

The other three challenges faced by Iberian and Latin American philosophers and theologians at this time similarly strengthened the ties among them and distanced them from the rest of Europe, supporting their historical interrelations and thus the development of a Hispanic philosophical universe. But this effect was accomplished differently, for the challenges of humanism, the Reformation, and skepticism did not facilitate the exploration of new themes that would draw Iberian and Latin American philosophers closer. Rather, these challenges alerted them to the need to come together in order to gather their forces and repel those whom most of them perceived as enemies. The need to defend what they considered to be the true Faith, to purge it from contamination by unorthodox or dangerous doctrines, and to vanquish those who threatened it, had the effect of drawing these philosophers together in a way which had not happened hitherto.[21]

The impact of humanism on the Iberian peninsula and its colonies was felt quite early. Although some Iberian and Latin American intellectuals were receptive to humanism, the movement was generally perceived by ecclesiastical and governmental authorities as a threat to the orthodox Faith.[22] The discovery of new literary, philosophical, and artistic works from the ancient world had given rise not only to a renewed interest in pagan ideas, but to a change of attitude in the intellectual community that was taken by many to pose a threat to the integrity of Christianity. Humanism was considered a threat, then, because it looked to pagan antiquity as an ideal era whose values had to be emulated. The Christian Middle Ages and Scholasticism in particular also looked to antiquity for enlightenment, but the attitude of the humanists was broader and less cautious. Scholastics borrowed from the past selectively, filtering what they borrowed through the sieve of Christian doctrine, and accepting only what they thought could be harmonized with that doctrine.[23] In spite of the mass borrowing that took place in the thirteenth century, a suspicious attitude concerning pagan antiquity was never absent, as the repeated condemnations of heretical and pagan doctrines illustrate.[24]

The humanists, by contrast, were attracted to the ancients and emulated less discriminatingly the forms and values of the period as displayed in art and literature. Their concern with beauty, the human body, ancient rites, literary style, and pagan religious ideas was a source of concern to ecclesiastical authorities. Although some humanists were devoted Christians and used their textual and linguistic skills for the service of the Faith, many were interested in the recovery of classical knowledge and art not for the sake of enriching the Christian faith, but for its own sake. This was certainly different from the attitude of medieval Scholastics and, moreover, appeared potentially dangerous to those in the Iberian peninsula and its colonies who wished to preserve the medieval worldview.[25]

Another challenge, the Reformation, had an effect on Iberian and Latin American philosophers and theologians similar to that of humanism. Indeed, it posed an even greater threat than humanism to the Church, for it was a challenge within the Church's own ranks and involved theology, the Church's conceptual foundation. Moreover, this rebellion against institutionalized Christianity gained considerable political support in some parts of Europe. There had been heretical challenges to the Church from within its ranks during the Middle Ages. Large revolts had occurred in southern France, as happened with the Albigensians, for example. There had also been serious threats to Christianity from without, primarily from Islam. But the Reformation was a different sort of movement for various reasons, three of which stand out. First, it was a challenge based on criticisms concerning the corruption prevalent at the papal court; second, it had strong political overtones, which lent it power in a way that some of the earlier reform movements had lacked; and third, it was a theological challenge arising from within the Church itself. These factors combined to make the

Reformation a most powerful threat and one that endangered the stability and future of the Church.

The final challenge which helped to draw Iberians and Latin Americans together is less defined than the others, but not for that reason less effective. This was the rise of skepticism. Skepticism had not been strong in the Middle Ages. It was known primarily secondhand through Augustine, who had argued against it in *Contra academicos* in particular. In fact, skepticism had a bad name among Scholastics, who used it to accuse and condemn their opponents.[26] Yet there were many Scholastics who adopted a skeptical or somewhat skeptical stance in order to defend those tenets of the Faith that they thought could not be defended if reason were held to be the ultimate arbiter of belief. Thus, there was a background to the skepticism that developed in the sixteenth century with authors like Montaigne which was to affect decisively the course of early modern philosophy. The skepticism of Montaigne, however, went far beyond that adopted by some Scholastics and did not aim to support the Faith. Montaigne's question, *Que sais-je?*, combined with a tolerance of what ecclesiastical authorities considered an easy morality, was regarded as an unwelcome development by those who considered themselves champions of the Christian faith.[27]

The response of the Church to humanism, the Reformation, and skepticism was swift. First, there was a movement toward reform led by members of the Church hierarchy which aimed to stamp out corruption and also to regularize Christian doctrine, rites, and laws. The most effective instruments used to achieve these aims were the Council of Trent (1545–63) and the Inquisition. The Council took care of doctrinal matters, whereas the Inquisition, originally established in the Middle Ages, was now charged with a new task, that of enforcing the new standards. Second, the movement of renewal affected also the rank-and-file members of the Church. Among grassroots efforts, the most successful was the foundation of the Society of Jesus by Ignatius of Loyola (1491–1556). This religious order became the symbol of reformed Roman Catholicism and one of the most effective instruments of the Counter-Reformation.

In the Iberian peninsula and the Iberian colonies the reaction of the ecclesiastical establishment to humanistic, Reformation, and skeptical ideas was also quick. Humanists, reformers, and skeptics were portrayed as mixtures of grammarians and heretics whose influence had to be eradicated.[28] This was achieved in various ways, including the exercise of strict controls on the publication and distribution of books and the general discouraging of book learning.[29]

The intellectual climate in which the Iberian thought of the sixteenth and seventeenth centuries flourished, therefore, was a defensive one. The Church was under siege and felt it had to fight its assailants. The result among Roman Catholic intellectuals was a great effort to rethink and defend traditional Christian theology. Hence, we find an abundance of literature dealing with doctrinal controversies cast both in apologetic and theological modes. Both modes are amply documented in the history of the Church prior to this time, but in the sixteenth and seventeenth centuries there was a renewed interest in them. Moreover, the polemical and defensive tone of some of these writings contrasts with the tone of many earlier Scholastics. The Iberian and Latin American thought of the period mirrors these characteristics. The effect of humanism, the Reformation, and skepticism in the sixteenth and seventeenth centuries, then, was to make Iberian and Latin American philosophers and theologians close ranks so that they might overcome these challenges to the established Church.

As noted, the attitude developed by the Roman Catholic Church in response to the challenges of humanism, the Reformation, and skepticism was not peculiar to the Iberian countries and their colonies. Its response extended to every place where the Church had a foothold: Italy, Germany, France, and so on. But the leadership of the Church's response fell largely to Iberians – to the government of the peninsula where arms were required, and to its philosophers and theologians where intellectual weapons were in order. Spain, in particular, became the military champion of the Roman Church in the religious wars in Europe, and its intellectuals became the Church's apologists. Latin Americans, of course, did not participate as actively in this affair, but their activities were regulated to a great extent by what was taking place in the peninsula, making them dependent and subsidiary to it. Nowhere is this more evident, for example, than in the controlling of reading materials allowed into the colonies. Although there have been some exaggerated claims concerning the control exercised by peninsular authorities over the circulation of books in America, it is evident that efforts were made in this direction, and thus to a certain extent the peninsula established the intellectual parameters within which intellectuals from Latin America were supposed to work.[30] This, naturally, tended to separate Latin America from intellectual developments occurring beyond the Pyrenees, and to tie it closely to peninsular concerns and news.

Apart from the four challenges discussed (namely, the encounter, humanism, the Reformation, and skepticism) there are two other factors that need to be mentioned because they also helped shape the course of Iberian and Latin American thought and thus the development of Hispanic philosophy. These two factors are the relatively late emergence of Iberian Scholasticism and the close relations between Church and State that developed in the Iberian peninsula.

The relatively late emergence of Iberian Scholasticism meant that this movement was influenced by well-established traditions associated with various religious orders. From the thirteenth century onwards, religious orders, particularly the powerful Franciscans and Dominicans, had appropriated certain ideas and authors, and they promoted them with extraordinary zeal. The Franciscans devoted themselves to the study and dissemination of the thought of Augustine (345–430) and John Duns Scotus, whereas the Dominicans worked under the spiritual tutelage of Thomas Aquinas and, through him, Aristotle. This commitment to a certain set of ideas and to certain authors became accentuated in some writers as time went on, lending the later Middle Ages an overall ideological tone. However, this feeling of partisanship decreased in the early sixteenth century, perhaps as a result of the influence of humanism and the overall rebellion against the excessive technicality that characterized the practice of philosophy in most European universities, and particularly in Paris, at the time.[31] Such partisanship quickly reasserted itself after the rise of the Jesuits and the subsequent growth of rivalry between them and the Dominicans.

The respect for well-established conceptual traditions, together with the large literature inherited from the thirteenth and fourteenth centuries, helped develop an encyclopedic attitude in which recovery and exposition became central to the Scholastic enterprise. Not that this attitude had been lacking in earlier stages of Scholasticism. From the very beginning, the Middle Ages displayed a concern with the recovery and preservation of the past. Thus we find throughout the period many encyclopedias of knowledge. The earliest successful attempts in this direction were the *De institutione divinarum litterarum* of Cassiodorus (477?–570?) and the *Etymologiae* of Isidore of Seville (d. 636). Both of these were indebted to earlier classical sources and were highly successful, the first owing to its elegant and easy style, and the second because of the mass of material it contained.[32] The effort continued with the *Speculum majus* of Vincent of Beauvais (1200?–64?) produced in the thirteenth century, *Lo Crestià*, undertaken by Francesc Eiximenis (1340–1409) at the end of the fourteenth century, and other works.

In the sixteenth and seventeenth centuries the encyclopedic emphasis on gathering all available information surrounding a topic became more pronounced. So much had been produced, and it was of such high quality, that it was natural for late Scholastics to feel they had to preserve it and at least take it into account in their own thinking. For this reason we find during the period much that is primarily expository, and many works whose character is informative. This attitude is displayed even in the work of the most original Iberian Scholastics, such as Francisco Suárez. In many ways, and in spite of their originality in many areas, Suárez's *Disputationes metaphysicae* (1597) constitute an encyclopedia of metaphysics in which every topic, every author of importance, and every relevant argument is carefully presented, examined, and evaluated.[33] Unfortunately, this emphasis on the past sometimes obscures the brilliant contributions of the period and has mistakenly led some historians to characterize it as sterile.

The second factor that played a major role in shaping the Hispanic thought of the period was the close relationship that developed between the Roman Church and the Iberian states, particularly the Spanish state. In the fifteenth century the Roman Church became the State Church in Spain, and the Pope granted the Spanish kings the right to appoint the highest members of the Church hierarchy in the country. This extraordinary development made Spain a *de facto* theocracy in which the interests of the State and the interests of the Church were inextricably connected.[34] It is easy to understand the reasons for this situation. First, Spain had become the main defender of the Faith against the threat of Islam. Having successfully expelled the Moors from Iberian soil after a 700-year struggle, Spain was in a favorable position to continue the defense of Christianity throughout the Mediterranean. Moreover, Spain was poised to become, and in fact did become, the first and most powerful European modern nation. Its kings, who also became emperors of the Holy Roman Empire for a time, controlled not only the Iberian peninsula but also territories in

Italy, France, the Netherlands, and Germany, and thus exercised extraordinary power.

Second, the Spanish struggle against Islam had been both national and religious; the Spanish kings had fought in the name of the Cross both for territory and the spread of Christianity. Therefore, it made sense to extend this political, military, and religious struggle against the reformers.

Third, Spain had recently encountered America and this provided an unusual opportunity for both colonization and missionary work. Since the Church had no means to organize the indoctrination of the newly discovered lands, it was natural that the Spanish Crown be entrusted with the task, strengthening once more the bonds that united Church and State in the peninsula.

Fourth, the preoccupation with the *Reconquista*, that is, the 700-year war against the Moorish invaders, had to some extent kept Spain away from the intellectual developments associated with the early Renaissance, making it an ideal base of operations for the defense against humanists, reformers, and skeptics. A militant faith was needed to defeat the challenges faced by the Church, and Spain certainly had such a faith. Spain had the faith, the power, and the means to conduct the struggle, and so it was to Spain that the task fell. Consequently, philosophical thought in the Iberian peninsula became subject to political influence and functioned in many instances as a tool of the Spanish government.

As a result of the two factors identified (late emergence of Scholasticism and close relations between Church and State), and the four challenges it faced (the encounter, humanism, the Reformation, and skepticism), the philosophy of this period in Iberia and its colonies developed close ties, which separated it from the rest of Europe and made it chart a course of its own, but it also developed some characteristic features which tended to distinguish it from prior and subsequent European thought. It was, for example, more encyclopedic, expository, and eclectic; it had a defensive, apologetic, and theological emphasis; it had the State and its power behind it and, consequently, was partly influenced by political considerations that affected the State; and it developed a set of new issues dealing with international law and human rights.

For our purposes, the most significant aspect of all this is the separation of Hispanic philosophy from the mainstream of European thought, for in spite of considerable popularity at the time, most of the Hispanic philosophers of this period have been largely forgotten. Suárez, Vitoria, Rubio, and many others were common names in the philosophical controversies of the time. Suárez's *Disputationes metaphysicae*, for example, was printed in more than 17 editions outside the Iberian peninsula between 1597 and 1636, whereas Descartes's *Meditations* appeared only nine times between 1641 and 1700.[35] Yet Descartes is considered a major figure in the history of philosophy, whereas Suárez is hardly known. Indeed, if we were to ask the more than 11,000 philosophers who teach in the United States today to tell us a few facts about Suárez, I am sure that no more than a couple of hundred would be able to do so. Yet Suárez is without a doubt the most important and well-known Hispanic philosopher of the period. Only a dozen American philosophers have ever heard of Briceño or Rubio.

We may ask, then, a final question: Why have these philosophers and the unity they comprise been forgotten? The answer is to be found in the very points I have been making concerning the development of Hispanic philosophy. For the reasons given, the philosophy of the Iberian peninsula and its Latin American colonies became increasingly isolated from European philosophy, thus losing the historical ties it had with it. Hispanic philosophy turned in upon itself, became concerned with the peculiar and pressing problems faced by Hispanic society and – fearing European developments that threatened its political and religious stability – it looked for support in the past. Thus it not only became isolated from mainstream philosophical developments in the West, but consciously rejected these developments in favor of its medieval foundations. The result was to be expected. European philosophy continued on its own way and came to regard the philosophy practiced in the Iberian peninsula and its colonies as marginal and regressive. For a while, the political and military power of Spain ensured that Iberian voices were taken seriously outside the peninsula, but the decline of Spain in political and military power in the seventeenth century contributed to the view of Iberian philosophy as stagnant and retrograde. This view slowly extended to all Hispanic philosophy and thought, leading to the general perception that there is little of importance to be found in it.[36] Thus were forgotten the original and extraordinary contributions to philosophy of the Hispanic authors of the sixteenth and seventeenth centuries.

3 Conclusion

In chapter 3 I argued that "Hispanic" is a useful term to refer to Iberians and Latin Americans from the sixteenth century onwards and also later to some members of the American community. This does not entail that there is anything all of us have in common; the unity we have is similar to the unity families have, the unity of historical, contingent relations. There are, then, no common properties which function as necessary and sufficient conditions for the achronic, synchronic, or even diachronic identity of all Hispanics, but there is a historical reality which unites us, and which is lost if we divide ourselves into groups and lose sight of the past that binds us.

The strength of my argument becomes clear when we look in particular at the history of our philosophy. Any account of our philosophical thought which does not consider it closely tied together from the sixteenth century to the present misses much that is important and fundamental. To speak of Spanish philosophy, Latin American philosophy, Mexican philosophy, Iberian philosophy, and so on, always omits something essential from the historical account of the philosophical thought which developed in Iberia and Latin America after 1492. This does not mean that these ways of organizing and looking at the history of our thought are necessarily inaccurate and must be abandoned. My point is only that they are incomplete and sometimes misleading, and that we need the category of Hispanic philosophy to complete the picture. The conceptual window that the notion of Hispanic philosophy opens for us is indispensable for seeing aspects of our thought which would otherwise be missed. But this concept, this window into history, does not entail, as some have tried to argue, that there is a set of properties common to Hispanic thought throughout history. Hispanic philosophy, just like Hispanics in general, constitutes rather a family united through changing historical relations. This is the key to understanding its identity.

5

Where Do We Come From?

Encounters, Inventions, and Mestizaje

Let us assume, as I have proposed, that we can speak meaningfully of Hispanics. Let us assume, furthermore, that by Hispanics we mean the community of persons who, since the end of the fifteenth century, has become a kind of family, not always, or necessarily, tied politically, racially, linguistically, culturally, genetically, or by class, but rather historically, by a web of relations that distinguishes it from other communities and explains some of the features which characterize it at various points in history. This is a community constituted by Iberians, Latin Americans, and Hispanic Americans. Even if all of this is granted, however, we still have an important question to answer: How did this community come about? After all, those who became members of it do not seem to have been particularly suited to form a community or wanted to do so, for that matter. Indeed, the majority of its members suffered greatly in the process, and joined the community only by force. The native population of America, and the Africans who were brought to America as slaves, became part of the Hispanic community only as a result of violence and exploitation. Nonetheless, here we are, tied by our history.

There are three other reasons why we should investigate our historical origins. First, in order to know ourselves and our present reality, we need to go back to our history not only because we are its product, but also because our identity is fundamentally historical.[1] Second, in order to liberate ourselves and open the doors to future change and development, we need to study the conditions that govern our present existence and put those conditions in context.[2] We must look back in order to look forward; our past horizon is part of our future horizon insofar as they meet in an intangible and ever moving present.

The third reason is also important, although more complex. I suspect that the desire of many subgroups of Hispanics to distinguish and separate themselves from other Hispanic subgroups, and sometimes even to disparage and discriminate against them, is motivated both by a misunderstanding of who we are as a group and who they are as a subgroup. They want separation for two reasons: they feel there is a conflict between their subgroup identity and the larger group's identity; and they hold on to the misguided belief that their subgroup is somehow pure in a racial or cultural sense. In both they are sadly mistaken. They are also misguided in that no genuine identity can be pulled out of a hat: we must recognize who we are, whether we like it or not. A healthy identity is one constructed on historical fact, not on ideological or psychological subterfuges. We must begin, then, by recognizing and accepting our racial and cultural heritage in all its historical complexity. And our reality, as Hispanics, is one of *mestizaje*, of mixing in every possible way. This is why any barriers between subgroups are largely artificial inventions, the product of ideology or nostalgia, and should not be used to discriminate against, or disparage, others. The lack of a proper recognition of our common identity forces us to choose sides, to identify with one or another, creating not only dissension, but also a sense of alienation and confusion in others and in ourselves.[3]

The beginning of our community is the moment in history which used to be known as the "discovery of America" and which is more appropriately called the "encounter between Europe and America." "Discovery" is a term justified only from a European point of view. Its use entails that somehow, although America existed before Columbus arrived on its shores, it was unknown. To discover is to uncover what was covered before, that is, to come to know what was there but still unknown. To speak of the discovery of America implies that the knowledge its inhabitants had of themselves and the places in which they lived does not count. And this is to say that these peoples were of no consequence, which is only justified from a Eurocentric point of view. "Encounter" is a much better term insofar as it appears to neutralize the European bias and to make both parts of the relation equal. "Discover" makes sense only insofar as it describes what Europeans thought had happened, not what actually happened.

Even the expression "the encounter between Europe and America," however, is not completely neutral, for the very name, "America," comes from Amerigo Vespucci, an Italian cartographer who made maps of America widely used at the time. "America," then, is European in origin, and was given by Europeans to the lands they thought they had discovered. Still, there is no other name we could use for the whole of what we know as America. Amerindians did not have a name for the whole of America.

Let me begin, then, with the Iberian peninsula, for it was the peninsula that initiated the encounter.

1 La Madre Patria

La madre patria is the name inhabitants of former Spanish colonies in America use to refer to Spain. It is an odd name. *Patria* comes from a Latin term that looks just like it and means exactly the same: fatherland. *La madre* means the mother, and added to *patria*, forms an expression which means the mother fatherland. Presumably, this allows the distinction of a fatherland, say Uruguay, from the mother fatherland, that is, Spain. Does this mean that there is also a father fatherland? If there is, I have never heard of it. But the idea behind this terminology is clear: there are daughters, *las patrias* or various fatherlands of Spanish America, and a single mother, *la madre patria*. But is there a *madre patria* for the whole of Latin America, not just for former Spanish colonies and their inhabitants?

If we look at the question from a political point of view, the only time in which one could speak of a single *madre patria* of Latin America was a relatively brief period in the sixteenth and seventeenth centuries when the whole Iberian peninsula was politically unified under the King of Spain. At all other times, *la madre patria* turns out to be at least two political units: Spain and Portugal. Moreover, at the time of Ferdinand and Isabella, when the encounter took place, Castile and Aragon had not yet become a single political unit. So in principle there could have been three *madres patrias*: Castile, Portugal, and Aragon. However, Aragon was in fact left out of this picture, for there was an agreement between Isabella and Ferdinand that America was the concern of Castile, whereas the Mediterranean was the concern of Aragon. Leaving this aside, however, we still have two *madres patrias*: one, the mother of Spanish America, and the other, of Portuguese America. But were there in fact only two?

Politically the answer is yes, with the qualifications which have been introduced. Culturally, however, Iberia was quite diverse. The Iberian peninsula was, and is, a conglomerate of very different peoples. When the Romans arrived on the peninsula they found many groups of peoples: Celts, Iberians, Basques, Phoenicians, Greeks, and Africans (Egyptians, Carthaginians, Berbers, and others) settled in various places and mixed in various ways. After the Romans came Vandals, Suebi, Visigoths, Moors, and Jews. Some of these groups were themselves products of mixing. Consider the Moors, for example. These were a mixture of Arabs, Syrians, Egyptians, Nubians, Berbers, and so on, who had been brought together under Islam. The Vandals seem to have gone through the peninsula in a relatively short time, leaving no discernible traces of their presence, but the Visigoths remained and established a kingdom which functioned effectively for a couple of centuries until the invasion of the Moors. The domination of parts of the peninsula by the Moors lasted more than 700 years, from 711 when Tariq crossed the strait that has been named after him, to 1492, when the last remnants of Moslem domination in Granada fell into the hands of the Catholic Kings. Many Jews remained even after their official expulsion in 1492, and so did many Moors after their expulsion in 1502.

During the Middle Ages the peninsula was divided into several political units which often reflected important cultural and linguistic differences. Catalans had the Kingdoms of Aragon and Valencia, the Principality of Barcelona, and the Balearic Islands.[4] Basques had the Kingdom of Navarre, which spanned both sides of the Pyrenees in the north-east. Castilians had the Kingdom of Castile in the north and center of the peninsula, creating a wedge between the other kingdoms which was progressively expanded at the expense of Moslem territory. The Portuguese had the Kingdom of Portugal in the north-west. And so on. The picture that one gets of Iberia at this time, then, is one of great cultural diversity, including linguistic and sometimes political diversity.

Political diversity had been drastically reduced by the time of the encounter, but cultural differences remained and are still very evident today. It is not just that Galicians, Catalans, Portuguese, Castilians, and Basques speak different languages; it is also that their outlooks on life and their customs are sometimes hardly compatible. There is not one place in the peninsula that can be considered a true melting pot of all the different peoples that comprise it. In Iberia, perhaps Madrid might be the exception, although most of the culturally different groups of the peninsula continue to be largely segregated and located in the areas where they have lived for centuries: Basques in the north-east, Catalans in the east and the Balearic Islands, Galicians in the north-west, Portuguese in the west, Andalucians in the south, and Castilians in the north and center. In this century, owing to increased mobility and the search for jobs, there has been considerable migration of these ethnic groups into other territories. Andalucians and Galicians have moved to industrialized cities like Barcelona and Bilbao in search of economic opportunities. Entrepreneurial Catalans have settled in non-Catalan areas for business reasons. And so on. Still, Iberia was, at the time of the encounter, and remains to this day, a collection of peoples who display varying degrees of cultural differences. Neither at the time of the encounter, nor today, is there one Iberia, or even one Spain. There are in fact many Iberias and many Spains, as a well-known expression confirms: *Por esas Españas.*

In 1492, in particular, it is even more difficult to speak of the Iberian peninsula as constituting any kind of unity, for there was not even political unity then. Ferdinand had succeeded in bringing under one rule political units which had at one time or another been independent of each other: the Principality of Barcelona and the Kingdoms of Aragon, Valencia, and the Balearic Islands. Isabella also reigned over areas that had not always been unified: Galicia, Castile, and Andalucía. But complete political unification did not take place until later, in the sixteenth century. There was, moreover, no territorial unity to speak of. There was a constant shifting of territorial boundaries within the peninsula, and politically, boundaries were extended beyond the Pyrenees, for example, to the area of Perpignan. In terms of culture, matters were even more confusing.

For these reasons it makes no sense to speak of Iberia, or even Spain, as a unit before the sixteenth century. The only period of history before the encounter for which one could argue that there was some unity centered in the peninsula was during the Visigothic domination (*ca.* 560–711). But this can hardly qualify as anything but a passing phase for several reasons. First, the Visigoths ruled over a relatively large territory, but the peoples over whom they ruled continued to be a motley of different peoples, with different customs and not much relating them beyond an enforced political structure . The proof of this is that as soon as the kingdom became politically weak it fell to the Moorish invasion. And when the Moors were finally defeated, the peninsula remained what it had always been, a collection of rather disparate elements.

Yet, one cannot ignore that there were some elements of unification at work which, together with the encounter, contributed to the development of the familial historical unit I have proposed – the world of Hispanics. Those most interesting from our point of view have to do with the *Reconquista*, the war that reclaimed peninsular lands from the Moors. This was an extraordinary process which took nearly eight centuries and which touched everyone in Iberia. One has to keep in mind when trying to understand Iberia and its peoples that every part of the peninsula, except for small territories in Asturias, in the north, and what came to be called the Spanish March in the north-west, came under the control of the invading Moors. Tariq crossed the Straits of Gibraltar in 711, and by 715 the Moorish forces were in France. They were defeated at the legendary Battle of Poitiers by Charles Martel in 732 and as a result retreated into the peninsula, below the Pyrenees. The *Reconquista* began at that very point in time with the two foci of resistance in Asturias and the Spanish March, which were expanded into larger fronts as time went on.

There are several things about the Moorish invasion that should be kept in mind. It was an invasion of forces with a different religion, language, and culture than the population of Iberia at the time. It resulted in the dispossession of land from those who had ruled in the peninsula, and it introduced a different form of government and civil organization. But the Moors did not make great efforts to convert Christians to Islam. The reason often given as an explanation is that Islamic law is tolerant of other religions, particularly people of the Book – Christians and Jews – provided they pay certain taxes, and the revenue from such taxes was often welcome. In any case, in spite of much mixing and cultural exchanges, the Christians of the peninsula never identified with the invaders, whom they considered foreigners who had unlawfully and unjustly taken their lands away from them.

It is now generally accepted that military activity related to the

Reconquista was intermittent. There were relatively long periods of time in which the Christian kingdoms and the Moslem caliphates lived in what can only be described as peace. But this was a *de facto* peace, not a *de jure* one. Christian kingdoms always seem to have regarded themselves in a state of war against the Moors, and the Christian population never forgot that they had been dispossessed of lands they considered to be rightfully theirs and that their religion was only tolerated. They shared, then, two important goals: the recovery of land and the reestablishment of Christianity as the religion of the land. The *Reconquista* was not just a matter of land recovery; it was also a religious mission.

The *Reconquista* had other important consequences. For example, it kept the Iberian kingdoms engaged in activities which separated them from the rest of Europe. In France there was also some concern with what was happening in Iberia. After all, the French were not too far away from the area of action and they kept the memory of the Battle of Poitiers alive. Indeed, the great medieval French epic, the *Chanson de Roland*, narrates events related to the struggle against the Moors. In southern Italy there was concern because of the power of Islam in the Mediterranean. But the concern receded in the minds of the English, Germans, and other Europeans. The Iberian kingdoms, then, became largely isolated from the political and intellectual issues which mattered for other Europeans. Two other factors emphasized this isolation. One was the Pyrenees. At the time, this range of mountains functioned as a mighty natural obstacle to any exchange between the Iberian kingdoms and the rest of Europe. Another was the fact that the center of activity in Christian Europe had shifted from the Mediterranean to the north–south axis Italy–France–England. Largely Mediterranean countries like the Iberian kingdoms, separated from the rest of Europe by the Pyrenees, were bound to experience isolation.

The *Reconquista* also promoted and in fact established a peculiar ethos. Four elements of this ethos are particularly pertinent. One of these was the emphasis on the purity of blood. In a country that is in a permanent state of war, family lines become extremely important, for they are the basis of loyalties and alliances. The purity of blood refers, of course, to blood that is uncontaminated by either Moorish or Jewish elements. Purity of blood became the requirement of any important position or office; it was an insurance against treason and betrayal. A key factor in social relations in the peninsula, the emphasis on purity of blood, reached extraordinary levels. Keep in mind that the expression "blue blood" in English is a translation of the Spanish *sangre azul*. The expression comes from the color of veins, visible through the skin, of those who have uncontaminated blood, in contrast with those whose skin, because of mixing with Moors or Jews, is too dark to allow the veins to be seen.

This emphasis on purity of blood reveals an even more fundamental fact about Iberians at this time: an extraordinary degree of racial *mestizaje*. Purity of blood became an issue precisely because it could not be taken for granted, because the mixing of blood lines was widespread. As Camilo José Cela states, referring in particular to Spain: "No one of Spanish ancestry is free of Moorish and Jewish blood, no concentration resided in one or another part of Spain. All modern Spain bleeds three bloods (not really three but thirty or forty)."[5] The need to reconquer territory and reestablish a Christian kingdom necessitated that blood lines be kept pure, but blood lines had become hopelessly mixed.

To this must be added the cultural *mestizaje* that permeated the peninsula. The inhabitants of this area were exposed to an extraordinary cultural variety. Consider that the culture the Islamic invaders brought into Iberia was itself a product of massive borrowing made possible because of the unification of very different peoples and cultures under Islam. From Persia and India to Greece and Egypt we have a rich mixture of customs, ideas, and values, all of which were brought into Iberia and adopted in various ways by the population. There was, then, a veritable cultural mixing and exchange in the peninsula at the time of the encounter with America. This constitutes a second, and most important element, which played a key role in the encounter and the future of both Iberia and America.

A third element of this ethos is the notion of *caballero*, a man on horseback. In a country where distinction was achieved in the battlefield, it was the knight on horseback who was most highly regarded. From this came a devaluation of all other activities, and particularly of commerce, manufacturing, and farming.[6] Commerce was frowned upon because of the biblical laws against usury, and manufacturing and farming were rejected because they involved manual labor. Manual labor was generally considered distasteful and unworthy of an *hidalgo*'s life. The *hidalgo* (literally, the son of somebody; high born) was slated for more important pursuits: the defense of the country or the Faith. Commerce, manufacturing, farming, and other similar occu-pations were left either to Jews or Moors living in Christian territories. When the Jews were thrown out of the peninsula at the end of the fifteenth century, and the Moors at the beginning of the sixteenth, an enormous vacuum was created which adversely affected the economic future of all the Iberian kingdoms.

Finally, the *Reconquista* ensured the preservation and expansion of the medieval feudal system. A society based on war, alliances, and territorial conquest, while poor in manufacturing, agriculture, and commerce, tends to be organized feudally.[7]

This was Iberia at the point of encounter with America. Moreover, the end of the *Reconquista* left many Iberians without jobs. The con-clusion of a 700-year war creates unemployment, and it also creates a vacuum. Moreover, when this vacuum has a religious dimension it is even more dramatic. What could these *caballeros* do? Fortunately, America appeared on the horizon and the process of conquest and colonization continued, filling in the emptiness left by the end of the *Reconquista*. The *caballeros* had new lands and peoples to conquer and new territories to settle and govern. Not that all Iberians who came to America were *caballeros* and *hidalgos* who had been engaged in the *Reconquista*. Most were peasants or members of a small, low bourgeoi-sie, and some were derelicts who were given the opportunity to start a new life, but they all shared the general ideals of Iberia at the time and were soon to claim the prerogatives and privileges of the upper classes.[8]

The idea of feudal estates could be exported to America and the wealth of the new territories could support a largely unproductive society at home. In America there was opportunity for everybody. Iberians were psychologically well prepared for the task, so it was easy for them to take up the new challenge and channel their energies toward America. Finally, let us not forget that there was no unity in the Iberian peninsula before its encounter with America. Iberia was characterized by an extraordinary variety of peoples and cultures, and both racial and cultural *mestizaje*. In spite of the traits to which I have referred, Iberians had no conception of themselves as one people; there was no single Iberian identity; not even a single Spanish identity.

2 La Hija Adoptiva

La hija adoptiva, the adopted daughter, is Latin America. I say "adopted" to emphasize the fact that Latin America is not a natural daughter of *las madres patrias*. Latin America is not composed simply of descendants of Spaniards or Portuguese. Iberians did not give birth to Latin America but adopted what was already there: a vast land populated by many different peoples. Indeed, just as we have spoken of not just one but many Iberias, we should speak of not one but rather many pre-Columbian Americas. So, strictly, we should refer to *las hijas adoptivas* rather than to *la hija adoptiva*.

One of the most salient facts about pre-Columbian America, as about Iberia, was its diversity. At the time of the encounter there were several millions of peoples in America, but they had no overall unifying traits other than the fact that they lived in America and not in Europe, Africa, or Asia. Language specialists tell us that the linguistic map of pre-Columbian America is a veritable tower of Babel, with hundreds, if not thousands, of languages, mostly different and often largely unrelated to each other.[9] To these languages corresponded an appropriate number of cultural and political units, tribes, and peoples who organized themselves differently and lived very different lives from those of others, sometimes even when those others dwelled in close proximity. Some were complex and well-developed civilizations, whereas others had only achieved a basic level of subsistence; some were on the rise, whereas others were in decline; some were composed of numerous peoples who lived throughout extensive territories, whereas others included no more than a handful of members and lived in small areas; and so on.

The diversity of pre-Columbian America is quite understandable when one considers two factors. First, its population appears to have come into the area in several waves; and, second, America is composed of two vast continents which take in all possible climatic zones and types of terrain. The different waves of immigration ensured a diverse population with some differences in languages, customs, and cultures. But even if the various people that crossed the Bearing Straits had been the same genetically and culturally, the isolation ensured by the topography of America over very long periods of time would have led to the development of major differences among various communities.

Indeed, some scholars have gone so far as to see the topography of the continent as the single determining factor in the history of Latin America and the identity of its people.[10]

Both North and South America are divided by great mountain ranges. The Andes is the second mightiest range in the world, after the Himalayas. These mountains divide South America into two parts, the west and the east, between which communication is generally difficult and in some places impossible. There are also vast inhospitable deserts, three of the largest river systems in the world, and the largest, most impenetrable rain forest anywhere. Moreover, the south-western part of North America, the part that is most significant for the question of Hispanic identity in the United States, is largely distant and isolated from the more populated area of Meso America.

In this extraordinarily diverse natural and cultural terrain a few peoples had been able from time to time to establish military hegemony over others and create larger political units. But even great civilizations of like-peoples were frequently decentralized. The Maya, for example, appear to have organized themselves in city-states, each of which, as a result, developed idiosyncrasies over time which further separated it from the others.[11]

At the time the Spaniards arrived on the shores of San Salvador there were two major empires in America. In the central plateau of Mexico the Aztecs had been able to establish a substantial political unit based on military strength and political alliances. On the western side of the Andes of South America and the Altiplano, the Inca also had been able to establish an empire among many different peoples. There seem to have been important economic reasons, apart from military and political ones, for the Inca's success in establishing and maintaining a grip on the different cultures and inhabitants of the region. But in both cases the grip of the Inca and the Aztecs was sufficiently loose for the cultural identity of those who were held by it to be to a great extent preserved.[12] Indeed, it is well established that the success of Cortés and Pizarro in conquering these empires was more a result of the weakness of the empires than the ability of the conquerors. Dissatisfied tribes and cultural units which considered the Aztecs in particular to be foreign, tyrannical, and oppressive masters, saw in the coming of the Spaniards an opportunity for liberation and lent considerable support to the invaders.

This does not mean, of course, that there were no close relations among the peoples who inhabited America before the Spaniards set foot on its shores. The existence of the Aztec and Inca empires is sufficient to prove the contrary. It means that the relations between these peoples were such that they had not obliterated the identity and cultural distinctiveness of many of the diverse groups that lived there. Amerindians had not one but many identities.

This conclusion can be easily illustrated by means of Amerindian art. To the casual observer, Amerindian art might look pretty much alike. A bas-relief from Chichen Itzá and one from Teotihuacán might appear similar, yet closer examination reveals profound differences. Amerindian art displays many strains, styles, and techniques. It is true that there are cross-cultural feedings and influences. Some elements of Aztec art can be traced to the art of the Toltecs, for example. And the Mayan Chichen Itzá displays the clear influence of peoples from Meso America. Yet it is also clear that the arts of the Toltecs and of the Aztecs are very different, and the same can be said about the arts of the Aztecs and the Maya, let alone that of the cultures of Meso America and those of South America. It is in the languages of these peoples, however, that these differences become most pronounced, for many of these differences were sufficient to prevent intercommunication.

The point of all this is to make clear that there was no unity in America before Iberians arrived. The idea of the American Indian so popular in the first half of this century is largely a myth concocted by whites and *mestizos* engaged in a program of nation building.[13] America displayed an incredible array of peoples and cultures. Amerindians had no conception of themselves as one people; there was no single Amerindian identity. This does not mean, however, that there were no unifying elements, but these were not even as strong as those we find in the Iberian peninsula.[14] There is no counterpart to the *Reconquista* in America. Still, the histories of the different groups native to America do have some common elements. Their histories are intertwined in various ways. Indeed, the very isolation of all America from Asia, Africa, and Europe tended to give its inhabitants a certain unity.

Surprisingly, in spite of vast differences, there were also some elements of similarity between Iberia and America. It does not take much to see that certain parts of Mexico and Peru, for example, resemble the topography of much of Spain. And we have already referred to the cultural and political diversity of both Iberia and America. But, more important than these, there were also common cultural traits. For example, the fusion of State and religion into a theocracy and authoritarian forms of government were common to both Iberia and several societies in America. Indeed, even the emphasis on the purity of blood and blood lineage, which appears to have been a key, and idiosyncratic, element in Iberia, seems to have been shared by some cultures in America, such as the Maya.[15]

3 The Encounters

The encounter between Europeans and Amerindians was one of the most cataclysmic and catastrophic events – especially for Amerindians – in the history of humankind. Here were two groups of peoples who did not know about the existence of each other, suddenly crossing paths. Here were two worlds which were really not just two, but multiplicities of worlds, and which, as a result of the encounter, became first two – the world of the conqueror and the world of the conquered – and then one – the Hispanic world. The birth of this world was drenched in the blood of America and degraded by suffering and disease.

Nothing like this had ever happened in the history of humankind and, although there had been antecedents here and there, there had never been an event of this sort on such a large scale. The encounter cannot be compared with Alexander's conquests in antiquity, for example, because Alexander was conquering lands he knew about and with which there had been contacts throughout long periods of time. Nor can it be compared with the conquests of Genghis Khan or the Romans, for similar reasons. Nor can it be compared with anything in the history of Egypt or with the Norman conquest of England. Only a future encounter with an extra-terrestrial civilization on some far-away planet about which we know nothing, not even its existence, could possibly compare with it. The encounter is a unique event in history and its significance is so great that it can never be overestimated.

But was there really *one* encounter? When we look at it more closely it becomes clear that there is no such thing as *one* encounter. One encounter requires two or more peoples who meet on one occasion, and nothing like this happened. The reality is that different groups of people met other different groups of people in a variety of places and times. We have already seen that there was not just one European people – the Iberians – and not just one pre-Columbian people – the Amerindians – before 1492. Now we see that there was not even one time and one place of meeting. The variety and multiplicity of Iberia and America met in a corresponding variety of times, places, and circumstances. This has enormous consequences for our history, for it undermines any rigid, essentialistic, and simplistic account of who we are and how we came to be. Instead of one encounter, we should speak of many encounters; instead of one time, we should speak of a drawn-out process that extends over centuries; and instead of one place, we should speak of multiple locations.

In spite of these pluralities, a major consequence of the encounters was the development of two identities – American and European – and two lands – America and Europe. A single identity was superimposed on the native inhabitants of America by Europeans. They were all lumped together into the same category and mislabeled "Indians." We all know that this term came into use because Columbus and those who accompanied him thought they had arrived at the shores of India. But this is not the most significant aspect of this phenomenon; the most significant fact is that Amerindians became one people in the eyes of Europeans. Likewise, the vast and variegated territories Europeans had "discovered" became one land: America. Suddenly, the multifaceted reality of the Amerindian worlds was changed by a group of conquering adventurers based on the false assumption that it was what it had never been: one place with one people. And this not only in the eyes of the conquered, but also in the eyes of some of the conquered. I do not say all of the conquered because there are to this day many people in Latin America who have no consciousness of themselves as one people other than in some very regional sense. And even for those who have come to think of themselves as one people in America, in addition to whatever they are specifically, the formation of this category was slow and difficult, unlike for the conquerors and Europeans.

Mind you, it is perfectly understandable why the formation of a single Amerindian identity was forged. First of all, it was difficult for most Europeans to distinguish between the different cultures they found in America. Amerindian cultures looked alike to them because European senses were not discriminating enough, refined enough if you will, to see the subtle but significant differences that would have been evident to more sophisticated observers. The languages of Amerindians sounded alike to them; their clothing looked similarly exotic; their food tasted equally spicy; their art appeared altogether too alien; and their religion was pagan. Moreover, the invading Iberians did not devote much time to examining the art objects and artifacts of these different cultures because, in their zeal to eradicate what they believed to be idolatrous gods, or to appropriate the precious materials of which some of them were made, they proceeded to destroy or melt down most of them. The complexity and sophistication of Amerindian cultures was too foreign for Europeans to grasp.

The lumping together of all Amerindians and the creation of a place for them also resulted from the necessity to comprehend them and the desire to dominate, exploit, and evangelize them. Humans need to conceptualize in order to act in an orderly fashion, and such conceptualization is based on finding unity where sometimes there appears to be little or none. We understand cats thanks to the concept cat, which lumps all cats together regardless of the differences among individual cats and various kinds of cats. It was necessary for Europeans to give an identity to the native population of America, and to America itself, in order to make these peoples and this place objects of understanding. Moreover, although the original purpose of Columbus's journey was trade, this was soon changed to conquest, profit, and evangelization. And all these things require identification and labeling. Conquest implies domination and domination requires identifying and labeling. Naming is the first required step toward domination. Evangelization also requires understanding and action, and these in turn necessitate conceptualization and naming.

In a sense, then, rather than the discovery of, or even the encounters with, America, one could speak of the *invention* of America. America was the creation of Spanish and Portuguese explorers, adventurers, and conquerors who passed on their invention to the rest of Europe and even to the peoples of America themselves. The encounters gave rise to a new concept, a new people, and a new land, the so-called New World.[16] "New," again, to Europeans, for its components had been there as long as most Europeans had been in Europe. And a "world" also to Europeans, for until they arrived at San Salvador there had not been any one world, or even a world at all, which encompassed everything which came to be called America.

To talk about the birth of this world, as is sometimes done, is again a misinterpretation of historical fact. The New World was not born because it is not a natural entity, like a cat or a dog. The New World was rather an artificial invention founded on need and greed.

Recently, much has been made by some authors about the fact that the concepts of Indian, America, European, and Europe are inventions following the encounters rather than realities preceding them.[17] The argument is that Europeans themselves became lumped together and objectified with the identity they hold to this day as a result of the encounters; Europeans did not exist before they became contrasted with American Indians. Europeans became one people as a result of the comparison between themselves and the inhabitants of America carried out by both Europeans and the inhabitants of America. The encounters, then, gave birth to the Indian and the European. And, of course, just as there are no American Indians without America, so there are no Europeans without Europe. Europe also was a result of the encounters, of the need by both the explorers and Amerindians to think about, and act toward, what came to be called Europe.

The notion that there is no Europe without America and no America without Europe is based on the philosophical doctrine which claims there is no I without a Thou, and no Thou without an I. There is no self-identity without other-identity; or, to put it differently, there is no isolated identity or identity by itself. Two points need to be made here, however. One is that one must distinguish between the consciousness of an I or the consciousness of a Thou and the existence of an I or the existence of a Thou. It is one thing to claim that an I cannot exist unless a Thou exists, and vice versa, and another to claim that consciousness of an I cannot exist unless there is consciousness of a Thou and vice versa. One must also distinguish between these claims and the claims that an I cannot come to be without a Thou, and a Thou cannot come to be without an I, on the one hand, and the claims that consciousness of an I cannot come to be without consciousness of a Thou, and vice versa, on the other.

The distinction between consciousness of X and existence of X is a counterpart of the distinction, made in chapter 2, between identity and identification. Recall that identity has to do with the conditions that make something what it is independently of time (achronically), at a particular time (synchronically), or at two (or more) different times (diachronically). Identification has to do with the conditions that make us aware of what something is independently of time (achronically), at a particular time (synchronically), or at two (or more) different times (diachronically – in which case it is a case of reidentification).

The distinction between consciousness of America and Europe and the existence of America and Europe assumes that Europe and America are different from the concept of Europe and the concept of America. This is a common-sense view which is rejected by many philosophers today. As improbable as it may seem from an ordinary standpoint, this position has become popular among post-Kantians. For some of them "the world" is nothing more than our conception of the world.[18] They reject the common-sense Aristotelian position in which the world is something extra-mental.[19]

Now, in principle, the view that Europe cannot exist without America is absurd and, therefore, its contradictory makes a lot of sense. Logically at least, there seems to be no need to agree with it. Of course, one could argue that, if we are talking about Europe as a physical territory, then the existence of America is intrinsically tied to it because the natural forces that brought about Europe are also responsible for America and vice versa. But there is no logical impossibility in becoming conscious of Europe without becoming conscious of America, unless thinking of Europe necessarily includes, or must necessarily be contrasted with, thinking of America. But this does not seem to be right, for I can think of Europe without thinking of America, even if the generation of each of these concepts requires contrasting them with other concepts.

If instead of Europe and America we are speaking about the *concept* of Europe and the *concept* of America, it seems that it is possible to hold that the concept of Europe is possible without the concept of America; the concept of Europe does not seem to necessitate in any way the concept of America as long as there are concepts such as Asia, Africa, Near East, and so forth with which it could be contrasted. Still, there is something to this point of view insofar as the encounters with America dramatized in a very strong way the concept of Europe, whether Europe is conceived geographically, culturally, or in some other way. Moreover, it may have also modified it in important ways. There is evidence that, until the consciousness of America resulting from the encounters, Europeans did not have as clear a conception of themselves *qua* Europeans as they did later. It is not that the reality of Europe was produced by the encounters; but it is true that Europeans saw themselves as different from others as a result of the encounters.

This process of differentiation and identification, however, had a paradoxical and peculiar twist, for it helped alienate some Europeans, namely the Iberians, from Europe, joining them to America in their own eyes and in the eyes of the rest of Europe.

4 Africans

African slaves were brought to America to make up for what were perceived to be the deficiencies of the native population. Hard work and European diseases had quickly decimated the Amerindian population. A new work force was required and Iberians found it in Africans. African slaves had already been used in Europe and they were not foreign to Spain and Portugal. Contacts with Europeans had strengthened the African resistance to European diseases and made them a more reliable work force.[20] The first license to bring slaves into America was granted by the Crown in 1518 and the process continued until the nineteenth century. The estimates of the number of slaves brought into America are almost pure guesswork, and they differ substantially, but all studies conclude that the figures had to be in the millions.[21]

It is common to speak of the Africans who were brought to America as if they formed a single population, a racially and culturally homogeneous group of people. Yet nothing is further from the truth. They were neither racially nor culturally homogeneous. Africa itself at the time was as varied as America.[22] Indeed, even West Africa, the source of most African slaves, displayed extraordinary multiplicity. Racially, all these people were classified by slave traders as *negros*, i.e. black, because of their dark skin. Moreover, their languages, religions, and cultures in general appeared the same or very similar to the untrained eyes of Europeans. For most Iberians they were the same, just as the Amerindian population was the same. But in reality there was extraordinary variety both in color of skin and other physical characteristics among the Africans slaves. Their skin color ranged anywhere from a coffee tone to a very dark, almost bluish tint. The shape of lips and mouths, the texture of the hair, height, and complexion varied according to the group to which they belonged. And culturally the differences were even more striking. Keep in mind that there was not a large political unit that encompassed all these people in Africa, and that most of them formed part of relatively small tribes and kingdoms, which kept themselves more or less separate from each other. Frequently they spoke different languages and worshiped different gods. The unity of the Africans that were brought to America, then, is as much a myth as the myths of the unity of Iberians and the unity of Amerindians.

The extraordinary variety in the African population was multiplied as a result of the process of enslavement. Africans were captured at different times and places, sometimes in groups, sometimes individually. Then they were put together in ships and sent to America, where they were sold to different people in different places. The original commonalities that could have survived in cases where the slaves had belonged to the same cultural and political groups were shattered when the slaves were scattered among different masters and territories. Individuals found themselves in foreign places, among peoples who spoke different languages and had different cultures. Even among themselves, the slaves found that, more often than not, they could not communicate. The language of the masters became the only vehicle of social intercourse.

All this makes the situation of Africans different from that of Iberians and Amerindians. There were great differences among Iberians, but some elements of unity were found in their history, both as individuals and as groups. There was even a political unity and certain cultural traits that united most of them, such as religion. The Amerindian population, likewise, had some elements of unity. They had been defeated and they had been conquered, but they remained largely who they were. They had not been scattered among foreign peoples. They still had their own languages and most of their own cultures. Their temples were destroyed and their religion forbidden, but their daily customs survived, and many continued living in the places where they had lived before the encounters. And then there was the matter of their numbers. Even though these decreased substantially as a result of abuses by the conquerors and the diseases they introduced in America, in comparison with the invaders there were still enough Amerindians to preserve some of their own character. Not that they were not divided and diverse. We saw that they were not one people by any means. But the groups that they had constituted before the encounters with Iberians largely survived.

None of this is true of the Africans brought to America. Indeed, the only thing that Africans had in common was the fact that they were brought as slaves. This is the only unifying factor to the whole African population in America, and it is the preeminent factor that makes them different from Africans who remained in Africa. The unity of American Africans, then, is in their history, and begins, like the unity of all Hispanics, in their encounters with Iberians and Amerindians. Their identity is a function of this cataclysmic process and is tied inexorably to the identity of Iberians and Amerindians.

5 Hispanics

I have rejected the notion of America as a New World discovered or even created by Europeans, and I have rejected the notion of Europe as a byproduct of the encounters. But there is an important sense in which the notion of a New World is correct in the context in which we are speaking. In this sense, the New World is not America, but the Hispanic world produced by the encounters. This is a world which amounts to more than the sum of its parts: Iberians, Amerindians, and African slaves. And if there is a New World, there is also an Old World. The Old World is not Europe, however, but rather the world which existed before the encounters. For Iberians, Amerindians, and African slaves it was a multifaceted world of many groups and cultures. The New World is the world of Hispanics, where all these cultures and peoples became increasingly interrelated and progressively separated from other cultures and peoples in general and from Europe, Africa, and Anglo America in particular. Before the encounters, there were the Portuguese, Castilians, Catalans, Aztecs, Yoruba, Inca, Congolese, and so on. After the encounters and the events they precipitated, there are in addition Hispanics.

Iberians, Amerindians, and Africans continued to exist, and so did Aztecs, Mayans, Castilians, Yoruba, and Catalans, but their identities became increasingly integrated into the web of interrelations that characterize the Hispanic world. This new reality, consisting of the old realities immersed in a new set of relations, engendered in time an identity different from those outside this world. Even the bitter fight for independence of the Spanish colonies in America did not cut the ties which had been established during more than 300 years between Iberians and Latin Americans. The encounters, then, gave birth to a new child, the Hispanic world.

This new world, this child of the encounters, did not appear suddenly. It is a product of a long, drawn-out gestation that still continues. Its first phase was constituted by the encounters themselves. These produced immediate changes. For Iberians, a most important one was that the original aims of trade were substituted by the goals of conquest and evangelization. Profit, of course, was the ultimate guiding principle of both, but conquest is very different from trade. Trade can be peaceful and often implies some equality among traders. Conquest, on the other hand, is always violent and requires inequality between the conqueror and the conquered.

The case of evangelization is similar and also different. It is supposed to be non-violent – and indeed many philosophers and theologians at the time argued for non-violence[23] – but in practice it did frequently involve violence. Moreover, evangelization also presupposes inequality between those who give and those who receive, those who "have the truth" and those who are "deprived of the truth."

The conquest was swift and thorough. By the middle of the sixteenth century most of what we now know as Latin America had been subjugated and brought under the control of Iberian powers, either Spain or Portugal. With conquest came consolidation and colonization. These lasted by and large until the colonies became independent. Altogether, these three phases take up more than 300 years of our history.

These 300 years constitute the cauldron in which the New World of Hispanics was created. This world is best understood through the notion of *mestizaje*. Immediately after the first encounters *mestizo* was used primarily in a racial context to refer to a mixture of Iberian and Amerindian. The origins of the term go back to the Latin word *misticius*, which simply meant mixed. The term mulatto was reserved for the mixture of Iberian and African, and sambo (sometimes zambo) for the mixture of Amerindian and African.[24] Later, however, *mestizo* was extended to include any kind of mixture and more recently to a mixture of cultures.[25] The most generic conception of *mestizo*, then, is simply that of racial mixture, although this statement must be qualified in two important ways. First, the notion of race in Latin America, as in the United States, is not always separated from the notion of ethnicity. There are sociological, anthropological, and psychological factors in the classification of people belonging to one or another race. Among other things, this is reflected in the imprecision of census figures.[26] For example, to be an Indian does not always mean, or mean primarily, to be of pure Amerindian descent. Most often, it means simply that the person in question has not yet adopted non-Indian ways. These non-Indian ways are the ways of city dwellers, of *mestizos* or of Europeans, such as European-style dress and European language. To be an Indian, then, is to be ethnically Amerindian rather than racially Amerindian, although the racial connotation is often present as well.[27] In areas and countries where the European racial element is very large, such as Argentina and Uruguay, "Indian" tends to have racial connotations which it does not have in countries where the European racial element is small. In the latter, the term is primarily understood ethnically. Something similar can be said about terms like negro, *mestizo*, and mulatto. There is always a combination of physical appearance and ethnicity. A slave is a negro even if light in skin color, but a free person is a negro only if he or she looks dark. In Latin America the American notion that someone who has a drop of black blood is black never took hold. Whether one is black, Indian, or white depends very much on how one looks and acts. Indeed, in the early 1900s the Cuban Fernando Ortíz had discarded the biological bases of race for cultural ones.[28]

The second important qualification to the conception of *mestizo* given above is that *mestizo* does not necessarily entail homogeneity or amalgamation. The *mestizo*, whether racially or ethnically, is a mix, but not an amalgam. Homogeneity and amalgamation produce a result in which the original elements are not recognizable. There is a similar consistency to all that is homogeneous, a fusion which prevents distinction. This does not apply to *mestizaje*. *Mestizos* come in all sorts and mixtures, and the elements of the mixes are often quite obvious. There is a new product, but the product is not of equal consistency.

Although *mestizaje* does not imply homogeneity, this does not mean that the elements mixed in the *mestizo* are actually separable. We cannot separate someone's copper-colored skin from her curly hair, or someone's taste for Mexican tortillas from his taste for refried beans. The concept of *mestizaje*, then, if understood in the way I have proposed here, fits nicely the non-homogeneous mixing that characterizes the Hispanic world. It can be a principle of union without implying the kind of homogenization which obliterates the contributions made by different ethnic and racial elements.

This conception of *mestizaje* is contrary to that used in much of the

Latin American discussion where *mestizaje* is often used to eliminate, or at least to obscure, differences.[29] The resulting mixture is conceived in homogeneous terms, where the elements that gave rise to it lose their original character and become unrecognizable. As Antenor Orrego puts it, the result is a biological, psychological, and spiritual amalgam.[30] Making this world one through unification and integration seems to be the overriding result of mixing.[31] A similar notion was developed in the United States, the notion of a "melting pot," first used in 1909, where all differences become blended into a homogeneous product. In the United States the myth of the melting pot was used to create a sense of nationality, but it functioned oppressively with respect to African Americans and Hispanics for they and their traits were excluded from this national amalgam.[32] Although the motivation varies for the use of the homogeneous notion of *mestizaje* in Latin America, one of the most frequent motivations is the perceived need for nation building.[33] In this sense, the notion of *mestizo* was used in some countries of Latin America in ways similar to those in which the notion of melting pot was used in the United States.[34]

Mestizaje should be distinguished from assimilation, with which it is sometimes confused. To assimilate or become assimilated implies, first of all, to make or become similar. In this sense, the assimilated become like the group who assimilates them and therefore lose what they had that was different; they are absorbed so that the boundaries between the assimilated and the assimilating disappear.[35] *Mestizaje* is different from assimilation in this regard insofar as *mestizos* preserve differences. To assimilate or become assimilated also implies a dominant group and a subservient group. *Mestizaje* may also involve this bifurcation, but need not do so. *Mestizos* could be mixes of groups which are not related as dominator–dominated. This is another reason why assimilation cannot be regarded as the same as *mestizaje*. Finally, the assimilated become part of the group into which they are assimilated and cease to suffer from an identity crisis. But *mestizos* continue to live an ambiguous social and psychological life that causes them to suffer a constant crisis of identity.[36] Clearly, there are socially positive and negative consequences of *mestizaje*.[37]

Mestizaje is based on a process characterized by adoption, rejection, and development. Adoption is part of it insofar as there could be no mixing without the adoption of something not originally present in the premixed components. There is rejection insofar as a racial or ethnic mixture frequently presupposes elements which, although unlike each other, serve the same function. One cannot be both black haired and blond haired. And there is development, because in order for there to be a true mixture, the mixture must function as a whole, and in doing so, the new whole will do something that the separate elements could not have done.

In the mix produced by *mestizaje* we find elements from the original components which remain largely the same, even though they are not in fact separable; elements from the original components which remain largely the same and are separable; elements from the original components which have been modified but are still recognizable as having belonged to the original components; elements which have been so consolidated and changed that they cannot be recognized as having belonged to the original components but whose origins can be traced to them; and, finally, elements which are new products resulting from the mix. All these can be easily illustrated with cultural or racial traits, so we need not cite particular examples.

Mestizaje, then, is the opposite of purity, whether ethnic, racial, or national. I mention the last three because they are distinct from each other, although they are frequently confused. Race is supposed to be physically based; ethnicity involves the cultural character of the group, at least in part; nationality has to do with political organization. The confusion between these three has been a constant source of grief for humanity. Indeed, the attempt to understand nations as races or cultures has caused no end of trouble. The confusion between nation, race, and culture was the basis of many of the claims of National Socialism and Fascism, for example. It has been the source of trouble in many countries such as Canada, the former Yugoslavia, Spain, and the United States, where there are ethnic or racial minorities. The suppression of ethnic traits and the elimination of racial minorities in an attempt to achieve national unity have been constant features of human history. The notion of *mestizaje* I have proposed undermines these attempts, for it recognizes the value of diverse elements originating in different cultures and races. A mix implies rejection, but also adoption.

There is a well-known culinary metaphor used by Fernando Ortíz to depict Cuba which is perhaps appropriate here. He describes Cuba as a cultural, ethnic, and religious *ajiaco*.[38] The *ajiaco* is a Cuban dish with roots in the Iberian *puchero*, but it is quite different to it in substantial ways. It is a kind of stew of many different vegetables and meats: corn, potatoes, squash, plantain (both ripe and green), a local variety of sweet potato, ñame, manioc, malanga, chicken, beef jerky, pork, and so on. All these ingredients are cooked together and produce an interesting mix with an idiosyncratic flavor, but the original ingredients remain discernible, even though the sauce they produce is distinctively new. One can still identify the corn, plantain, malanga, and so on, and not only identify them visually, but taste their particular flavors, although even then their immersion in the common sauce and cooking together with the other ingredients modifies their taste. There is no homogeneity in the *ajiaco*, although it is a mixture which could not exist without the diverse ingredients that compose it. *Mestizaje* is like this. Homogenization and amalgamation would result only if we made a purée of the *ajiaco* by putting it in a blender. But then we would not have *ajiaco* any longer. And the same goes for *mestizaje*.

The kind of *mestizaje* about which I have been speaking affected every dimension of the lives of Iberians, Amerindians, and Africans, from religion and race to food and language. There is no homogeneity among Hispanics, but there is a world of close interactions that produced, and is still producing, an extraordinary variety of combinations and new results. Moreover, this is not a one-way street; it did not come from Europe to America, or vice versa. The mixing affected the populations of Iberia and America, including all those who have settled in these places voluntarily or involuntarily.

Consider, for example, political organizations. One could argue that the consolidation and survival of the Spanish and Portuguese States and their political prominence in Europe in the sixteenth century, particularly of Spain, were the result of the conquest of America. America's gold made possible Spain's European military adventures and gained the country the power it had. At the same time, because America was primarily the business of Castile, it contributed to the consolidation of Castilian power over Catalans, Basques, and other peninsular groups which had been previously independent or semi-independent.

On the Latin American side, the dominance of Spain and Portugal divided Latin America into two political hemispheres that functioned independently to a great extent, but at the same time consolidated and unified these separate hemispheres in ways unlike any before. Moreover, administrative divisions introduced by Spain seem to have had a decisive influence in the formation of what later became the Latin American nations. Consider the case of Mexico. This country is largely the result of the administrative decision by the Spanish Crown to bring under one administration the many lands that we call Mexico today. Thanks to this decision, peoples who had different cultures, languages, religions, traditions, and who had never belonged together politically, were gathered into a single unit. Indeed, the repercussions of this Spanish decision are not only still felt in Mexico itself, but also in the former Spanish colonial territories in the United States. Some Native Americans from the south-west consider themselves Mexican American, when in fact their Mexicanity was non-existent prior to the Spanish decision to gather them together with all the peoples living in the colonial Viceroyalty of New Spain.[39] Similar things could be said about many other countries in Latin America.

Of course, in principle one could argue that the way Spain cut up the American territorial pie was a result of lines already there: pre-existing natural, cultural, and political boundaries. Although this might be true in some cases, it is just not so in many, perhaps most, cases. There is no reason, for example, why New Spain should have included Mayans, Aztecs, and Pueblo Indians.

Economically, the conquest of America brought drastic changes in Iberia and America. America's gold transformed Spain and Portugal into the richest countries in Europe and made possible the congregation of intellectuals and artists from all over Europe in the Iberian peninsula. It also transformed the economies of these countries in drastic ways. Inflation exploded and manufacturing, agriculture, and commerce suffered irreparable damage. Indeed, in most ways the Iberian economies became hostages to America, preventing any independent developments.

On the other side of the equation, a largely feudal system was imposed on America. Vast territories were awarded to individual persons, and native inhabitants were made virtual slaves through the system of *encomiendas*, whereby they were made charges of the owners of land granted by the Spanish Crown.[40] The *encomienda* was not a land grant, but was *de facto* entrusted only to landowners. Pre-Columbian economic systems were largely destroyed and new systems developed as the result of compromises between the demands of the past and the present, the needs of Amerindians, the greed of Iberian conquistadors, the demands of the Church, and the relentless thirst for cash of the Iberian Crowns.

In this context, mixing became the rule. Racially, Iberian men came to America without wives for the most part and used the native women at will.[41] Moreover, the Roman legacy may have left a more tolerant attitude toward different ethnic and racial groups in the peninsula than in other places in Europe.[42] Unlike Anglo-Saxon settlers in North America, who were generally unfamiliar with dark-skinned peoples and therefore less prone to develop intimate relations with Amerindian women, most Iberians were accustomed to darker-skinned people, and did not look at them with the repugnance that other Northern Europeans did. Indeed, they considered the Moors to be rivals and heathen, but nonetheless had to recognize, even if only grudgingly, their superiority in many ways – in learning, technical advances, and so on.[43] There is also the fact that Portuguese sailors had extensive knowledge of Africa. The proximity of the Spanish Canary Islands to Africa made for frequent exchanges between Spaniards and the continental African population. Indeed, male immigrants from the Canary Islands to Cuba came to be known as *blanqueadores* (whiteners) because of their preference for dark-skinned women.

Of course, there was racism. One does not have to look very closely into the literature of the period to see racist comments, attitudes, and actions.[44] In spite of all this, however, there is some justification for saying that, as a result of their historical situation, Iberians had less prejudices to deal with and the prejudices they had were more easily overcome (or their needs were more critical) when it came to sexual intercourse with native women.

Mixing was so widespread that laws were enacted at various times during the colonial period in order to introduce some measure of control over intermarriages and interracial relations,[45] but they proved ineffective.[46] Indeed, the scale of this process has led one scholar to note that "No part of the world has ever witnessed such a gigantic mixing of races as the one that has been taking place in Latin America and the Caribbean since 1492."[47]

Considering the large Amerindian population and the comparatively small number of Iberian settlers and African slaves, one would have expected such mixing to have been rather limited and disproportionate. But there was a major factor which must be taken into account, namely, the demographic disaster which resulted from the encounters. By some estimates, in central Mexico alone the native population at the beginning of the sixteenth century numbered four and a half million, whereas 150 years later it was almost one million less.[48] Regardless of the credibility of these figures, no one disputes that the Amerindian population decreased drastically in the first century after the first encounter. The reasons given vary. Some emphasize mistreatment at the hands of Iberians, whereas others emphasize the new diseases to which the population was exposed. Both undoubtedly occurred, but it is now generally accepted that only the second can explain the extent of the disaster.[49]

The encounters produced, then, substantial changes in political structure, economic organization, and racial composition in both Iberia and America. But more important than this, surely, is the cultural *mestizaje* that slowly permeated Iberia and America. There are few aspects of pre-encounters cultures of Iberia and America that were not affected by this *mestizaje*. Religion, art, architecture, food, language, music, and social mores became intertwined in extraordinary ways. Some of the most commonly associated cultural icons of the countries that now compose the Hispanic world are the result of this *mestizaje* and are inconceivable without it. It is not hard to think of examples, from the pedestrian to the sublime. Consider foods. Can any one imagine the Iberian cuisine without the common bean, or the Spanish tortilla without potatoes? Yet the common bean is an Iberian import from America. There are some Iberian bean dishes, like the Catalan *muñeta*, that look surprisingly similar to pre-Columbian dishes, such as the Mexican refried beans. And potatoes are something Spaniards did not have before the encounters; potatoes are native to America.[50]

Consider music. Does anyone doubt the influence of African rhythms on Iberian music and the influence of Iberian themes on Latin American music? Could the Cuban *danzón* exist without Iberian and African elements? Can one make sense of the Mexican *jarabe tapatío* (Mexican hat dance) and the Iberian *zapateo* independently of each other? Does not the history of the *habanera* show the close interdependence of America and Iberia? The very instruments used to play music are often the result of cultural *mestizaje*. The *charango* is a string instrument made up of the carapace of the armadillo. In fact, several of the musical instruments that have become essential for regional music in various parts of South America are adaptations of European musical instruments.

Keep in mind that there were no stringed instruments in America before Iberians landed there, and yet much of what is now regarded as typically folkloric music relies on stringed instruments.

Architecture is another area where the legacy of the Hispanic world is eminently mixed. There is little doubt that the best pieces of Iberian baroque are found in Mexico. Not even Salamanca can rival Tepotzo-tlán, Querétaro, and Taxco. But some of the baroque jewels of Mexico are inconceivable without the Amerindian component. What would Zacatecas and San Miguel de Allende look like without the Amerindian contribution? Did not the tile-style architectural decoration which is generally associated with Portugal actually originate in Oro Preto?

Art is no different from architecture when it comes to *mestizaje*. From colonial painting to the Mexican muralists of the twentieth century, there is clear evidence of mixing of themes and techniques that characterize all expressions of culture in the Hispanic world. Perhaps the best example of this deep and widespread *mestizaje* is the famous beaded *zemí* in the Pigorini Museum.[51] This small religious idol combines African, Amerindian, and European techniques, materials, and styles. The African influence is so strong that until 1952 it was identified as an African fetish. It is now established that it was a product of Taíno craft that incorporates European and African elements. The *zemí* was made at the beginning of the sixteenth century, perhaps as early as 1513, which indicates how early *mestizaje* set in after the first encounter. The same applies to recent artworks as well. Mexican murals owe as much to Iberia as to their Amerindian past. The works of Orozco, Siqueiros, and Rivera are eminently *mestizos*. Even if one were to argue that their art is Mexican and not Iberian insofar as it is a rebellion against Iberia, this very reference to Iberia confirms my point.

More pedestrian examples of the phenomenon of *mestizaje* can be found in clothing, particularly among Amerindians. The typical dress of many of them incorporates native and Iberian elements. Consider, for example, the traditional dress of some Andean groups where the women's *pollera* (a Castilian term for skirt) is an essential component. The *pollera* is a result of certain native elements (for example, a wrap-around used by native women), a rule instituted by Spaniards that the wraparound should not have an opening, and some elements borrowed from Spanish skirts. The Cuban dress of the *rumbera* incorporates elements from the dress of Andalucian flamenco dancers and certain elements of African origin. The traditional Brazilian *carioca* dress again includes elements brought to Brazil from Africa and Portugal.

In religion, the beliefs of many were drastically affected, and their religious behavior incorporates elements from different religions. In Cuba, for example, many members of the population jointly hold beliefs and engage in practices which belong to Roman Catholicism and some of the African religions which slaves brought with them to the island. This has led some to argue that religion in Cuba is syncretistic, a claim which has caused a debate among specialists. Whatever the truth of this, it is beyond doubt that the same persons hold beliefs originating from different religions. For example, a person might believe that Our Lady of Charity is the Virgin Mary and at the same time that she is Changó, an African deity. Likewise, they may engage in practices which originate from different faiths. On Sunday morning they may attend a Roman Catholic mass, but in the evening they may make an offering of an apple and tobacco to some of the statues of saints they keep in an altar at home. This, again, illustrates *mestizaje*: two beliefs and two practices, each arising from different religions and which are clearly distinguishable as such and do not lose their character. But these beliefs are integrated into a single body of beliefs and the practices are made part of the person's religious behavior with no felt incompatibility.

Mestizaje in literature is pervasive and inescapable. There may be some works of literature produced after the encounters in Iberia and Latin America that can be regarded as purely Castilian, Catalan, Portuguese, Mexican, or Chilean, but they are hard to find. The overwhelming majority of the literature of Iberia and Latin America is anything but pure. Great literature is particularly significant in that it springs from a lived reality, and the reality that most great literature from Iberia and Latin America reveals is a Hispanic reality, a mixed reality. Think of Gabriel García Márquez, Jorge Amado, Alejo Carpentier, Pablo Neruda, Octavio Paz, or Federico García Lorca. Is the world of their works anything but a Hispanic world? Besides, literature is made up of language and the language of every place in the Hispanic world owes much to other places of this world. Perhaps the basic grammar is Castilian or Portuguese – and I am not quite sure of this – but this is where purity stops. When it comes to vocabulary and accent, the linguistic mix everywhere in the Hispanic world is quite evident.

It is obvious that some of the examples I have given of the influence of America on Iberia are not unique, in the sense that their impact has gone beyond Iberia to other areas of Europe. This is particularly obvious with the use of such staples as potatoes, tomatoes, and tobacco, all native to America. What is Italian cuisine without tomatoes? Or Irish, British, and German cooking without potatoes? Or European culture in general without tobacco? My point is not only that America changed Iberia and Iberia changed America. Rather, my point is that the interchange that went on between Iberia and America has been so extensive and profound that it created a new identity. The impact of America on the rest of Europe and of non-Iberian Europe on America does not alter this fact. That tomatoes changed Italian cuisine does not alter the fact that they also influenced Iberian cuisine and, together with many other things, contributed to the cultural *mestizaje* prevalent in the Hispanic world.

The reality of Hispanic *mestizaje*, then, is this two-way street, and is founded on the tacit acceptance of what the other has to offer, even in cases in which it originates in a relation of dominator–dominated. This is a fact that has escaped many of those who have analyzed this phenomenon. They concentrate on the fact that the dominators imposed their ways on the dominated and the dominated, out of a sense of servitude and a deep inferiority complex, developed a desire, almost a need, to adopt the ways of the dominator.[52] They see the *mestizaje* that resulted from the encounters as a non-reciprocal relation, affecting only the dominated. *Mestizaje*, understood thus, is based on inequality and inferiority.

There is much truth to this way of looking at the situation, but it is not the complete picture, for *mestizaje* also affected Iberia, and even in Latin America it affected not just the conquered but also the conquerors. Both *criollo* and Iberian culture, ethnicity, and even race – if one can still speak meaningfully about race – became *mestizas*, even more than they already were. And this *mestizaje* did not come from a sense of servitude and inferiority. In this case the dominated imposed their ways on the dominator, a fact which cannot be interpreted in terms of servitude and inferiority. Iberians, whether in Europe or in America, took from America because they found in it things they wanted or needed, and they did not feel inferior because of it. The phenomenon of *mestizaje*, then, is not necessarily based on inequality and inferiority. To take what one does not have but wants or needs, does not imply inferiority. It does imply a kind of inequality, but not an inequality of value or worth; it implies an inequality of having rather than being; I do not have what you have and I want it or need it. This want or need does not ipso facto make me inferior or unequal to you as a being.

Mestizaje can be egalitarian and self-assertive,[53] and in fact it has been so in the Hispanic world in many cases, even if in Latin America it has been based, more often than not, on a sense of servitude and inferiority. The Inca Garcilaso de la Vega took pride in being a mixture, even when others regarded his being *mestizo* with contempt.[54] We need not reject *mestizaje*; we need only recognize it for what it is.[55] Indeed, the rejection of *mestizaje* is precisely a sign of a sense of inferiority if those who reject it are the borrowers, and a sense of superiority if those who reject it are the lenders. It reveals that they still consider a particular culture, ethnicity, or race superior to another, and thus that they have a desire to preserve it pure and unmixed.

I hope it is clear that I am not advocating cultural relativism. If anything, I am advocating the reverse, for I am proposing the need for borrowing and lending while arguing that these do not imply inferiority or superiority in culture or ethnicity, let alone race. Those who draw a different inference miss the point.

The few examples of *mestizaje* I provided earlier are not meant to exhaust a list which seems endless, but to illustrate a phenomenon which has permeated the reality of Iberia and Latin America since the first encounter. Moreover, this reality has become stronger rather than weaker with time. As means of travel and communication become more common, the relations between the variegated members of the Hispanic world become stronger and closer. Common projects – intellectual, cultural, and political – are increasing. At one time, isolation was the permanent status quo of Latin American societies, but this isolation has been decreasing steadily in the last few years. The process of globalization that is taking place is forcing the members of the Hispanic world to come together to form a block of resistance and defense against other cultural, political, and ideological blocks. Union seems a requirement of survival. Even deep ideological disagreements have not been enough to sever ties between countries and societies in the Hispanic world. Consider that Franco's Spain never broke diplomatic relations with Castro's Cuba in spite of an enormous ideological gulf between the two. And consider that Latin American countries frequently resisted the extraordinary pressures brought to bear on them by the United States to isolate Cuba after 1959.

The overwhelming fact of *mestizaje* among Hispanics does not mean, however, that it has not been resisted or blamed for all sorts of ills. Indeed, Latin American positivists at the end of the nineteenth century and the beginning of the twentieth frequently identified *mestizaje* as the cause of what was wrong with Latin America at the time.[56] But this does not alter the fact of its all-pervasive presence.

In closing this section, let me remind the reader that I am not arguing for a conception of Hispanic which involves a particular property common to all Hispanics since 1492. *Mestizaje* is not to be construed as a property peculiar to Hispanics which sets them apart from other people. Many other peoples are *mestizos*; indeed, perhaps all peoples are so to some extent. *Mestizaje* implies no unique property, but a constant changing reality whose unity can be found only in the continuity provided by historical relations. My point is rather that our identity cannot be understood apart from *mestizaje*.

From all that has been said several consequences follow. One is that anyone who wishes to go back to some distant point of origin to recover some ethnic, cultural, or racial purity – whether Iberian, Spanish, Amerindian, African, Mexican, or whatever – that pertains to one of the groups or subgroups that constitute the Hispanic family, will be sadly disappointed. The task is impossible, first of all, because 500 years of *mestizaje* cannot be undone. There is no purity of blood or culture left in the Hispanic world; there are only elements traceable to the past which are currently inseparable from other elements. But the task is also impossible because none of the points of origin to which those who search for this purity want to go back ever existed as pure and unmixed. The Spanish, the African, the Iberian, the Mexican, the Inca, the Amerindian – all these are myths if we mean by those names something pure, unmixed, and separable. Indeed, they are at best abstractions and at worst nothing but fictional creations of the present based on nostalgic longings for the past or on political manipulation by power-seeking opportunists.

The reality of our *mestizaje* was already too evident in the nineteenth century to be denied. In the well-known words of Simón Bolívar, in his message to the Congress of Angostura,

We must keep in mind that our people are neither European nor North American; rather they are a mixture of African and the Americans who originated in Europe. Even Spain herself has ceased to be European because of her African blood, her institutions, and her character. It is impossible to determine with any degree of accuracy where we belong in the human family. The greater portion of the native Indians has been annihilated; Spaniards have mixed with Americans and Africans, and Africans with Indians and Spaniards. While we have all been born of the same mother, our fathers, different in origin and in blood, are foreigners, and all differ visibly as to the color of their skin: a dissimilarity which places upon us an obligation of the greatest importance.[57]

Indeed, the aim of recovery is not only self-defeating, it is also dangerous. The ideals of racial, ethnic, or cultural purity have been responsible for countless atrocities all over the world. And these ideals are not the exclusive property of Europeans, Iberians, or Caucasians; but it is particularly unfortunate if they are adhered to by Amerindian Latin Americans, African Latin Americans, or Hispanic Americans, for those who have been oppressed because of their race, ethnicity, or culture should know better than to adopt the ways of the oppressors. Racism, ethnicism, and cultural bias are bad in all cases, but they are particularly pernicious in the case of oppressed minorities. Their consequences – exclusion and discrimination – are bad no matter the source. It is as bad to exclude some Mexicans and Puerto Ricans from the group of Hispanics (as we saw the Spanish American Heritage Association doing) because they are *mestizos*, as it is to exclude some Brazilians from the group of Brazilians because they look white.[58] This is unacceptable and can only be described as a kind of oppression which must be avoided at all costs. Our ultimate goal, after all, should not be to exchange oppressors; it should be to prevent oppression. Oppression breeds resentment and leads to conflict and violence. To exchange oppressors does not put a stop to this conflict and violence. Only the termination of any kind of racism, ethnicism, and cultural centrism will do this. Let us welcome, then, racial, ethnic, and cultural promiscuity. Forget about racism, ethnicism, and cultural centrism. These are destructive to the core. Let us take what we can from wherever, irrespective of the source, as long as it is good. Promiscuity in this sense is based on the appreciation of what the other has to offer and, therefore, should be considered a virtue and encouraged. In this, we Hispanics are a model for the world to follow.

6 Other Sources: Latecomers

I have challenged the notions of Iberian identity, Amerindian identity, and African identity. I have also challenged the idea of a single encounter whereby Iberians, Amerindians, and Africans all came together. Instead, I have proposed the notion of many diverse peoples coming together at different times and different places, increasingly binding themselves together in various ways and forming, in addition to whatever other identities they had, an overall Hispanic identity. A corollary of this view is that not everyone who is now a Hispanic entered the world of Hispanics at the same time. Indeed, not all Iberians, Amerindians, and Africans did. Some entered it in 1492, some in 1561, and some in 1935, for example. Some Iberians came to America in the sixteenth century, but others arrived in search of work and opportunity in the twentieth century. Some Amerindians encountered the invading Iberians in the first years after the first encounter, but some lived isolated from this cataclysmic process for years or even centuries. Indeed, some Amerindian groups were not touched by this process until fairly recently. Moreover, the Africans who have become part of the Hispanic world were brought to America over a period of several centuries. There is no reason, then, to exclude from this process more recent immigrants to Iberia and Latin America. They too are part of the Hispanic world; they too went through various encounters; and they too have contributed, and are contributing, to the development of a Hispanic identity.

I am speaking, of course, of Europeans, Africans, and Asians who have emigrated to Latin America and Iberia in the recent past. Good numbers of Africans have settled in both Spain and Portugal; Asians in Spain, Portugal and various countries of Latin America; and Europeans in Spain, Portugal, and Latin America. Their numbers in some cases are very large and have changed the composition and character of the societies they joined. For example, between 1880 and 1930, more than 3 million immigrants came to Argentina. Of these 43 percent were Italian, 34 percent Spanish, 2 –6 percent Jewish, and the rest a motley of Anglo-Saxons and others. The results of this largely European immigration were evident as early as 1887. By that year the blacks in Buenos Aires, who had composed 25 percent of the population in 1838, had dropped to 2 percent.[59] Something similar happened in

Cuba. Between 1900 and 1929 approximately 900,000 Spaniards and Canary Islanders and 150,000 Haitians and Jamaicans emigrated to Cuba.[60]

Some of these immigrants have tried to preserve their original ethnicities and cultures and to avoid mixing, but generally they have not been successful. The Japanese have mixed with native Guarani; Germans with *criollo* Chileans; Welsh with Argentinians of diverse origins; Chinese with African and non-African Cubans; and so on. The mixing has been so pervasive that, even when some of them have left the country to which they had originally emigrated because of political or economic reasons, they have kept elements of their Hispanic identity. One needs to look no farther than New York City, where there are several Chinese–Cuban restaurants where both Cuban and Chinese food, customs, and language mix indiscriminately.

Of course, this immigration, like all immigration, has been uneven. Immigrants of one sort have gone to some places and immigrants of another to other places. Germans have gone to Argentina, Brazil, and Chile in greater numbers; Italians to Argentina; Chinese to Cuba; Japanese to Peru and Paraguay; Indians from India, Angolans, and Mozambicans to Portugal; North Africans to Spain; and so on. And this has added new flavors to the different areas into which they have immigrated. The immigrants have contributed to the mixing and variety of the Hispanic world, but their integration into it has not been an obstacle to Hispanic identity. On the contrary, it has contributed to its enrichment and often has strengthened it.

7 Hispanic Americans

So far I have been speaking about Hispanics in general, but now let me turn to Hispanic Americans in particular and see how we fit into the picture I have painted. Who are we, and how are we different from, and the same as, other Hispanics?

Clearly we are not Iberians, or Latin Americans, or Cubans, or Colombians, or Argentinians, or Mexicans. Some of us were one or more of these at one time, but now we are not quite that any longer. It is not clear I am a Cuban any longer. To use an example close to home: I am sure if I were to visit Cuba, I would not feel as at home there as I used to feel at one time. I have become something more, if not something entirely different. And this, whatever it is, identifies me as different from Cubans living in Cuba.

Suzanne Oboler has an interesting anecdote which is pertinent to the question of our identity as Hispanic Americans. Not long ago, a Mexican scholar was speaking at a panel on Mexican writers and she was asked how she defined "Mexican writers." The question was very important for this audience, for its members were anxious to hear something about themselves that tied them to Mexico. They wanted to hear themselves called Mexican. Yet the answer was disappointing to the audience, because it was given in national terms: "Mexican writers are either writers born in Mexico or writers who have been raised there since a very young age."[61] Clearly, this person (and I venture to say Mexicans in general) does not consider Hispanic Americans to be Mexicans, even if they are of clear Mexican descent, let alone those who are native to the American south-west.

This anecdote dramatizes in an interesting way the fact that Hispanic Americans are not Mexican, or Cuban, or even Latin American; we are Americans with more or less close links to Mexicans and Mexico, Cubans and Cuba, and so on. Indeed, Hispanic Americans are Americans with links to many other Hispanics; this is why we also qualify as Hispanic Americans. To have these links, to be related in these ways to other Hispanics, that is, Mexicans, Cubans, Iberians, and so on, is to be Hispanic and, in the United States, to be Hispanic American. We come from different places and have different backgrounds, but nonetheless we maintain relations with other Hispanics which are different from those we maintain with other Americans. Let me begin, then, by saying something about our particular origins, because those origins are part of the historical relations that tie us to other Hispanics.

Hispanic Americans have very diverse origins. Long before the Pilgrims landed in North America, Spanish explorers and missionaries had traveled in Florida, some of the southern states, and the south-west.[62] As a result of these travels, some communities were formed – mixtures of Spaniards and Native Americans – who learned Spanish and adopted some of the ways of the Spaniards, including the Catholic faith. From the beginning there was mixing, both racial and cultural, so that these communities could not be identified as purely Spanish or purely native. Although there were some members of the communities who tried to keep themselves racially unmixed, none was immune from racial and cultural mixing. The ideal of racial purity based on unmixed Spanish descent in this context is no more than a "fantasy heritage," as Carey McWilliams has appropriately called it.[63] Both Spaniards from Spain (i.e. Castilians, Catalans, Andalucians, etc.) and untouched groups of Native Americans would have found significant differences between these communities and themselves.

In the south-west in particular, these communities were regularly supplied with missionaries and later administrators and bureaucrats from New Spain. Indeed, Spain claimed both Florida and the south-west, and Mexico lost the south-west to the United States only after the Mexican–American War in 1848. This loss, however, did not stop the population of this area from considering itself different from Anglo Americans and from maintaining strong ties to people who lived across the Río Grande.

An important event in the history of the Hispanic American community in the United States was the acquisition of Puerto Rico by the United States as a result of the Spanish–American War. This was important not only because it substantially increased the number of Hispanics in the United States, but also because it made possible for Puerto Ricans to enter the continental United States legally and to remain there (Puerto Ricans were granted United States citizenship in 1917). Puerto Rico became an increasing source of Hispanics for the continental United States, and one that has strongly resisted assimilation and acculturation. There are many reasons for this resistance, but one no doubt is the facility with which Puerto Ricans can return to Puerto Rico. Puerto Ricans living in Puerto Rico and those living in the continental United States have been able to maintain close ties. This, in turn, has allowed the Puerto Rican population to maintain an identity distinct from that of other Americans, and has also kept Puerto Ricans in close touch with Hispanic countries outside the United States, particularly with Cuba, the Dominican Republic, and Spain.

Another important group of Hispanics in the United States are Cubans. These began immigrating into the United States for political or economic reasons in the nineteenth century. Even the greatest Cuban poet and national hero, José Martí, spent some time in the United States. But the largest immigration of Cubans came in the 1960s as a byproduct of the Cuban Revolution. Approximately half a million Cubans came into exile in the United States and most of them settled in Florida, particularly in and around Miami. This community has grown considerably since then, and in the 1980s increased even further as a result of the so-called Boat-lift, when around 120,000 Cubans were brought into Florida in a flotilla organized by Cuban exiles.

Apart from these major groups of Hispanics, there has always been a steady, if small, immigration of political exiles and people from a variety of other countries in search of better economic opportunities. Argentinians, Brazilians, Chileans, Venezuelans, and others have joined the Hispanic American community in the United States from time to time. More recently, they have been joined in greater numbers by Dominicans, Colombians, and Central Americans. Moreover, some Portuguese immigrants settled long ago along the north-east coast.

Most large groups of Hispanics tend to congregate in certain areas: Mexican Americans in the South-west, Cubans in Florida, Puerto Ricans and Dominicans in New York City, and Portuguese along the eastern coast of the United States. But most large cities in the United States have substantial populations of Hispanics of various origins. Hispanics also tend to congregate in more rural areas where there is agricultural work to be done, whether seasonal or permanent. One can find nuclei of different Hispanic groups throughout the United States.

The different locations of these Hispanic groups have resulted in a certain isolation from each other and sometimes in the development of rivalries and jealousies between them.[64] The siege mentality produced by their minority status and their marginalization in American society has sometimes been translated also into a suspicious attitude among themselves. In the abstract also, there is a sense of ethnic identity and ethnic nationalism that seeks to separate each group not only from Anglo Americans, but also from other Hispanic groups. Hence, there exists a sometimes passionate call for the rejection of a common name and the adoption of more ethnically parochial epithets. These groups maintain strong ties to certain countries of Latin America: Cuban Americans with Cuba; Mexican Americans with Mexico; Dominican Americans with the Dominican Republic; and so on. But the relations between them, *qua* groups, in the United States are not strong. Nonetheless, at the more personal level, and in spite of the rhetoric used by some of their self-proclaimed leaders, there is considerable affinity among the groups. And there is also the undeniable fact that there is considerable mixing among members of these groups. Indeed, there is so much of this that there have been calls for the United States Census to take into account mixed categories of ethnicity.[65]

The rivalries among these groups are in part the result of their peculiar situation and do not reflect the national rivalries that sometimes exist between some countries or groups in Latin America or Iberia. Serious conflicts have erupted from time to time between Latin American countries and between ethnic groups in Latin America and Iberia. In the nineteenth century Latin America saw several national wars and there have been conflicts of various sorts between different segments of the population both in Latin America and Iberia. The wars have been to a great extent artificially manufactured by *caudillos* and groups seeking power in particular countries. They usually exploit ideas and feelings of "national pride" based on territorial disagreements, mostly about useless pieces of land. Indeed, one grows tired of the repeated flare-ups between Argentina and Chile, and the ease with which the governments of these nations manipulate those disputes to distract attention from serious internal stresses that threaten to destabilize the governments.

These national conflicts have little import when it comes to personal relations among the people themselves. There is, of course, some good-natured and sometimes not so very good-natured criticism of the ways of other countries in some Latin American and Iberian countries. These criticisms, however, are not very deep and do not undermine the many ties that exist among the people. Neither the manufactured national conflicts, nor those that exist between inhabitants at the grassroots level, can be taken very seriously, and they certainly cannot be compared with some of the resentment and rivalries that seem to be developing among some Hispanic American groups in this country.

Closer to these are the conflicts and rivalries that sometimes exist between ethnic groups in Latin America and Iberia, some of which go back to pre-encounter times. In Iberia, for example, there has been a serious conflict between Catalans and Castilians since the sixteenth century. In part, this is a political conflict because Catalans had political independence before that century, but were incorporated into the Spanish State afterwards. But there is also an ethnic element to it, for the Catalan's native tongue is not Castilian and there are many cultural differences between Catalans and other ethnic groups in Iberia. Yet the reasons for these rivalries and conflicts are primarily political. They stem from the desire of a group (in this case the Castilians) to establish hegemony and domination over others. Matters are made worse because Castilians have tried to extend their hegemony and domination to culture. The Spanish government repeatedly tried to suppress Catalan cultural traits, such as the language, in order to break any political resistance to centralization under Castilian rule. This has created many bad feelings and also has been the cause of much spilled blood.

In Latin America, also, there are ethnic conflicts within larger political units. Often these conflicts have been between so-called Indian groups and the dominant *mestizo* population. The most recent example of this phenomenon is the case of Chiapas in Mexico. The indigenous population of the area feels oppressed by the *mestizo* power structure, and this has caused much conflict, disruption, and violence. These conflicts originate in feelings of oppression and inequality, and are fed by the rhetoric of ethnic and national identities.

In the United States, also, some of the subgroups of Hispanics consider themselves marginalized and discriminated against, if not directly oppressed, by other Hispanic groups who treat them as inferiors. This has resulted in the development of resentment in some groups against others. Moreover, this resentment has been fed by the rhetoric of ethnic and national identities. The general sense of marginalization and isolation from mainstream American society has added to the bitterness, and in some cases has been used against other Hispanic groups instead of against the real oppressors. This, of course, is not an unusual phenomenon. It is frequent that the oppressed turn against each other rather than against those who oppress them. This is in part a consequence of their inability to affect the oppressors and the divisiveness that oppressors create among the oppressed in order to control them more effectively. The case of some Mexican Americans in the south-west, to whom we referred earlier, who reject the label "Mexican" because of the way they were treated by the conquering Anglo Americans, is a classic illustration of this phenomenon.

Let me summarize. Hispanic Americans are Americans, but Americans who have a history of relations with other Hispanics within and outside the United States. And this history makes us members of the historical family of Hispanics. Unlike members of Latin American nations, we do not have political ties to other Hispanics outside the United States. But political ties are only some of the ties that unite Hispanics. The ties that unite Hispanic Americans with other Hispanics have to do more often with origin, culture, and values. Like other

Hispanics, moreover, we are the product of *mestizaje*. These ties constitute the elements of our identity as Hispanics and Hispanic Americans.

8 Conclusion

I hope it has become clear how the Hispanic identity was forged. It is an identity resulting from a cataclysm which cannot be characterized in benevolent terms by any stretch of the imagination. Yet there arose from this cataclysm something new, a new people, who are related in important ways and constitute a historical family. These people do not share common properties throughout history. Rather, we are eminently diverse, but our diversity has produced a non-homogeneous mixture which nonetheless has an identity that warrants a common name. In the next chapter, I explore the conscious search for identity in one segment of the Hispanic community: Latin America. It will serve to make explicit various dimensions involved in the search for a Hispanic identity.

6

The Search for Identity
Latin America and Its Philosophy

The search for identity among Hispanics takes three forms pertinent to our discussion: the search for identity in the Iberian peninsula; the search for identity in Latin America; and the search for identity among Hispanics in the United States. The first two have been under way for a long time. In Spain it became critical in the nineteenth century with the group of intellectuals known as the Generation of '98. The event that prompted it was the loss of Cuba, Puerto Rico, and the Philippines in the Spanish–American War. Spain had considered itself a world power for the previous 400 years. Its navy sailed throughout the world and its will was imposed on a vast empire where the sun never set. During the nineteenth century this empire was greatly reduced with the loss of the continental colonies in America; nonetheless, Spain continued to maintain a significant presence in the Far East, the Caribbean, and Africa. Defeat in the Spanish–American War, however, made Spain realize how weak it in fact was. The vast Spanish empire was no more, and the country found itself poor and marginal, not just in the world, but even in Europe.

Another factor aggravated the situation. Spain had become so closely tied to its American colonies that it had not only forgotten its connection with Europe, but had forged an identity which included these colonies. After the Renaissance and the loss of its European possessions outside the Iberian peninsula, Spain's efforts were channeled almost entirely toward America. Now, having lost the last remnants of its former American empire, Spain found itself in an entirely new situation: the country lost its mission and the image it had of itself was shattered. Who or what was Spain? Was it part of Europe after all? What kind of connection could Spain maintain with its former colonies? The colonies that had become independent earlier in the nineteenth century had in part shunned Spain; they had turned to France, Britain, and the United States for commerce and intellectual inspiration. If the newly independent colonies followed their example Spain would become completely isolated. Moreover, internal forces within the Iberian peninsula itself were threatening the political unity the country had enjoyed since the sixteenth century. Basques, Catalans, Galicians, and other ethnic minorities found new voices and claimed new rights which undermined the centralized power Castilians had enjoyed largely because of their control of the country's American colonies.

Reflection on these facts led the Generation of '98 to address the question of Spanish identity in depth. This is an important chapter in the history of the search for identity among Hispanics, but one that we will have to ignore for the moment for three reasons: it is parochial to the Spanish situation; it is somewhat removed from the issues of identity that face Hispanics today; and its proper discussion would require the kind of treatment for which we have no space here. For similar reasons, I shall ignore the discussion of identity in Portugal and among the various ethnic groups within the Iberian peninsula.

The search for identity among Hispanics in the United States has barely started and, therefore, has no history to speak of; its history is in the making. There are only a few studies that have explicitly raised this question, and most of their perspectives are limited to particular social sciences, such as anthropology, psychology, and sociology. Practically nothing has been done from a more general point of view and certainly nothing from a philosophical perspective.[1] Indeed, those Hispanic American philosophers who have discussed issues of identity have done so with respect to Latin Americans rather than Hispanic Americans.

Instead of dwelling on Iberia or the United States, then, I believe we can learn more about the question of Hispanic identity if we turn our attention to Latin America. This effort serves our purpose better because the search for identity in Latin America extends to many countries with different populations and conditions. Latin Americans have always been keenly aware of the enormous differences that separate them and the challenges involved in finding common ground. Latin America is closer to the United States than Iberia, and its population is more tightly related to the Hispanic population in this country. Moreover, the conscious search for identity in Latin America began quite early and has received considerable attention at almost every level of intellectual activity.[2] Finally, this has been a topic of discussion not only for Latin Americans, but also for some Hispanic Americans.

The most conscious effort to find a Latin American identity has been made in philosophical contexts. Not that such a search has not been undertaken in other contexts. We find it in many other cultural expressions, but it is in philosophy that efforts have been most constant and extensive. Indeed, most discussions of identity have been carried out by philosophers, and the centerpiece of most of these discussions has always been philosophical identity. Even in cases where an explicit discussion of philosophical identity is missing, the position adopted generally presupposes views about it. For this reason the focus of our discussion will be philosophical.

1 The Issue

The search for philosophical identity has been one of the most pervasive and characteristic preoccupations of Latin American thinkers for the past 100 years.[3] Discussions of this issue are frequently introduced with the question: Is there, or can there be, a Latin American philosophy? But this question is ambiguous insofar as it can be interpreted in various ways. For example, it may be taken as asking whether there are Latin American philosophers, or whether philosophical works have been and are being produced in Latin America. If the question is interpreted in this way, then its answer is quite clear, for there are many Latin Americans who practice philosophy and produce considerable philosophical writings; it is no more than an empirical question that is easily answered in terms of the evidence available. As such, it lacks philosophical interest, belonging to the realm of history.

In order for the question to have philosophical bearing, it must be concerned with something more than historical fact; it must address the issue of whether it is possible for there to be a peculiarly Latin American philosophy. Moreover, in order to resolve this matter, three things must be established, the first of which is the nature of philosophy and the nature of what is purely Latin American. Once this is done, one can determine, second, whether the nature of philosophy allows for the acquisition of characteristics that may qualify it as Latin American and, third, the relationship that such characteristics may have with philosophy. This type of inquiry, in contrast with the former, is philosophical, insofar as it involves an analysis of the notions of "philosophy" and "Latin American," and the establishment of their relationship. And this is, indeed, what has preoccupied those philosophers who have discussed the problem of the philosophical identity of Latin America.

Although Latin American philosophers have adopted many positions on this issue, their views may be classified under three headings: universalist, culturalist, and critical. The universalist position is inspired by a long tradition that goes back to the Greeks. According to this view, philosophy is a science (be it a science of reality, concepts, or language). As such, the principles it uses and the inferences it makes are meant to be universally valid; consequently, it makes no sense to talk about Latin American philosophy, just as it does not make any sense to talk about Latin American chemistry or physics. Philosophy, as a discipline of learning, cannot acquire peculiar characteristics that may, in turn, make it Latin American, French, or Italian. Philosophy, strictly speaking, is simply philosophy, or philosophy "as such," to use an expression in vogue in the literature.[4]

When one speaks of French and Italian philosophy, one does not mean that philosophy as such is any different in these two cases. Categories like "French" and "Italian" are used as historical designations to refer to the historical periods that include the thinking of the time or place one wishes to discuss, but this does not mean that philosophy in a particular period is in itself any different from philosophy in another period. What may be considered peculiar to the philosophy of a given period is not an essential part of philosophy, but simply the product of circumstances surrounding the development of the discipline at the time. As a result, then, such peculiarities are not part of the discipline, and are not included in its study; they are only part of historical studies concerning the period in question, just as a mathematical error is not part of mathematics, and just as the study of Egyptian physical theories is not part of physics. Philosophy, like mathematics and other disciplines of human knowledge, consists of a series of truths and methods of inquiry that have no spatiotemporal characteristics. Their application and validity are universal and, therefore, independent of the historical conditions in which they are discovered. The conclusion, for instance, that rationality is part of human nature is true or false anywhere and at any time. And an *a priori* or an *a posteriori* method of procedure is what it is, independently of historical location.

From this perspective, then, the answer to the question of whether there is a Latin American philosophy is negative. Furthermore, this universalist view not only denies that there is a Latin American philosophy, but it also rejects that there could be one, for it sees an intrinsic incompatibility between the nature of philosophy as a universal discipline of learning and such particular products as culture.

To this, the culturalist responds by contending that the universalist makes a serious mistake. Philosophy, as everything else based on human experience, depends on specific spatiotemporal coordinates for its validity. There are no universal and absolute truths. Truth is always concrete and the product of a viewpoint, an individual perspective. This can be applied even to mathematical truths, as Ortega y Gasset, a philosopher favored by many culturalists, suggests.[5]

Orteguean perspectivism, introduced in Latin America by many of Ortega's disciples and particularly José Gaos, is to a great extent responsible for the popularity of the culturalist view in Latin America. A philosophy that emphasizes the value of the particular and idiosyncratic lends itself quite easily to supporting the views of culturalist thinkers.[6] Consequently, many of them adopted this view unhesitatingly, adapting it to their conceptual needs. This is how the idea of a Latin American philosophy as a philosophy peculiar to Latin America came about; a philosophy different from that of other cultures and particularly opposed to Anglo-Saxon philosophy. This philosophy is supposedly the product of Latin American culture, which is in turn the product of the perspective from which Latin Americans think. This view has given way to the search for an autochthonous philosophy that can unambiguously reflect the characteristics of Latin American culture.

From this perspective, it is not only possible to find a Latin American philosophy, but also one is led to conclude that any genuine philosophy produced in Latin America must be Latin American. If it is not, then it is simply a copy of philosophies produced elsewhere, imported and imposed on Latin America. As such, these alien ways of thinking do not constitute a genuine philosophy when they are adopted in Latin America because they do not have any relation to Latin American culture, being, as they are, the products of perspectives completely foreign to those of the region.

Many of the thinkers who adopt this view conclude that, at present, there is no Latin American philosophy because the only philosophy that has been practiced in the area is imported. But, at the same time, they trust in a different future. Others, on the contrary, point out that there are some Latin American philosophical perspectives that can be classified as Latin American, and although they may be few, they are sufficient to justify the use of the term "Latin American philosophy" with a culturalist connotation.

A third view adopted by Latin American philosophers in relation to this problem may be described as critical; it has been put forward as a reaction against both universalism and culturalism, although it takes some elements from both. This view, like the universalist, rejects the existence of a Latin American philosophy, but not because the concept of "Latin American" is incompatible with the concept of "philosophy." Rather, it rejects it because it claims that until now philosophy in Latin America has had an ideological character, that is, it has not been a free pursuit. Philosophy has been used and is used in Latin America, according to the proponents of this view, to support ideas conducive to both the continuation of the status quo and the benefit of certain interest groups. Followers of this point of view offer as examples the cases of Scholasticism and positivism.

In relation to Scholasticism they stress how the Spanish Crown made use of Scholastic philosophy to maintain its political and economic hegemony over its colonies. Scholastic philosophy, they argue, became an instrument to sustain an otherwise ideologically untenable position. In the case of positivism they emphasize how certain Latin American governments used this philosophical viewpoint to justify both their conception of social order and the supremacy of a ruling elite. The most frequently cited case is that of Porfirio Díaz's government in Mexico, which adopted positivism as the official doctrine of the regime.

The inference drawn, on the basis of this and other examples, is that until now there has not been, and in the future there cannot be, a genuine Latin American philosophy so long as present social and economic conditions prevail. Only when this situation changes, and philosophy is no longer used ideologically to justify the *modus vivendi*, can there be an opportunity for an authentic Latin American philosophy to develop. Some of those who defend this view think that this Latin American philosophy will be the product of a peculiarly Latin American perspective, adopting therefore a culturalist view with respect to the future. Others, on the contrary, take a universalist position, and suggest that this non-ideological philosophy will be universally valid and purely scientific. They all coincide, however, in viewing the role of philosophy at present in a critical light.

These three views have advantages and disadvantages. To begin with the critical view, for instance, it is undoubtedly true that in many ways several philosophical systems popular in Latin America have become ideologies used to defend and maintain the status quo. In this, the followers of the critical view are right. They are also right in suggesting that this ideological defense of certain positions has precluded the development and originality of philosophy in Latin America. Apologetic concerns, along with other considerations alien to philosophical endeavors, have prevented the free development of philosophy and the results that could otherwise be expected from it. But, on the other hand, the critical view makes two serious mistakes. The first is to conclude that all philosophical work produced in Latin America is ideological. This type of assertion requires historical foundation, something that so far has not been given. It is true, as mentioned before, that there are many cases in which philosophy has been used ideologically, but this does not mean that it has always been so or that it has to be so. The second mistake is to maintain that Latin American philosophy will not be free from ideology until social and economic conditions change in Latin America. As can be clearly seen, this is an assumption based on a very particular conception of philosophy, one which understands the discipline as an expression of social and economic conditions. But this is far from indubitable. Indeed, the very existence of the claim concerning the ideological character of all Latin American philosophy seems to invalidate the universality of the claim.

Something similar happens with the culturalist view. It is obvious that philosophy functions in the context of a given culture, receiving from it impulse and direction. Philosophy does not exist in a vacuum; it is the product of human reflection, which is in turn always particular, belonging to one person or another in specific situations and cultures.

But this does not mean that the content of philosophy – that is, the claims that it makes, the arguments it uses, and the conclusions it reaches – is necessarily relative to this or that person, or to the conditions where it is produced. This can be illustrated by referring to four different types of declarative sentences which can be used to express different claims: absolute, relative, universal, and particular.

A declarative sentence is absolute when its truth value does not depend on factors other than those described in it. Note that I am not saying *all* factors, for there are many sentences whose truth depends on particular facts, even though they are absolute. An obvious case is the sentence, "Cuba is approximately 1,200 kilometers long." The truth of this sentence does not depend on the meaning of its terms, but on the length of Cuba, which is a fact in the world. But, at the same time, the sentence is not relative, because its truth value does not depend on factors other than those described by the sentence. Regardless of the actual truth value of the sentence, its truth value is independent of any perspective, or point of view, associated with the proponent of the sentence.

In the case of relative declarative sentences, on the contrary, their truth value depends not only on factors described by the sentence, but also on factors external to them. The sentence, "The coffee pot is to the left of the coffee cup" is relative, because its truth value depends on the relative position of the observer with respect to the coffee pot and the coffee cup. The observer may be in such a position that the coffee pot may appear to be behind, or to the right, of the coffee cup, rather than to its left. In this case, the truth value of the sentence depends in part on something other than what the sentence describes. This something other varies from case to case. It can be a scale of some sort, or it can be a principle, and so on. In all cases, however, the perspective or principle at work operates from outside what the sentence describes, although it plays a role in determining the truth value of the sentence.

Apart from absolute and relative, declarative sentences may be classified into universal and particular. A sentence is universal when its subject term refers indistinctly to every member of a given class. (I assume we are speaking of classes with more than one member.) For instance, the sentence, "The whole is equivalent to the sum of its parts" is universal, because the whole to which it refers is not any particular one; the subject term of the sentence refers indistinctly to every individual which falls under the category "whole." Universal sentences are opposed to particular ones.

A sentence is particular when the subject term refers to some members of a class but not to every member. (Again, I assume we are speaking of classes with more than one member.) The sentence, "Some islands are over 1,200 kilometers long" is particular because the subject of the sentence refers to some members of the class of islands, rather than to every member of the class.

The great majority of philosophical conclusions are expressed by universal declarative sentences, but the premises which constitute the bases for such conclusions are frequently expressed by particular declarative sentences. "An infinity of physical entities is impossible" is universal, whereas "This universe is infinite" is particular. Furthermore, there are also many philosophical sentences which are absolute and many which are both universal and absolute. An example of a sentence which is both universal and absolute is: "Nothing can be itself and not itself at the same time." Finally, there are also relative universal sentences, such as "Communist governments are unjust." This sentence is universal, but also relative, because the unjust character in question depends on circumstances which are external to the claim made by the sentence, and which have to do with the criterion of justice used. For example, if justice is interpreted in economic terms, then it is not necessarily true that communist regimes be unjust, provided they satisfy the economic needs of their citizens. Other conceptions of justice, however, may render the sentence true.

Now, the culturalist position amounts to a view which holds that every philosophical sentence is relative and particular. They are relative insofar as their truth value depends on cultural circumstances, or a cultural perspective; they are particular insofar as their subjects refer only to certain members of a class, those with whom the philosopher is acquainted. But, from what has been said, it follows that culturalists are mistaken in this claim, for not all philosophy (i.e. every philosophical sentence) is relative and particular. There are philosophical sentences that are universal and absolute.

The source of the culturalist mistake is a confusion between what a sentence says and the conditions under which it says it. All sentences, when entertained or stated by someone, are necessarily historical to the extent that the person in question is historical. This is what I like to call the *extensional historicity* of sentences, because the historicity in question refers to the sentences themselves considered apart from their content, that is, from what they say. But not all sentences say something historical. Some, such as "Jorge Gracia was born in 1942," do; but others, like "2 + 2 = 4," do not. Those that do, I call *intensionally historical*, because they say something about history. The culturalist assumes that all philosophical sentences are intensionally historical because they are extensionally historical. But this is simply not the case. Most culturalists get away with this view because the opacity of the language they use allows them to profit from this ambiguity.[7]

This does not mean, however, that the universalist view is free from severe shortcomings. In fact, by taking the completely opposite approach to culturalism and implying that all philosophical sentences are universal and absolute, universalism also falls into an intolerable extreme. Its main mistake consists precisely in refusing to accept that philosophy originates from particular conditions and that, therefore, every philosophical generalization is based on particular situations. The description of the situations on the basis of which generalizations emerge is as legitimate a part of philosophy as the general conclusions harbored by the discipline. This is why in philosophy we find not only universal and absolute sentences, but also particular and relative ones, which in many cases provide the foundation for universal or absolute sentences. It is in the nature of science, philosophical or not, to proceed in this fashion, for science and philosophy are human endeavors, and we humans are historical and individual. Of course, this does not mean that we cannot transcend historical circumstances. Indeed, we do so the moment we formulate true universal principles and laws. But it must be remembered that philosophy also includes the sort of relative universal sentence we examined earlier.

What is the answer, then, to the question, can there be a Latin American philosophy? The answer, like most good philosophical answers, is both affirmative and negative. It is affirmative in three senses. First, as a discipline of human knowledge, philosophy begins from the set of particular circumstances surrounding the observer who carries out the inquiry. Second, some of the conclusions reached by philosophy, however universal, are still relative to the observer and his or her culture, making complete sense only when they are seen in the context in which they originate. This is another way of saying that philosophy includes relative and particular declarative sentences, whose truth value depends directly on historical circumstances. Third, in spite of the social pressures which strive to transform philosophy into an ideology in Latin America, in principle it still can overcome these circumstances and develop freely, for there is no logical reason that stands in its way.

The answer is also negative in three senses. First, the aim of philosophy as a discipline of human learning consists, at least partly, in transcending the particular circumstances surrounding the observer who carries out the inquiry. Second, a great many of its conclusions, although starting from particular data, are universal and absolute, and, therefore, (a) they can be applied to all cases of the same kind, and (b) their truth value is independent of the historical circumstances related to the observer. Third, ideological pressures are so strong in Latin America that it is quite difficult for philosophy to follow an independent course.

2 History of the Controversy

The division into the universalist, culturalist, and critical positions is useful for the purpose of providing a general sense of the historical development of this philosophical controversy in Latin America, but it is not sufficient. We also need to offer a more detailed account of the specific views adopted by the leading participants in the controversy in order to discover the internal mechanisms that originated and developed it. Also, a closer look at their views may help us determine what unity, if any, exists in Latin American philosophical thought.

Explicit questions about a Latin American philosophical identity were first explored in the writings of Leopoldo Zea (b. 1912) and Risieri Frondizi (1910--83) in the 1940s. The growth of philosophical literature until then justified, and perhaps even required, an investigation of this sort. The proliferation of specialized journals, the creation of philosophy departments in various universities, and the foundation of international associations that had started to coordinate philosophical activity in the region prompted the raising of this issue.[8]

The problem of the character and future of Latin American philosophy, however, had been raised much earlier. The first author to do so was the Argentinian Juan Bautista Alberdi (1810–84). As an outstanding member of the thriving liberal movement of his time, Alberdi put forth his ideas under the influence of a liberalism very closely allied with the philosophical rationalism, the anti-clericalism, and the optimism about industrialization that were so characteristic of nineteenth-century Latin America. His view of philosophy was not alien to the basic tenets of this movement. Alberdi, however, had a high degree of awareness of the connection between philosophy and cultural identity that, for good reasons, has drawn the attention of many philosophers who have subsequently focused on the theme of Latin American philosophy.

According to Alberdi, Latin American philosophy must have a social and political character intimately related to the most vital needs of the region. Philosophy is an instrument that can help introduce an awareness about the social, political, and economic needs of Latin American nations. This is why Alberdi categorically rejected metaphysics and other "pure and abstract" philosophical fields, which he viewed as alien to urgent national needs.[9]

Alberdi showed no interest in glorifying "Americanism" through philosophy and did not consider the discipline anything idiosyncratic or culturally peculiar to Latin America. On the contrary, he saw philosophy as a means of providing arguments to eliminate cultural and economic models based on the alleged prevalence of Spanish colonial institutions in nineteenth-century Latin American society. Alberdi proposed the implementation of an industrial society based on the democratic–liberal features he perceived as characterizing the political organization of the United States.[10]

To this effect, Alberdi believed it necessary to eliminate the cultural legacy of Spain and dilute the peculiar racial characteristics of segments of the Argentinian population. Just like his liberal peers Domingo Faustino Sarmiento and José Victorino Lastarria, Alberdi blamed existing national characteristics for the economic disadvantage of the region in relation to Europe and the United States. To eliminate such crippling traits, Alberdi proposed industrializing the region, importing European and American capital, and encouraging massive Anglo-Saxon immigration. In this group he saw a work ethic largely absent in the native population.[11]

It is significant that Alberdi explicitly opposed technology to cultural identity. The industrialization of the region, Alberdi hoped, would effectively eliminate the backward cultural features of Latin American society. It is thanks to his advocacy of industry that one realizes how far Alberdi was from being an ardent defender of "Americanism" and the culture of his time.[12] On the contrary, he was an outspoken enemy of this culture because he believed that it prevented the industrial development of Latin America. Philosophy had, henceforth, a double purpose: to oppose, on the one hand, the cultural legacy of the Spanish colonial past and, on the other, to direct the economic, political, and social development of the region. In this last respect, Alberdi's ideas coincide with the basic tenets of positivism, the most popular school of thought in Latin America in the second half of the nineteenth century.[13]

Positivism, in fact, at least in the Latin American version, advocated the development of science and technology, rejected religion and metaphysics, and saw the Latin American native population as responsible for the economic backwardness of Latin America. While fighting to introduce the teaching of science in the Latin American system of education, and defending the industrialization of the region, positivism also produced a series of racial theories which attempted to explain the "inferiority" of the native Latin American population.[14] The reasons for this emphasis on race are intimately connected with the identification, common at the time, made between technology and what many considered to be the Anglo-Saxon race. To many positivists, and also to many liberals, the great obstacle to the industrialization of Latin America came from the predominantly Latin and native populations and their alleged resistance to technology and the Anglo-Saxon character attached to it.

The positivist model for social and economic development received one of its first attacks from José Enrique Rodó (1871–1917).[15] This Uruguayan thinker understood the distinction between technology and culture in terms of the Ariel–Caliban distinction made popular by the French philosopher Renan, who had borrowed it from Shakespeare's play *The Tempest* and used it as an instrument for social analysis. Rodó represented a reversal of the Alberdian optimism with respect to industrialization, although he legitimized this phenomenon as a genuine concern for the Latin American philosopher. According to Rodó, technology not only embodies the gross features of Caliban, but it also represents the pragmatic democracy of the United States. Two years after the Spanish–American War, when the United States emerged as a triumphant world power, Rodó wrote *Ariel*, interpreting industrialization, mass politics, and the North American expansion into Latin

American territory as an expression of the advances made by the victorious forces of Caliban.[16]

Whereas Alberdi viewed the elimination of the backward features of Latin American culture by means of industrialization and technological development rather positively, Rodó was strongly opposed to it, favoring instead the development of the same culture rejected by Alberdi. Rodó underlined the positive features of the Latin American race, which he viewed rather romantically, and ascribed to it a spirituality capable of effectively opposing the pragmatic character of the industrial phenomena introduced by Anglo-Saxons.

The Uruguayan thinker moved the confrontation between technology and culture to a spiritual level, where Ariel, the representative of the Latin race at its highest, accepted the presence of Caliban but only in a very restricted and inferior role. According to this new dichotomy, Caliban and Ariel coexisted in a world in which the former lived in the merely economic sphere, whereas the latter dwelled in a loftier spiritual sphere.[17] By means of this imagery, Rodó rejected the Anglo-Saxon social and political model transferred to Latin America through industrialization, a model which he viewed as a threat to his spiritual and aesthetic goals. His rejection of industrialization and its cultural implications, however, did not lead him to defend, or identify himself with, the Latin American native population.[18]

Such a defense and identification, however, is central in the work of the Mexican philosopher José Vasconcelos (1882–1959). He adopted many of Rodó's views, especially the dichotomies technology–culture, Latin–Saxon, and foreign–autochthonous, turning them into the very core of the question of Latin American cultural identity. A proponent of a racial and cultural Pan-Americanism, Vasconcelos was confident that the region would find a cultural unity based on the amalgamation of its racial variety. The synthesis of the different cultures and races of Latin America provided the very basis of the region's cultural identity, a feature which he opposed to the Anglo-Saxon spirit embodied by the British and North American alike.[19] In fact, Vasconcelos believed this spirit to be limited to the white race. He thought that the Latin American race, because of its higher spirituality and racial richness, could successfully confront the narrow Anglo-Saxon spirit and its brain-child, technology.[20]

Vasconcelos interpreted the conflict between Latin and Anglo-Saxon as "a conflict between institutions, purposes, and ideals."[21] A critical point to this conflict is the white Anglo-Saxon's attempt to "mechanize the world," whereas the Latin strives to integrate the components and virtues of all existing races into the one ethnic synthesis which Vasconcelos called the "cosmic race."[22] Adopting Arnold Toynbee's view concerning the tendency of races to mingle, and, from Mendel, the belief that racial mixtures are for the better, Vasconcelos believed this "cosmic race" to be the agent for the creation of the highest possible level humanity can attain: a spiritual–aesthetic stage where technology plays only a subordinate role.[23]

Vasconcelos's ideas, like Rodó's, are part of the reaction against positivism and against the notion of progress defended by this school. According to Vasconcelos and many others of his generation, such progress was only a material one which suffocated spiritual and aesthetic values. Just as Rodó did, Vasconcelos presented his views on Latin American cultural identity as a response to the industrialization of the region. He understood the opposition between technology and culture in racial terms and suggested that the greater receptivity and interests of the "cosmic race" would supersede the narrow aims and the inherent weaknesses of the white Anglo-Saxon race.

Vasconcelos's emphasis on the cultural peculiarities of different ethnic groups attracted the attention of many intellectuals during the first half of the twentieth century, especially in Mexico, where the recent revolution was seeking to vindicate socially, economically, and culturally the native segment of the population. Not only art and literature, but also philosophy and the essay of ideas in general, began to concern themselves with the racial component of the region.

Samuel Ramos (1897–1959) was perhaps the leading figure among the intellectuals who were inspired by Vasconcelos's thought. Like Vasconcelos, Ramos rejected the positivism of pre-revolutionary Mexico, though not so much in spiritual and aesthetic terms as in humanistic ones. He pointed out that the conspicuous lack of humanism in Latin American thought was due to a large extent to the legacy of positivism.[24] The growth of this humanism, which he believed to be an essential component of any genuine Latin American thought, was impeded by "the universal invasion of machine civilization," by which he meant industrialization.[25] In this way Ramos opposed humanism, which he viewed as the vehicle for the liberation of Latin Americans, to the pervasive technology which was beginning to characterize modern civilization. This mechanistic civilization, according to him, rather than helping human development, was becoming a "heavy burden" which threatened to "denaturalize" men and women.[26]

Technology, just as Vasconcelos had conceived it, had a racial foundation for Ramos. The white man – but particularly the Anglo-Saxon North American – felt at home with the use of technology, owing to a "will to power" largely absent in the inhabitants of Mexico and of Latin America at large.[27] Ramos believed that his country was threatened by the increasing power of the United States in economic and technological terms. He urged his country to become aware of this penetration, lest its people become "automatons."[28] He did not have, however, an entirely negative view of technology, and he suggested that it has some positive aspects, especially when placed under control and used for the service of people. Its most beneficial aspect is technology's capacity to free people from physical labor, thus allowing them to use their time in pursuit of higher goals.[29]

Ramos inaugurated a new trend in Latin American thought which emphasized autochthonous and national characteristics as the basis for philosophical activity. In contrast with Vasconcelos, who understood cultural identity in Latin American terms, Ramos placed his emphasis on the national level, and only by inference on Latin America in general. The study of *lo mexicano* (the properly Mexican) acquired full expression with Ramos, providing the basis for the culturalist view of Latin American philosophy.[30] Students of Ramos's thought, however, have understood *lo mexicano* in more optimistic terms than those envisioned by Ramos himself.[31] Indeed, Ramos's view that an "inferiority complex" constitutes the fundamental feature of the Mexican character, and his skepticism concerning the integration of marginal segments of the Mexican population into the mainstream of Mexican society, are far from expressing an unqualified optimism with respect to *lo mexicano*.[32]

The contrast between Vasconcelos and Ramos, however sharp it may seem, is insignificant when their common view on the power of technology is considered. Both saw in technology a threat not only to the cultural identity of Latin America, but also, and very specifically, to spiritual life in general. They, as well as Rodó, opposed technology to spiritual life, and all three concurred in viewing the latter both as aesthetically oriented and separate from the mass-directed tendencies of contemporary technology. Ortega y Gasset, whose influence on Ramos was very strong, had made this view of technology popular in his *Meditación de la técnica*, where he suggested that the spiritual emptiness which he found characteristic of modern life was the direct product of the development of technology.[33] Both in Spain and in Latin America, intellectuals viewed technology not only with some skepticism, but also in some cases with open hostility.

Latin American thinking in relation to technology and its cultural impact on the region found a more balanced theoretical expression in Félix Schwartzmann (b. 1913). This Chilean thinker understood the cultural impact of the introduction of technology as a phenomenon which is not restricted to Latin America, but which affects the entire planet. Contrary to the positions taken by his predecessors, for Schwartzmann the reaction against the process of "technological Westernization" constitutes a cultural reality of its own.[34] Therefore, he suggested that the Latin American reaction against modernity and technology provides some of the most distinctive features which constitute the cultural identity of the region.[35] The loneliness of the Latin American man, his impotence of self-expression, his search for genuine human bonds, are some of the most important traits which Schwartzmann viewed as Latin American responses against the universal phenomenon of modernity, whose main feature is impersonalism.[36] This, however, is not restricted to Latin America, for even what appear to be peculiarly regional aspects, such as the emphasis on nature, characterize any cultural response to the universal phenomenon of modernity. In search of these peculiar traits, Schwartzmann analyzed literature, poetry, and essays of ideas in the region, and found that both autochthonous and universal traits combine to produce a unique cultural expression which he called "the sense of the human in America."[37]

Schwartzmann's location in the controversy concerning a Latin American identity, then, is both similar and different to Ramos's. It is similar in that both were searching for common features to explain a common phenomenon and both considered technology an important element in the discussion of those features. But it is different in other aspects. First, Schwartzmann's emphasis was on Latin America, whereas Ramos's emphasis was on Mexico. Second, Schwartzmann's analysis concerned expressions of so-called high culture, rather than particular socio-psychological phenomena, as was the case with Ramos. Finally, Schwartzmann took a different stand with respect to the extent and nature of technology than did Ramos.

The decade of the 1940s was a period in which intellectuals looked back on Latin American culture and attempted to use it as the basis for philosophical thinking. A generation of Mexican authors inspired by Orteguean perspectivism, made popular in Latin America by the *transterrados* or Spanish exiles, particularly José Gaos,[38] suggested that the cultural "circumstances" of the region provided the basis for the development of an original Latin American philosophy. Leopoldo Zea, the leader of these intellectuals, asserted that any type of philosophical reflection emerging in the region could be classified as "Latin American philosophy" by virtue of the intimate relationship between philosophy and culture.[39] He also suggested that this Latin American philosophy had a historical foundation, owing to the fact that the Latin American man had always thought of his situation from a vitally Latin American perspective.[40] In this sense, even philosophical reflection lacking originality, resulting from mere imitation, could qualify as Latin American philosophy by virtue of its historicity and the fact that it emerges in response to peculiar vital circumstances. Therefore, Zea categorically affirmed the existence of Latin American philosophy. It is significant to note, however, that he did not feel compelled to verify his theses, as Schwartzmann had, in the literature and the arts. He did not proceed by formulating his theories on the basis of the peculiar ethos manifested by the region's culture. Rather, like many others of his generation, his views were based on an *a priori* conception of philosophy – of Orteguean origin – which understands this discipline as a historical product always emerging from particular perspectives.

The nationalist sentiment that characterized the politics of most Latin American nations at the time, but particularly Mexico, helped to promote Zea's views concerning the existence and nature of Latin American philosophy. Advocates and opponents of this conception of philosophy made their voices heard quite quickly throughout the region. Abelardo Villegas, Diego Domínguez Caballero, and Guillermo Francovich were just some of the advocates of Zea's culturalist perspective.[41] Among the opponents, Frondizi counts as a leader. For him and those others who opposed Zea and his followers, philosophy must be distinguished from cultural nationalism and should be considered independent of geographical boundaries: one should speak of philosophy *in* America rather than a philosophy *of* America.[42] Philosophy, as Francisco Romero had pointed out earlier, has no last names, that is, it must be understood as a discipline with universal characteristics.

Vasconcelos himself, whose work in many ways reflected a culturalist perspective, adopted a universalist position when discussing the nature of philosophical activity. He went so far as to deny explicitly the existence of a peculiarly Latin American philosophy on the grounds that the discipline was universal in character, although he conceded that it was the prerogative of each culture to reconsider the great themes of universal philosophy. Philosophical nationalism had no place in his thought.[43]

The polemic that suddenly surrounded the question of the existence of a Latin American philosophy in the 1940s had the effect, in many cases, of undermining the focus on cultural identity that had characterized Latin American philosophical thought prior to the dispute, and which, in many respects, had prompted it. The controversy set a precedent for discussions of culture that became increasingly separated from the actual analysis of cultural phenomena. The culturalists themselves, who base their conceptions of a Latin American philosophy on a cultural perspective, have left few detailed accounts of the region's cultural ethos, and frequently refer to culture in very general terms.

Eduardo Nicol (1907–90), one of the members of the generation of *transterrados* to settle in Latin America after the Spanish Civil War, was among the first to return to the search for an ethos that would define Latin American culture. He proposed the notion of *hispanidad* as the core of both Spanish and Latin American cultural identity.[44] This concept, according to Nicol, unites linguistic and cultural aspects in both geographical areas, giving a distinctive character to these regions. Still, he did not see these regions as separate from the rest of the world. In a complete turnabout from the pessimism with which many intellectuals before him had viewed technology, Nicol suggested that whatever unity the world has is due to science and technology. Technology, in effect, provides an opportunity for world integration. Neither Orteguean perspectivism nor existentialism, products of a culture of crisis, are able to muster this integration. These philosophies, from Nicol's perspective, provide a rationale for cultural regionalism and separatism in the midst of a world increasingly unified by science and technology.

Nicol's attack on one of the byproducts of cultural regionalism, namely *indigenismo*, led him to justify and even minimize the politically sensitive question of the effects of Spanish colonization in Latin America. Echoing themes already sounded by Alberdi, he charged this movement with presenting an obstacle to the economic and technological integration of the region. Followers of this movement feel threatened, he suggested, by the integrating might of science and technology. And this integrating might cannot but produce a "mutation" or upsetting of the "vital foundations" prevalent in Latin America.[45] But Nicol did not see anything negative in this process. On the contrary, he saw it as a positive step leading to a "meditation on one's own being" which will ultimately help establish a cultural ethos based on *hispanidad*. This, in turn, will produce a positive attitude in relation to technology and a subsequent end to the economic backwardness of the region.[46]

Nicol's position, then, argues in favor of an overall Hispanic unity based, contrary to the position I defend in this book, on traits common to Spaniards and Hispanic Americans. From this group he excludes the Portuguese and Brazilians and leaves unexplained the basis for the unity of Iberian and Latin American ethnic groups. His view extends, moreover, to culture in general and philosophy in particular, a feature which also separates him from his predecessors in this controversy.

Phenomenological views of a Heideggerian variety, represented by Ernesto Mayz Vallenilla (b. 1925), have also been used in the philosophical analysis of Latin America's cultural identity. According to Mayz Vallenilla, Latin American culture is historically based on the Latin American man's "expectation to become."[47] This expectation provides a peculiar state of consciousness which defines the most fundamental nature of man in the region. Mayz Vallenilla's definition represents an attempt to understand culture in ontological terms, an attempt which exempts him from examining in detail literary, artistic, and social expressions. In a later work, however, he picked up the thread which explicitly relates technology and culture in Latin America, revealing a desire to apply his views to technology. In fact, he suggested that technology, which has among its outstanding features certain tendencies toward fostering "anonymity" and "homogeneity," is bent on destroying a Latin American ethos based on peculiarity, originality, and an "expectation" about the future.[48] Consequently, he understands the confrontation between the Latin American cultural ethos and technology as a true "challenge."[49] It is significant that this confrontation led him to address technological phenomena in philosophical terms. In doing so, Mayz Vallenilla went back to one of the basic themes of Latin American philosophical thought, which had been temporally displaced by the discussion on the precise nature and existence of Latin American philosophy.

None of the different interpretations of the cultural identity of Latin America has become established, a fact which should not surprise us. For neither the "inferiority complex" in terms of which Ramos used to refer to the Mexican character, nor the "cosmic race" of Vasconcelos, nor a particular sense of the human proposed by Schwartzmann, nor the *hispanidad* of Nicol, nor the "expectation" of Mayz Vallenilla, are subject to verification. There is, indeed, no consensus concerning the character of Latin American culture so far, and the definitions and descriptions of it which have been provided to date are frequently too abstract and general to gain acceptance.

The lack of a consensus about the notion of Latin American culture extends also to the notion of Latin American philosophy. This is one of the reasons why during the 1960s a number of authors readdressed this problem, although not in terms of either universalism or culturalism. It was at this time that the critical position discussed earlier arose. These authors viewed the general issue of identity in Latin America and the more particular issue of philosophical identity in the region in terms of social conditions, ideology, oppression, and domination.

Augusto Salazar Bondy (1926–74), for instance, regarded philosophy in Latin America as the province of intellectual elites. These elites have borrowed European cultural forms uncritically, lacking an identifiable and rigorous methodology and an awareness of the situation of other social groups. Considered in this light, the problems of culture and philosophy have been problems for only a small minority of intellectuals alienated from the rest of society, and from economic, social, and political problems.[50] This position, which has also been shared by Juan Rivano (b. 1926), suggests that the history of the controversy concerning the existence and nature of a Latin American philosophy epitomizes a lack of concern among intellectuals with the most urgent problems of their respective communities.

This last author, however, also discussed technology, suggesting that it is part of its very nature to precipitate a crisis of cultural identity. As Schwartzmann and Nicol before him, Rivano considered that this crisis is not restricted to Latin America. For him, it is in the nature of technology to extend its influence all over the world in a process which he termed "technological totalization."[51] Thus, he maintained that the question of the region's cultural identity must be considered in the context of the global phenomenon of technology. As Mayz Vallenilla had, Rivano developed categories which he viewed as fundamental for understanding technological questions in philosophical terms.

Those who favored the universalist position reacted quickly to this new philosophical position with respect to the problem of the philosophical identity of Latin America. Among them was Fernando Salmerón (1925–97), who, in spite of having developed "culturalist" themes at the beginning of his philosophical career,[52] in subsequent years rejected both the culturalist and the critical postures. According to him, two different conceptions of philosophy must be distinguished. The first conceives philosophy as "wisdom or a conception of the world and that, strictly speaking, it is nothing but the expression of a moral attitude."[53] In this sense, it is possible to adopt a position like that of Salazar Bondy, for example. But the word "philosophy" is also understood more strictly "to refer to a determinate intellectual enterprise, analytic and theoretical, which, guided by an appropriately scientific energy, confronts problems of various types – for example, logical, epistemic, semantic – making use of certain methods about which there is general agreement."[54] If philosophy is understood in this way, then neither the culturalist nor the critical position makes sense.

In recent years a new dimension has been added to the controversy surrounding Latin American philosophy: the attempt to understand and locate this controversy in historical terms, as well as to study its origins, limits, and themes. Francisco Miró Quesada (b. 1918) is among the most important thinkers who have propounded this type of study. He has analyzed the causes, results, and future of this controversy, as well as the views proposed by many authors. The situation which originated the issue of identity, according to him, is a so-called "sense of disorientation." The effort to overcome this disorientation, he suggests, "is the key for understanding Latin American philosophical activity."[55] His concern is not with the question whether there is, or can be, a Latin American philosophy, but rather with the study of the preoccupation with the topic and its future.[56]

The controversy has continued to grow and attract much attention among members of practically every philosophical tradition, with the exception of analytic philosophy. Existentialists, phenomenologists, Thomists, Kantians, and Ortegueans have felt compelled to explore this issue. But since none of the different interpretations of the cultural identity of Latin America has become widely accepted, it has been impossible in turn to establish a consensus on the notion of Latin American philosophy.

It is in this milieu that the movement known as the "philosophy of liberation" appeared in the 1970s. For philosophers like Enrique Dussel (b. 1934), Horacio Cerutti Guldberg (b. 1950), and Arturo Andrés Roig (b. 1922), the fundamental task of philosophy in Latin America consists in the social and national liberation from unjust relations, such as that of dominating–dominated, that have traditionally characterized Latin America. For Roig in particular, this implies an integration of the Latin American peoples based on the consciousness of the historicity of the American man and of the history of philosophy in Latin America. He rejects what he considers to be the formalism and ontologism characteristic of traditional academic philosophy, favoring instead a philosophy of commitment that seeks integrating concepts in Latin America. The novelty of this philosophy, according to him, will be founded in the political discourse of the marginal and exploited segments of society, developing an authentic thought that may serve to give rise to man's humanity.[57]

The last chapter of this controversy and one that is still in progress is being written by postmodernists. Following the venerable Latin American tradition of applying European ideas to Latin American issues, some Latin American authors have initiated a reflection *on* the reflection concerning the cultural and philosophical identity of Latin America. Their concern is with what the historical reflection on Latin American identity tells us. Their object of analysis, then, is not the identity of Latin America, or the history of Latin American thought concerned with that issue. It is the Latin American discourse on identity and what it reveals about itself.[58]

3 The Hispanic-American Contribution

An important chapter of this controversy which is of particular interest to us is to be found in the contribution of Hispanic-American philosophers. One would have expected that a polemic concerned with the identity of Latin American philosophy would have been ignored by Hispanics living in the United States. However, several Hispanic-American philosophers have addressed this issue, and not merely from a historical or scholarly point of view. Rather than detached erudite investigations, these philosophers have produced analyses which involve them in the controversy itself. Why? What does this tell us about Hispanics in the United States and their relations with Latin America?

Perhaps we should start with some facts which may have a certain relevance. There are only four Hispanic-American philosophers who have discussed the issue of Latin American philosophical identity in any depth. There are, of course, specialists in other disciplines who have done so as well, but our concern here is with philosophy and philosophical treatments, so I shall omit reference to the others. The four philosophers in question are Oscar Martí, Vicente Medina, Ofelia Schutte, and myself.

Several facts stand out about this group. All four are Cubans who emigrated to the United States. Three are over 50 years in age, and one is in his 40s. Two teach in graduate philosophy programs and two in undergraduate programs. All four teach in states where there is a heavy concentration of Hispanics: New York, New Jersey, California, and Florida. For two of them their primary field of specialization is Latin American thought; the other two work in other areas, although they maintain an interest in Latin American thought. From these facts not much can be inferred. One thing that may be significant is that all of these philosophers are foreign born; this may explain their interest in Latin American thought. Perhaps they feel closer to Latin America than Hispanic Americans born in the United States.

The earliest publication on the issue of Latin American philosophical identity in the United States is Oscar Martí's "Is There a Latin American Philosophy?" (1982). Martí's approach is to a large extent noncommittal. He distinguishes two ways in which one can understand the question: (1) Are there Latin American philosophers? (2) Is there a philosophy which is Latin American in character? The answer to the first is generally affirmative, and Martí concurs; the answer to the second, however, is controversial because it depends on one's conception of philosophy. Those who view philosophy in universalist terms answer negatively; those who view it in culturalist terms answer affirmatively.

Martí refuses to commit himself to one of these views of philosophy to the exclusion of the other and thus to any one answer to the question of Latin American philosophy understood in the second sense.

He prefers a middle ground where philosophy is taken both as "its history and the attempts to solve those problems we see as universal."[59] In the end he prefers to stay neutral with respect to the issue, although he grants that the way he has raised it already implies some commitments.

Almost contemporary with Martí's article was "The Problem of Philosophical Identity in Latin America: History and Approaches" written by Iván Jaksić and me (1984). This was followed by a section in a book on Latin American philosophy in the twentieth century which I edited in 1986, where I introduced the issue and included texts by Leopoldo Zea, Augusto Salazar Bondy, and Arturo Andrés Roig. Two other publications on this topic followed, but they appeared in Spanish: an anthology edited with Jaksić, in which we gathered most of the classic texts on this controversy, *Filosofía e identidad cultural en América Latina* (1988), and an article by me entitled "Zea y la liberación latinoamericana" (1992).[60]

The thrust of the first three publications has been summarized in the previous sections of this chapter. In the last article, however, I proposed a way of understanding Latin American philosophy through the idea of liberation. My argument is that the history of Latin American thought can be seen as a progressive search for liberation in diverse ways, culminating in the contemporary liberationist thought. The bases of the search are found in the long struggle for political and religious liberation known as the *Reconquista* and in the spiritual and civil liberation of Amerindians in colonial Scholasticism. This was followed by the more explicit awareness of the need for liberation in the political struggle for independence, in the economic struggle for development and progress promoted by nineteenth-century positivism, in the individual and moral struggle against positivist mechanicism and determinism at the beginning of the twentieth century, and subsequently in the cultural and intellectual struggle for the establishment of Latin American and national identities. This process took 500 years and culminates in the philosophy and theology of liberation, which propose to make the idea of liberation the central concept of Latin American thought and to extend it to all aspects of Latin American experience.

The desire for liberation, so I argued, is a constant in the intellectual life of Latin American thought and reveals both its marginal and subservient condition throughout history as well as the awareness of this condition. This does not mean, however, that this condition and awareness are idiosyncratically characteristic of Latin American thought; there may be other intellectual histories that may reveal a similar emphasis; but it does reveal an element of Latin American philosophy. The concern for liberation, then, is neither a sufficient nor a necessary part of Latin American philosophy; it is merely a feature based on a limited judgment of past Latin American intellectual history.

Following the work of Jaksić and Gracia, two pieces by Ofelia Schutte are of particular interest here. The first, "Toward an Understanding of Latin American Philosophy: Reflections on the Foundations of Cultural Identity," appeared in 1987; the second is a substantial monograph, *Cultural Identity and Social Liberation in Latin American Thought*, which integrates earlier work, including the 1987 article, and was published in 1993. It presents an original perspective which departs from standard treatments of this issue.

Schutte's concern is not primarily with the question of philosophical identity, but with the question of cultural identity, although she uses the discussion of cultural identity to present a new interpretation of the history of philosophy in Latin America in the twentieth century. This interpretation is presented from a socio-political perspective in which the point of view of some marginalized voices, such as those of heterodox Marxists like José Carlos Mariátegui (1894–1930) and women, take center stage and in which the idea of liberation has a key role. Schutte's subtle historico-philosophical analyses show how even self-proclaimed champions of Latin American liberation like Zea and Dussel fall short of what is required. They too frequently adopt European and masculine categories, precluding a true understanding of those they wish to liberate. True liberation must go deeper and adopt the cultural perspectives and conceptual categories of those who are to be liberated. The poor, the Latin American, women, and so on, must be allowed to speak for themselves and in their own terms. It is their identity that is at stake, and any understanding of that identity must come from within.

Schutte claims that there is an established tradition in Latin American thought dealing with questions of cultural identity and social liberation. To this extent her claim is descriptive and is not controversial. But she goes beyond this in showing that views of cultural identity too frequently have been used "to block the process of social liberation"[61] and in claiming, prescriptively, that this should be stopped.[62] Her view is that both identity and difference are rooted in the human need to give meaning to one's existence. But this search should aim for a flexible identity which is open to evolution and transformation. Rejecting any kind of essentialism, separatism, or cultural superiority, Schutte defends the Latin American right to borrow and integrate elements from other cultures in a true sense of *mestizaje*.

One of the most recent contributions to the controversy on Latin American philosophical identity is an article by Vicente Medina: "The Possibility of an Indigenous Philosophy: A Latin American Perspective" (1992). Medina points out that if the term "Latin American philosophy" has any clear sense at all, it refers to one or more of the following: (1) a body of literature which discusses the possibility of a Latin American philosophy; (2) some unique features that are generally true of Latin American philosophy; and (3) the so-called philosophy of liberation. The first, he claims, has no particularly interesting philosophical consequences; the challenge of the second is to find any idiosyncratic feature to Latin American philosophy; and the third is at least questionable and at most incoherent, because it involves an ideological and, therefore, defective understanding of philosophy which leaves no room for certain universal principles such as the laws of logic. The obvious inference from all this is that there is no philosophically interesting, unquestionable, coherent, and substantial conception of a Latin American philosophical identity. The only philosophically interesting and coherent conception of that identity, as one which involves certain common, necessary, sufficient, or necessary and sufficient, features, is yet to be justified.

What can the discussion of Latin American identity by Hispanics in the United States tell us? Several things. First, the approaches are varied, but they mirror some of the discussions in Latin America itself. Two are exclusively concerned with the discussion of philosophical identity (Martí and Medina), and the others are concerned with both philosophy and culture (Gracia and Jaksić, Gracia, and Schutte). Two are systematic (Martí and Medina) and the others include both systematic and historical elements. One (Martí) is largely noncommittal with respect to substantive issues, but the others make strong substantive claims. Some of the points made by these authors are similar to theses defended by Latin Americans in Latin America, but in all cases there are elements of originality.

There are important elements of difference with discussions of identity in Latin America. For example, in none of the Hispanic-

American discussions is there an emphasis on the contrast between Latin America and Anglo-America so frequently found in Latin American discussions. Nor is there the concern with technology so often present in Latin American treatments. Finally, they have a more dispassionate, less nationalistic tone which contrasts with the very passionate and nationalistic tone of many of the Latin American discussions.

The similarities and differences between Hispanic-American and Latin American discussions are not surprising. One could easily attempt to explain the similarities by the fact that the four authors whose views we have presented are all Latin American born and, therefore, share much history with other Latin Americans. The differences could be explained by the circumstance that all of them reside in the United States and were partially educated there. As Americans, they could hardly share some of the attitudes that permeate part of the Latin American literature on philosophical and cultural identity.

4 Conclusion

There is more in the history of the search for a Latin American philosophical identity than a simple aggregation of themes and authors. For one thing, the relationship between philosophy and cultural identity in Latin America provides one of the constant topics of study since Alberdi's time. In many cases, definitions of philosophy and culture lack precision, but nonetheless reveal an effort on the part of Latin American thinkers to address cultural problems with the aid of philosophy. The problem of the impact of technology on culture, for instance, has been a recurrent theme in Latin American philosophical writing. This reflection on technology in a geographical area that, to this day, is undergoing the impact of modernization, has captured the attention of many Latin American thinkers precisely because of the magnitude of this impact in the region's culture as revealed in its literature, poetry, and essays of ideas. This, in turn, has led to a variety of views on the nature and aims of Latin American philosophy.

The controversy concerning the philosophical and cultural identity of Latin America illustrates well some of the issues that do surface and must surface in discussions of group and cultural identity. Indeed, it fits well with the general theory defended in this book insofar as it shows that there is not one, clear property common to all Latin American thought that can be used to distinguish it from others. Furthermore, it illustrates well the close interaction between Latin American and Iberian thought. It would not be possible to explain the development of Latin American philosophy in the twentieth century without reference to Ortega, for example, or the *transterrados*. It provides, also, a good contrast between the life of our philosophical community and other philosophical communities, showing that there is some unity we have which is not shared with, say, the Anglo-American philosophical world. The constant references to differences between us and Anglo-America in discussions of our cultural and philosophical identity should carry the point. The emphasis on a kind of cultural and conceptual *mestizaje* also is displayed in Latin American intellectual history. The lack of agreement and uniformity, the diversity of approaches, and the richness of the views, all point to the absence of homogeneity and fusion within a historically related and vitally engaged community. The tension between more general categories and more particular ones, between Latin America and Panama or Mexico, reveals the same dialectic that applies to discussions of an overall Hispanic identity vs. the identity of Peruvians, Dominicans, South Americans, or Hispanic Americans. Moreover, the lack of clear definition, the absence of a common property to a historically and closely related family, leaves the doors open to the future. And, finally, we can also observe in it the same sense of marginalization and inferiority that permeates discussions of Hispanic identity at large.

7

Foreigners in Our Own Land

Hispanics in American Philosophy

A book about Hispanic/Latino identity written in the United States cannot ignore our situation in American society. But this is too large a topic to be treated comprehensively and adequately here. I propose instead a narrower focus that may help us with the larger topic: the situation of Hispanics in American philosophy. This should function as an effective illustration of our place in the United States at large.

Two facts are clear when one considers the question of Hispanics in American philosophy. First, the percentage of Hispanic philosophers in the United States is significantly lower than the percentage of Hispanics in the overall population. Second, neither non-Hispanic philosophers nor Hispanic philosophers themselves pay much attention to philosophical issues involving Hispanics or to Hispanic philosophy. In this chapter, I defend the thesis that an important reason for these facts is that Hispanic philosophers are perceived as foreigners and their issues and philosophical thought are regarded as belonging to a different, non-American culture.

1 The Problem

Let me begin by saying something about the number of Hispanics in philosophy in the United States. In recent years there has been an increase in the number of Hispanics working in philosophy, both at the faculty and the graduate student levels, but our numbers are still very low. The results of a 1992 questionnaire sent by the American Philosophical Association's Committee for Hispanics in Philosophy to 850 philosophy departments at four-year and graduate institutions, provides evidence of the small number of Hispanics in philosophy and, more specifically, of a dramatic fall in the number of philosophy undergraduate majors who continue graduate work in philosophy. Of the 316 departments that responded to the survey, only 31 percent (99 schools) reported that there were any Hispanics among their faculty, graduate students, or undergraduate majors. In these departments there was a total of 277 Hispanic undergraduate philosophy majors, 66 Hispanic graduate students, and 55 Hispanic faculty members (part- and full-time).[1] Even three years later, when I stepped down as Chair of the Committee for Hispanics in Philosophy, there were only 68 faculty members and 59 graduate students registered with the Committee.

These figures mean that because there are roughly 12,000 philosophers teaching in the United States today, the percentage of Hispanic faculty is around half a percentage point. This is a much lower percentage than that of Hispanics in the population at large, which is around 10.3 percent.[2] Indeed, even if one were to count only philosophers who are members of the American Philosophical Association (roughly 9,000) and tripled the number of Hispanic faculty registered with the Committee to account for many who may not have registered, still the percentage of Hispanics in philosophy comes out very low at 2.26 percent.

Particularly alarming is the low number of Hispanic graduate students in philosophy. The total graduate student population in philosophy in the US is roughly 1,700. This means that the percentage of Hispanic graduate students in philosophy is 3.8 percent. It also means that unless a dramatic shift in interest occurs among Hispanic undergraduates the number of teaching Hispanic philosophers will not increase sufficiently to match the proportion in the Hispanic population.

Other statistics confirm the low number of Hispanics in philosophy. The number of Ph.D.s in philosophy awarded to persons of Hispanic descent each year since 1974 appears to be the lowest of any discipline, except for English.[3] In a 1987 report on a survey of the profession by the American Philosophical Association's Committee on the Status and Future of the Profession, the number of Hispanic philosophers falls below even the extraordinarily low figures for the humanities in general.[4] A more recent survey of philosophy in the United States carried out in 1994 by the American Philosophical Association Committee on the Status and Future of the Profession does not show any significant amelioration of the situation.[5] And the situation with graduate and undergraduate students is not significantly different.[6]

So much for numbers and percentages. Consider an equally discouraging fact: currently, there are only half a dozen Hispanics who have become established philosophers in the United States and Canada, and all of them are foreign born. By "established" I mean philosophers who have full rank in philosophy Ph.D. programs and who are known in the profession for their work in some subfield of philosophy. Mario Bunge (b. 1919) was born in Argentina; Ignacio Angelelli (b. 1933) was born in Italy but considers himself Argentinian; Alfonso Gómez-Lobo (b. 1940) was born in Chile; and Ernesto Sosa (b. 1940), Ofelia Schutte (b. 1943), and I (b. 1942) were born in Cuba.[7] There is no other Hispanic in the over-50 age group who is established in his or her field, although there are some younger members of the profession who are fast developing a profile.[8]

There is another fact that needs to be taken into account. Many African-American philosophers who have achieved prominence have done so by working precisely in areas that are intrinsically related to the African-American experience and the condition of African Americans in this country. And the same goes for many women. Many of the best-known women in the profession are known for work related to the condition of women in society. The work of African Americans and women in these areas has earned them high praise and they have secured appointments at full rank in graduate philosophy programs or elite undergraduate colleges.[9] In contrast, only one of the aforementioned Hispanic philosophers, Ofelia Schutte, has as her primary field the study of the Hispanic condition. Two others, Angelelli and I, have done some work in areas related to the condition of Hispanics in philosophy, but have as primary fields of research other areas of philosophy and are known for work in the latter rather than in the former. All the others have had little or nothing to say about Hispanic issues and some of them in fact have publicly criticized those Hispanic philosophers who have.[10]

Perhaps just as significant, the philosophy curriculum in this country generally ignores Hispanic philosophy. There may be as little as a dozen universities and colleges that offer courses in Hispanic – either Iberian or Latin American – philosophy. The 1994 American Philosophical Association report cited earlier does not mention Hispanic, Latin American, Latino, Spanish, or any other kind of philosophy particularly associated with Hispanics. It does mention, however, the percentages of departments which offer courses at least every two years in Eastern/Asian (33 percent), Eastern/Indian (21 percent), Arabic/Islamic (5 percent), and African (27 percent) philosophy.[11] This leads one to conclude that either Hispanic philosophy is simply not part of the philosophy curriculum in this country or else those who carried out the survey were not sensitive to it. I believe it is the former, but even the latter would be a clear indication of little regard for Hispanic philosophy among American philosophers.

Of course, one should not be surprised at all this, for among the many historical and systematic fields for which the American Philosophical Association has Advisory Committees to the Program Committee, none is included that has to do with Latin American, Hispanic, or Latino philosophy. Yet there are committees for all sorts of other fields, including Eastern and African philosophy. And the same attitude is reflected in classroom materials. Consider, for example, *A Companion to the Philosophers* edited by Robert L. Arrington in 1999. This massive book of more than 700 pages includes articles on philosophers from Africa (8), China (18), Europe and the United States (122), India (26), Japan (11), and from the Islamic and Jewish traditions (8), but it has no articles on philosophers from *any* Hispanic country.

Add to this that the American Philosophical Association did not have a committee devoted to Hispanic issues until 1991, when Robert Turnbull, Chair of the Board of Officers, singlehandedly decided it was time for the Association to take us into account. By contrast, the Committee for Blacks in Philosophy has been in existence since 1968. Incidentally, when I contacted the National Office of the American Philosophical Association in the summer of 1997 to ask for information about Hispanics in the Association, I was told that the National Office could not help me because it had no information at all on this matter. I believe this response indicates quite clearly how invisible and unimportant Hispanics still are in the American Philosophical establishment.

This neglect, surely, has contributed to making philosophy an uninviting area of study and career choice for most Hispanic undergraduates. Political science, sociology, literature, modern languages, and religious studies appear – at least to students in introductory courses – to be more immediately and effectively relevant and welcoming to Hispanic undergraduate students.

There is a society devoted to Hispanic philosophy, the Society for Iberian and Latin American Thought (SILAT), founded in 1976 by a group of scholars concerned with the lack of attention given to Hispanic thought in this country. But its history does not show many successes.[12] Although the society is now over 20 years old and regularly organizes sessions at the meetings of the American Philosophical Association's Eastern Division, it has been a struggle to keep it alive, and the number of active members is not larger than a dozen.

This situation requires explanation. First, why is it that there are so very few Hispanics who have become established in the profession in the United States? Second, why is it that those few who have become established are foreign born? Third, why are there so very few Hispanic Americans in the profession at all? Fourth, why is Hispanic philosophy ignored in the philosophy curriculum? And fifth, why is it that Hispanic-American philosophers are not attracted by, and perhaps even avoid, areas that have to do with their identity as Hispanics, whereas African Americans and women do not?

2 Some Explanations

There are many reasons that may explain why few Hispanic Americans become philosophers. One of these is socio-economic status. Hispanics are still at the lower end of the socio-economic ladder in the United States.[13] This means that a smaller proportion of them go to college compared to other Americans, with the exception of African Americans, and thus the pool from which philosophers are chosen is very small.[14] This fact is also used to explain why there are so few African Americans in philosophy. And there is some truth to it. It is a fact that the Hispanic population in this country, considered as a whole, is poorer and less educated than the population of European background. Some Hispanics belong to the factory-working class, some are agricultural laborers, some are migrant workers, and many are involved in unskilled services (e.g. food service, cleaning, maid service). Various statistics support the view that a majority do not go to college, and a large proportion does not even complete high school.[15]

A factor that supports this explanation is that Hispanics who go into philosophy generally come from middle- and upper-class families where at least one of the parents is a professional person. Indeed, the statistics show a disproportionately high number of Cuban- and Argentinian-American philosophers. In the case of Cuban Americans, the explanation could be that most Cubans who live in this country are either political exiles or children of political exiles, and these are people who belonged to the middle or upper classes in Cuba and were professionally trained members of the bourgeoisie. The case of Argentinians is similar insofar as many of them came to this country in search of political freedom or professional advancement.

Another reason that may explain the meager number of Hispanics in philosophy is that language functions as a barrier to Hispanic Americans in philosophy. Language plays a key role in philosophy, and a good knowledge of it is required of the philosopher. But Hispanics, whether immigrants or children of immigrants, are at a disadvantage, either because their native language is not English or, if it is, their parents do not know it well and have not passed on to them the linguistic skills necessary for the practice of philosophy.[16]

There is clearly some truth to this. One can see, for example, that there are many Hispanics, both as faculty and students, in Spanish departments in universities and colleges throughout the United States, namely, places where knowledge of English is not so crucial as in philosophy. Moreover, there are even some specialists in the history of Hispanic thought who actually work in Spanish departments, indicating that lack of English proficiency is an important deterrent for working in philosophy departments and joining the American philosophical community.

Another reason often cited for the small number of Hispanics in philosophy is that Hispanic culture in general does not encourage philosophical reflection. After all, some argue, philosophers are rare in Hispanic countries and the number of Hispanic philosophers who have made an impact on world philosophy is very small. It would be odd, then, to find large numbers of Hispanics devoted to philosophy in the US.

I will not be convinced that this is a sound reason unless someone can produce evidence that there is something in Hispanic culture that is somehow anti-philosophical. First of all, it is questionable that one can speak meaningfully of one Hispanic culture for all times and in all places. Indeed, earlier I questioned the notion that all Hispanics, at all times and places, have something in common, and this extends to culture as well. A more accurate way of speaking would be to refer to Hispanic *cultures* or, as I have argued, to groups of people tied by historical events in special ways, some of which are cultural. But even assuming there were such a thing as a single Hispanic culture whose traits could be identified, I do not see any cultural trait associated with Hispanics that necessarily discourages them from pursuing philosophy. If anything, it seems that Hispanic culture is more amenable to philosophical reflection than, say, Anglo-Saxon culture.[17] There is considerable affinity in Hispanics for the discussion of issues that have to do with politics, religion, the meaning of life, and so on, and these issues are usually entering points into philosophy. In this sense, Hispanics have the same sort of general interest in philosophy that the French have, and they make it evident in the honor they bestow on philosophers. I do not know, for example, of major American philosophers who, in recent times, have been asked to be members of the president's cabinet, to be ambassadors, or to head specially appointed commissions. Yet these are fairly common occurrences in both Latin America and the Iberian countries.

To this must be added that the proportion of Hispanics that go into philosophy in countries outside the United States is much higher than that in the United States. Consider the case of Latin America, for example, a place where one would expect a low number of philosophers because of adverse conditions for the profession, the low level of education in the population, and the adverse social and economic conditions under which a large proportion of the population lives. Latin America today has a population of approximately 489 millions,[18] and the number of philosophers who teach in Latin American universities is at least over 2,000.[19] I say "at least" because the list provided in the *International Directory of Philosophers* of philosophers and even institutions where philosophy is taught is grossly inadequate.[20] Moreover, this does not take into account the large number of philosophers who teach philosophy in high school: in many Latin American countries philosophy is a part of the secondary-school curriculum. Even using this understated figure, however, the proportion of philosophers in the general population is much larger than in the US. Indeed, the US, with a total population of around 270 million and around 30 million Hispanics, has less than 100 Hispanic college philosophy teachers.[21]

A reason sometimes given for the absence of Hispanics in philosophy, but which I consider both malicious and groundless, is that Hispanics are not quite as intelligent as Americans of non-Iberian European background; that they lack the kind of capacity for abstraction that non-Iberian European Americans have and, therefore, cannot do philosophy well. This, by the way, is a reason also used by some to explain *mutatis mutandis* the relative absence of African Americans and women in philosophy.

There is no convincing evidence to support this claim. The fact that there are established Hispanic philosophers, both in this country and elsewhere, and that some Hispanics have done very demanding philosophical work, shows that the tasks of philosophy are not beyond Hispanics. True, one could argue that, because Hispanic Americans in general score lower than non-Iberian European Americans on standard tests,[22] the pool of Hispanics who can do the kind of thinking required in philosophy is smaller than that of Americans of non-Iberian European ancestry. Still, the evidence is not convincing for many reasons. For one, it is not clear that these tests are not culturally biased. And for another, the choice of philosophy as a profession does not appear to be determined by performance on standard tests. Certainly, a high score does not lead to an interest in philosophy, as is clear from the fact that Asian Americans have the highest scores in these tests and yet do not favor philosophy as a profession. Even if we were to accept that doing well in these tests does not increase the number of philosophers, whereas doing poorly decreases it, this does not explain how most Hispanics who perform well in them go into other professions than philosophy.

One could argue that very few Hispanics have become established in the philosophical profession because the pool of Hispanics is small, for the reasons already discussed; or one could argue that there are very few established Hispanic philosophers because their cultural background does not make the profession amenable to them, because they are not sufficiently intelligent, and so on. Moreover, socio-economic factors can be used indirectly to explain the smaller pool from which Hispanic philosophers are drawn.

None of these explanations, however, makes any sense when we ask why it is that Hispanics who go into philosophy (particularly those who have been most successful in their philosophical careers) are not attracted by – and may even avoid – anything that has to do with their identity. Part of the answer to this question, I think, does not rest with Hispanics themselves, but rather with the American philosophical community. Moreover, this answer also serves to explain the other issues we have raised, including the absence of Hispanic philosophy in the curriculum in American colleges and universities. Let me begin, then, by making a few comments about the American philosophical community.

3 The American Philosophical Community

The world of contemporary American philosophy is completely foreign to non-professional philosophers. From the outside it probably appears to be a rather cohesive and unified group of scholars devoted – as the name of the discipline so eloquently proclaims – to the pursuit of wisdom. Moreover, again from the outside, it probably looks as if the members of this group behave with disinterested deliberation and according to high principles in pursuit of an elusive, but lofty, object. To be a philosopher is not as prestigious in the United States as it is in Germany, for example, but there is a patina of respectability attached to the profession. For one thing, it is believed not to be lucrative, and for another, it is supposed to attract, if not all the best, at least some of the best intellects available in American society.

The facts do not quite confirm the appearance. The world of American philosophy is not composed of a unified, cohesive, and principled group of people in search of wisdom. Indeed, in some unflattering ways it resembles the non-philosophical world. For this reason, the examination of the place Hispanics occupy in it serves as a good illustration of our overall situation in this country. It confirms, for example, the fact that we are, as a group, alienated and marginalized; that we are considered foreign; and that we are stereotyped in various pernicious ways.

The first thing that is false about the outsider's view of American philosophy I have sketched is that it is cohesive and unified. The facts tell another story. American philosophy is more divided today than at any other period. Indeed, the American philosophical community may be more divided than any other philosophical community in history. One only has to attend the yearly convention of the Eastern Division of the American Philosophical Association to confirm this judgment.

These conventions, attended by roughly 20 percent of philosophers in the United States, have two programs. One is the official program of the Association. This program is organized into more than 80 sessions with more than 250 participants. In addition to the official program, there is also what can only be referred to as "the side show." This program is organized by the many specialized philosophical societies which are currently operating in the country. The number of satellite sessions is around a hundred, and there are more than 300 speakers who participate in them.[23] The philosophers who participate both in the official program and in the side show, moreover, do not always speak the same language. The tower of Babel would be an apt analogy. The result is that most sessions are poorly attended, both because there are so many concurrent sessions that the general convention population is divided into too many groups, and because of the diversity of interests, styles, and traditions of the different groups. The picture that the meetings of the Eastern Division of the American Philosophical Association presents, then, is anything but cohesive or unified.

Things have not always been this way, however. There was a time when the official program of the American Philosophical Association was more cohesive, when there were fewer sessions, and when attendance at each of the sessions was higher. Moreover, there was a time when there was no side show or, if there was, it was so small that the official program maintained a visibility and hegemony that gave unity to the meetings. The question is, how did we get where we are now?

The definitive answer to this question must be settled by future historians and sociologists of American philosophy; we are too close to the situation to provide a satisfactory answer. In my case there is a further disadvantage, namely, that I am not a historian of American philosophy. I speak merely as a philosopher who, as a member of the American philosophical community, has to share some responsibility for the present state of American philosophy. My knowledge is anecdotal, but based on three decades of experience as a Hispanic philosopher working in the United States. A deep commitment both to philosophy – as a discipline, profession, and way of life – and to my Hispanic identity, gives credibility to what I have to say.

In the 1980s a public brawl broke out between two groups of philosophers in the Eastern Division of the American Philosophical Association.[24] The American Philosophical Association is divided into three groups of which the Eastern Division is the oldest, largest, richest, and most distinguished. The other two are the Central Division (formerly called Western) and the Pacific Division. The Eastern Division has considerable clout and in many ways sets the tone for the profession. Now, on one side of the brawl were the so-called analytic philosophers; on the other, the so-called continental philosophers. The continental group accused the analytic group of monopolizing the power of the Association and threatened to walk out and form a new association. The number of philosophers was substantial and, therefore, a truce was reached and an arrangement was worked out whereby power would be shared at the Eastern Division. Committees would be appointed in such a way as to allow room for members of the continental group. Moreover, the slates of candidates for elected office would always include members of the continental group.

This system has been in place now for more than a decade and on the surface seems to be working well. Yet, in reality, matters are quite different. The naked truth is that American philosophers are still very much divided into two groups. On the one hand, there are the analysts. On the other, there is a large number of different groups with little to unite them except for their opposition to the analysts. Many of these philosophers still like to call themselves continental philosophers, although the term "pluralist" is also used. I shall return to the matter of the name later.

If one looks closely at the analytic group itself, there is not much that can be found, in terms of philosophical position and approach, that unites them. Indeed, many analysts even reject this denomination, claiming that they do not do anything different from what Aristotle, Descartes, and Kant did. Still, whether they like it or not, as Max Black pointed out a while ago, analysts do "share a common intellectual heritage."[25] This heritage involves certain assumptions: the concern with language and the clarification of its meaning; the interest in logic and its use in philosophical discourse; a positive attitude toward science; and the conviction that non-empirical claims of a non-syntactical nature are to be subjected to careful scrutiny.

The strongest bond of the group, however, is genetic. Present analysts were students of certain philosophers who in turn were students of certain other philosophers, and so on. In other words, present analysts have a common intellectual ancestry which goes back to certain key figures: the members of the Vienna Circle, Ludwig Wittgenstein, G. E. Moore, and Bertrand Russell.

If analysts have little in common beyond genesis, continental philosophers have even less in common, for the denomination includes widely different groups and genetically different families. Marxists, Thomists, Pragmatists, Peircians, Process Philosophers, Postmodernists, Hegelians, Phenomenologists, Neo-Kantians, Existentialists, Heideggerians, and a score of others fit into this group. It is not clear why philosophers of these different persuasions are called continental, for clearly some of the roots of the analytic movement are found in continental Europe (the Vienna Circle and Wittgenstein, for example), and some continental philosophers have never lived in continental Europe and their intellectual mentors never lived in continental Europe (Peirce, for example). Nor can it be argued that the group receives its name because analytic philosophy became dominant in Great Britain and the Anglo-American world, whereas continental philosophy flourishes only in continental Europe and there is no analysis in this part of the world, for analysis is the primary mode of philosophizing also in Scandinavia, and there are scores of continental philosophers in the United States and Great Britain.

The term "continental," then, makes no sense. And, indeed, for this reason some members of the continental group prefer the term "pluralist" to refer to themselves. By pluralist they mean philosophers who are committed to philosophical diversity and therefore tolerate, and even accept, modes of philosophizing very different from the ones they themselves favor. By the use of this term they seek to distinguish themselves from hard-core analytic philosophers whom they perceive as intransigently sectarian and exclusionary when it comes to non-analytic philosophy.

Regardless of whether one uses "continental" or "pluralist" to refer to this group, most of these philosophers are united in their aversion to analytic philosophers. Again, this aversion is not explained because continental or pluralist philosophers share anything in common, or even because, like the analysts, they are themselves related genetically. Their single unifying characteristic seems to be that they are opposed to analysts, although their opposition is not always for the same reasons. Some object to the analysts' emphasis on language; some object to their anti-metaphysical bias; some, to their scientism; some, to their rejection of the use of metaphorical language in philosophy; some, to their use of symbolic logic; and so on. Perhaps, more than anything else, their opposition is political: continental/pluralist philosophers believe that analysts have monopolized power in the profession, relegating them to a marginal role, and they accuse analysts of philosophical intransigence and provincialism.[26]

Within this panorama it is particularly ironic that the group of historians of American philosophy who are members of the Society for the Advancement of American Philosophy (SAAP) consider themselves marginalized and have joined forces with other groups to oppose analysts. The irony lies particularly in that many of them devote their efforts to the study of the thought of analysts. Of course, these philosophers are not genetically tied to the analytic group, their interests are primarily historical, and their attitude is tolerant of diverse philosophical approaches, factors which do not endear them to many hard-core members of the analytic family.

This, then, is the schizophrenic world of contemporary American philosophy. This situation, united to the pervasive competitive nature of American society, has made philosophy another field of competition. Unfortunately, the competition is not often for truth, to see who has more of it, who has better access to it, or who can get it faster; the competition is frequently for power and intellectual immortality.

Plato noted long ago that human beings have an insatiable thirst for immortality; we want to live forever. Most non-philosophers satisfy this thirst through a religious belief in the afterlife, the erection of economic empires that will outlive them, or the establishment of a strong and numerous progeny. Most philosophers, however, do not believe in the afterlife; they despise wealth (at least some do); and they want an immortality associated with them individually, not with their family name. Because philosophers believe in ideas, their strong desire for personal immortality translates into a desire for the immortality of their own particular point of view. They want the world to think like them and acknowledge that it thinks like them.

In this process, truth often gets lost somehow and the power to impose and disseminate one's views becomes the all-consuming objective. Some philosophers will do anything to get others to read their publications, to discuss them, to acknowledge them. No matter that they themselves may become the object of ridicule; no matter who gets hurt or how hurt someone gets. Indeed, most philosophers would rather be ridiculed or condemned than ignored. What counts is who has more students and who can place them in positions of power, so they can continue to be instrumental in the dissemination of the views of the master. Grants, jobs, and publications become of the essence, necessary instruments for the goal of intellectual immortality.

Obviously, the preservation of power requires the annihilation of the power of others: there can be only one cock on the walk. Moreover, once in a position of power, more power accrues. We can more easily block the publications of those who disagree with us; we can more easily get our students in the right places; and we can more easily make possible the publication of materials that support our own point of view or at least support our general perspective, method, and philosophical family. For this system to work, there must also be a network of faithful associates; we must build IOUs; we must block others and encourage allies. In short, we must build and maintain an ol'-boy's network, or, in political terms, a philosophical machine.

In the United States this is facilitated by the fact that the profession works through a system of referees, specialists who give opinions on the merits of proposals and manuscripts submitted to presses, journals, and foundations. Presses and foundations are run by non-specialists who need advice from specialists. Journals are run by specialists who do not know much about the fields of a large number of the manuscripts they receive. Once these specialists are named to the boards that assist non-specialists or other specialists in different areas, they tend to perpetuate themselves, their students, the students of their friends and associates, and their allies and supporters. Moreover, they are in a position to recommend other referees for particular projects.

Books are generally not subjected to blind refereeing. This means that the referees know the author of the book they are refereeing, a fact which facilitates the elimination of rival scholars and points of view. A standard procedure in the profession is to block the publication of materials that do not make reference to the work of the referee. Another is to eliminate texts critical of the referee's work.

An unfortunate aspect of this process, which is in part the result of the feuding among philosophical families in their search for power, and which tends to discourage many from pursuing a career in philosophy, is the unusual nastiness and vitriol that is frequently found in the reports of referees. There is some nastiness in other disciplines as well, but in my experience I have never encountered the degree of vitriol, even cruelty, that is used by some philosophy referees. I edit an interdisciplinary series of books and, because of my work, I am also associated with several journals, some of which cater to materials from other disciplines. Seldom do I see referee reports in other disciplines that contain the level of callousness, sarcasm, and plain sadism I find among referee reports from philosophers. It is as if their intent were not merely to reject the work submitted for publication, but to humiliate the author and discourage him or her from ever attempting to publish anything else. They seem to be intent on the kill, and sometimes not just the kill, but torture. Indeed, I know several cases of young scholars in which such vicious attacks have succeeded in destroying their confidence and dissuading them from pursuing the practice of philosophy. Only very sturdy egos, or egos covered by many layers of skin, survive some of the attacks I have witnessed. As should be expected, the attacks are particularly nasty when the person whose work is under review does not belong to the family to which the reviewer belongs. In cases where both persons belong to the same family, the tendency is to be nice and sweet, even in situations when rejection is recommended – the most frequent scenario is one in which constructive, rather than destructive criticisms, are offered. But in other cases, there is frequently no truce, no compassion, not even respect. The situation is particularly bad for those who do not belong to any established family, for they are attacked from all sides.

Certainly, none of this is done "maliciously." I do not know anyone in the profession who blatantly acknowledges doing it. Most philosophers actually believe that they are doing a service to the profession when they block the publication of texts that do not refer to themselves or are critical of their point of view. If these works do not refer to their own work, they reason, it must be because the author is not well acquainted with the pertinent sources and, therefore, they judge the work to be immature. If the work is critical of their own views, it must be that the author is wrong, or confused. Naturally, referees have a professional, even a moral, responsibility to block the publication of works that are immature, insufficiently researched, wrong in perspective, or confused in presentation. Philosophers are not less efficient when it comes to self-deception than the rest of the population, and perhaps even more so because of their frequent isolation from the world at large.

The situation with articles is somewhat similar to that of books, except that most often the identity of the author is not known to the referee. Most articles are supposed to be refereed blindly. All the same, editors of journals have much to say about the publication of articles. I remember the editor of a leading journal of philosophy telling me in confidence that when he received a manuscript he did not want to publish, he used himself as one of the referees. The editor of another journal, of slightly less prestige than the one mentioned, told me, when I mentioned this practice to him, that he was not so crass. His procedure was to send the article to referees that he knew would be unsympathetic to the point of view or the methodology of the article he wanted rejected. And this, considering the many and deep divisions in the profession, was not difficult to do.

Some editors are not so subtle. I know the organizer of a conference who set up a rather elaborate system of blind refereeing for the selection of the conference papers. However, after the referees had made their selection, he proceeded to disregard their opinion in those instances where he disagreed with their choice. What makes this case particularly appalling is that his decision was not based on subject matter or paper quality – he did not bother to read the papers he rejected. The decision was based exclusively on the identity of the authors. I suspect that the real reasons for rejection had to do with the advancement of his personal career, but this is a conjecture.

Of course, one must keep in mind that some of the most prestigious journals receive large numbers of articles of which they can publish only a small fraction. Under these conditions, when they must reject a high percentage of the manuscripts they receive, are they not entitled to use all the means they have at their disposal, including personal preferences, to reject some of them? Besides, do not editors of journals have the prerogative, and some would say the duty, to set the tone for the journal, to encourage a certain philosophical style, and even to promote a certain point of view?

This is all very well, but it has the extraordinary consequence that much of what is published in philosophy is published for reasons which are not entirely philosophical. Certain points of view and certain styles of doing philosophy are excluded merely because they are not in accordance with the views and styles favored by the group that dominates the journal, or the press.

The same applies to grants. Once a particular group gets hold of a grant mechanism, it is almost impossible to get it open to others. The genetic factor sets in and prevents any other family of philosophers from participating. There are extreme situations. In some subfields of philosophy, a single person practically dominates it. True, it is difficult to keep this machine oiled, and fortunately, some disciples are sufficiently open to allow some non-genetically related persons to participate, but breaking down machines takes time, and most of them work quite efficiently. Particularly unfortunate is that many "successful" philosophers tend to go on working well into their 70s and thus keep their machines in order for decades. Moreover, sometimes they are successful in passing them on to younger favorites, who ensure a still longer period of operation.

Prior to the rebellion of continental philosophers against analysts, the latter held the reins of power in the profession. Analysts had built a network which was almost impregnable. The network would have continued to be impregnable but for the kinds of excesses described above. These were so egregious that they made possible what otherwise would have been impossible: the alliance of many other rival philosophical groups into a united front against analysts. Fed up with marginalization, the inability to secure jobs in elite institutions, to publish in certain presses and journals, to acquire national grants, and to participate in the life of the American Philosophical Association, these groups got together and decided to protest. They understood that the situation called for political action rather than conceptual discussion. And they were successful to a certain extent, although their success proved clearly that American philosophy has become something other than philosophy and truth has been forgotten for the sake of power. Indeed, we could say that American philosophy today is largely ideological. It is so because it is too often practiced for reasons which have nothing to do with philosophy: power and immortality. But how has this happened?[27]

Paradoxically, this change has been made possible in part because of a fundamental agreement between analytic and continental philosophers. Most members of these groups have adopted what can only be regarded as a form of skepticism toward truth. On the side of analysts, we need not go farther than the most important American philosopher of our times, W. V. O. Quine. His philosophy is based on two extraordinary doctrines. According to one, we can never be certain that we mean the same thing as someone else means when we use the same word.[28] Naturally, if this is the case, then how can we aspire to certainty in anything, and how can we believe in the possibility of truth? According to the other doctrine, our language is theory laden, so that we can never adopt an independent, neutral point of view with respect to the nature of the world.[29]

On the side of the continentals, we need only mention Martin Heidegger, perhaps the most influential continental philosopher in the twentieth century and one who has had an extraordinary impact on American philosophers. A capstone of his philosophy is the so-called hermeneutic circle. In his version of this conundrum, we can never acquire certainty because knowledge of the whole depends on the knowledge of the parts, and knowledge of the parts depends on the knowledge of the whole. Hence, all our knowledge is interdependent and ultimately circular.[30]

With truth gone, what is there for philosophers to pursue? One thing is power. And, indeed, Michel Foucault and other postmodernists suggest that the search for power is the primary force that moves philosophers.[31]

Three important results followed the truce worked out between analysts and continentals/pluralists. One was the return to fragmentation among continentals/pluralists. They were united in opposition to analysts, so when these retreated and made room for them in the American Philosophical Association, they returned to their original state of fragmentation. But not only that, they seem to have gone into even greater fragmentation. For now the doors of the Association were open to endless divisions among different groups with different interests. The multiplication of specialized societies provides evidence for this extraordinary phenomenon. Apart from larger groups, like those composed of Marxists, Thomists, and Phenomenologists, there are societies for individual philosophers and interest groups, including very minor philosophers indeed. There are societies for gays and lesbians, animal ethics, Christian philosophers, technology, genocide and the Holocaust, machines and mentality, ancient philosophy, medieval and Renaissance philosophy, Jesuit education, Marcel, Jaspers, Santayana, Zubiri, Nietzsche, Scotus, Maritain, the history of philosophy, Eriugena, neo-Platonism, and so on. There seems to be no end to this process of multiplication. It looks as if every philosopher wants to establish his or her own society tailored to his or her own particular philosophical interests so that he or she can have and exercise some power. Andy Warhol mentioned a future in which everyone would enjoy fifteen minutes of fame. Well, the future of philosophy appears to be one in which every philosopher will preside over a philosophical society at some point in his or her career.

Together with the first result comes a second: a greater toleration and active encouragement of the study of the history of philosophy. One of the bones of contention between analysts and continentals/pluralists is precisely that many analysts have a rather contemptuous disregard for the history of philosophy. After all, many of them consider themselves scientists, and scientists have always been inattentive to the history of science.[32] Continentals/pluralists, on the other hand, seem to make the history of philosophy an essential part of their philosophizing.[33]

The renewed interest in the history of philosophy among continental/pluralist circles, and indeed, not just the interest, but the belief that philosophy must be done historically, that is, as a commentary on what past philosophers have written, makes sense in contemporary philosophy.[34] The reasons are twofold. First, the general skeptical attitude with respect to universal philosophical truths, that is, the belief that knowledge of philosophical truths is impossible, leads philosophers away from the task of trying to find it and into the path of historical studies. If philosophical truth is not possible, one thing philosophers can nonetheless do, apart from criticizing those misguided persons who still believe that philosophical truth can be known, is to engage in the study of the history of philosophy. The study of the history of philosophy becomes indistinguishable from philosophy. Second, many continental/pluralist philosophers have been influenced by historicism and perspectivism, which claim that whatever truth we can gather is always historical and the result of a unique perspective; our point of view is always colored by our history. Consequently, any attempt at understanding ourselves must go back to that history and uncover the historical presuppositions under which we work.[35]

A third result of the truce between analysts and continentals/pluralists was, paradoxically, another offensive by the analysts. In part as a consequence of the renewed fragmentation of the continentals/pluralists, and the concentration of many of them on the history of philosophy, analysts have mounted a come-back, although a more subtle one. There are many signs of it. For example, in response to the opening of the official program of the American Philosophical Association to continental/pluralist philosophers, the *Journal of Philosophy* ceased to publish abstracts of symposia. Another example is the malicious rumor that attendance at sessions of the official program decreased after the opening occurred. A more insidious example still is the circulation of an unofficial ranking of graduate programs entitled "The Philosophical Gourmet Report." This ranking is available on the Internet and given considerable credibility among analysts, even though it is gossipy, inaccurate, and biased in its judgments.[36] But it serves a useful ideological purpose: to maintain power in the hands of a few members of the profession. Finally, in recent years continentals/ pluralists have been unable to elect a president to the American Philosophical Association, and often even their favorite candidates to the Executive Committee of the Association have failed to get elected. This is a consequence in part of their own divisions, but also no doubt of the renewed closing of the ranks among the analytic establishment.

In short, then, the American philosophical community does not seem to live up to its reputation. It is not united and cohesive; philosophers are not always devoted to the search for truth, and they can hardly be regarded as polite scholars who engage in careful, disinterested deliberation and follow high principles. Moreover, this community is composed of families who are quite protective of their members, hostile to outsiders, and fight fiercely for their turf.

A further result of this state of affairs in the American philosophical community pertinent for us is the widespread use of typecasting. In the current climate, philosophers tend to be typecast early in their careers in terms of families and traditions. No one is just a philosopher. One is an analyst or a continental, an Aristotelian or a Peircean, a Scholastic or a Kantian, and so on. Moreover, once someone is typecast, nothing that the person does is ever considered except in the context of the stereotype under which it has been classified. This means that once an analyst, always an analyst; once a medievalist, always a medievalist. This is a very interesting phenomenon indeed. Consider my case, for example. I began my career as a medievalist, but most of my work in the last ten years has been in systematic metaphysics and historiography. Nonetheless, practically everyone (who thinks about me in a professional capacity) thinks about me as a medievalist and nothing else. Typecasting, of course, has very serious consequences. One of these is that it serves to put aside and marginalize. He is X, and X is not good, or not important, or not pertinent, or whatever, therefore I do not have to bother with him. Typecasting fits nicely within the family feuding of contemporary American philosophy and contributes to the emphasis on some of the features I have been describing.

Still another result of the organization of the American philosophical community in families favors the development of dynasties and a certain philosophical aristocracy. As happens with all aristocratic systems, questions of blood purity – for philosophers, intellectual orthodoxy and pedigree – surface, and quarrels about degrees of purity and lineage become important. How faithful is X to Y? How much of a Ynian is X? Is she a student of Y or Z? Any philosopher knows how concerned philosophers are with questions such as this, and with the gossip that such questions tends to generate. Of course, aristocracy involves exclusion and censure. Those who do not have the same blood or who mix it indiscriminately, are rejected and condemned. He is not really a Ynian! He does not belong with us. The technique of dismissal, so prevalent in American philosophy today, is put to good use in this context, and this in turn engenders resentment, anger, and warfare.[37]

This characterization of the American philosophical community is quite dismal and should not be applied to all American philosophers, of course. Some qualifications are in order. First of all, not all American philosophers are ideologues and most of them do not consider themselves to be such, even if many of them act as if they were. The characteristics of the whole do not apply to every member, and we must keep in mind the many American philosophers who fulfill to a high degree the expectations generally associated with the philosophical life. Indeed, and this is an important second qualification, the work of many American philosophers today is of the highest quality, and the best of it compares well with anything produced in the past. Philosophy is undergoing an extraordinary renaissance. There are more philosophers today and more philosophical publications than at any other time in the history of the discipline. And the center of this renaissance is the United States. I can only think of two other places in history where such philosophical ferment took place: Athens in the fourth century BC and Paris after AD 1250. Third, the work of philosophers who are not only unconsciously ideological, but consciously so, can be as good as, and even better than, that of those who are not. And we must recognize that some of the work of some of the most partisan philosophers in the United States today is of the highest quality. In fact, my point is not about the quality of the philosophical work being

179

produced in the United States today, but about the sociological factors in the American philosophical community which affect the place of Hispanics in it.

Finally, in all fairness we should keep in mind that some of the xenophobia and familialism which characterizes American philosophy is not different from certain attitudes of the population at large. I remember how mystified I was when I first came to this country and people kept asking me what I was. My usual answer was Cuban. But this did not satisfy most people. They wanted to know where my ancestors came from. After a while I got so tired of their insistence that I simply told them my ancestors came from a certain place, leaving out the fact that this was true only of some of them – my ancestors came from so many places that any other answer would not have shut them up. At any rate, once I told them about my ancestral origin, then they quickly classified me: Oh, I see. Then you are not Cuban; you are X. This was completely foreign to me. In Cuba I thought of myself as Cuban and not as belonging to the nation, country, land, or continent of my ancestors. Yet in the United States I became something I had never thought I was, and there was very little I could do about it. The United States is obsessed with origins and lineage, and American philosophers are no different.

Let us turn now to the relation between what has been said about American philosophy and the place of Hispanics in the American philosophical community. Furthermore, let us see how this can serve to answer the questions raised earlier.

4 Hispanics and the American Philosophical Community

The questions we want to answer have to do with the limited number of Hispanics in philosophy, the small number of established Hispanic philosophers, and the general indifference of non-Hispanic American philosophers and Hispanic-American philosophers to issues particularly related to Hispanics and Hispanic thought. My suggestion is that one reason behind all these facts is that Hispanics in general are perceived as foreigners; we are not thought to be "Americans."[38] Whereas African Americans, in spite of their differences with European Americans, are identified with this country, and both they themselves and other

Americans think of them as belonging here, Hispanics are thought of as belonging elsewhere.[39] We are considered ethnic; African Americans are not. African Americans constitute a minority, but their ways are considered to belong to the United States, not to a foreign culture or a foreign people. As a result, we are not considered quite American; in fact, we are not thought to be American at all and this affects the way we are perceived by the American philosophical community.

This situation is exacerbated because of the current state of American philosophy. The divisions and rivalries among different philosophical families and the fragmentation of the community make it very difficult for individuals and groups who are not perceived to belong to established philosophical families, and are not considered to be part of the so-called American tradition, to be accepted. This naturally works against Hispanics, for we have no clear pedigree, aggravating our estrangement. Moreover, the emphasis on the history of non-Iberian European and of American philosophy excludes Hispanic thought. And the renewed dominance of analysis leaves out anything that has to do with Hispanic culture. Hispanic philosophers are marginalized in the profession, and Hispanic issues and philosophy are regarded as alien to the interests of American philosophers. Indeed, even philosophers as important as George Santayana for the history of American thought are somewhat marginalized, primarily because of the feeling that they do not belong.

One would think that the fragmentation of the American philosophical community would have made room for Hispanics and Hispanic philosophical issues. And it has. Hispanics now are allowed to have a place in American philosophy if we wish, but our place is marginal, one among the many interested groups vying for attention in the American philosophical community. But attention we cannot get, because we are perceived as alien. Only if we abandon our cultural heritage and become "Americanized" can we have a significant place in the American philosophical community.

It would be impossible for me to recall the number of times that my European-American, and even African-American, friends have spoken of me as if I were not an American, a true American, or quite American. Indeed, I do not think a week goes by without my hearing some comment or other which confirms this view. This judgment is appropriate in their eyes because I have an accent, or they think I look different, or they perceive my cultural idiosyncrasies as different, although I find it questionable. Why is it that having a Hispanic accent is not American, and having a southern, or an African-American, accent is? Haven't some of the people who have a Hispanic accent been here as long as the others, or even longer? What do we make of the descendants of Mexican Americans who lived in California, Texas, and New Mexico before the United States decided to annex those territories? And what about the look? Why is it that the European or African look is American, but the Hispanic look is not? Finally, why should someone be excluded from the "American family" because he or she likes to comb his hair in a particular way, or smiles at certain times, or moves his or her hands more than European Americans do?

None of this makes sense, but it makes even less sense when referring to Hispanics who are American born, have no accent or foreign mannerisms, and look as European or as African as any European or African American. Yet the same standard is applied to them. Hispanics, regardless of how we actually speak, look, or behave, are perceived as foreigners, as belonging elsewhere, and as not being true Americans.

This perception of foreignness is a major obstacle to Hispanics in the philosophical community. The American philosophical community is cliquish, xenophobic, and tilted toward Europe. If one is perceived as not being part of one of the established American philosophical families, European in philosophical tradition, or part of the American community, then one is left out; one is thought to belong elsewhere or what one does is thought not to be philosophy. These are the two ways of disenfranchising philosophers: locating them in a non-European or non-American tradition, or classifying what they do as non-philosophical. Hence, Hispanics in general are excluded unless we can prove that we truly belong to one of the accepted groups, think in European terms, or are part of the American community. And we can prove this only by forgetting most of what has to do with our identity as Hispanics, by becoming clones of American philosophers, and by joining one of the established philosophical families. We must forget who we are; we must forget where we came from; and we must forget our culture and values. Don't wave your hands; don't speak enthusiastically; speak slowly and make frequent pauses; adopt the Oxford stuttering technique; look insecure; be cynical and doubtful; buy yourself tweed jackets if you are a male, and try to look like Apple

Annie if you are female. In short, become what the others want you to become, otherwise there is no place for you.

Hispanics who are fast and articulate in conversation are perceived as glib and arrogant. Hispanics who have a strong sense of humor, and laugh freely, are regarded as not serious. And Hispanics who speak with an accent are thought to be uncouth and unintellectual. I can vouch for this in my personal experience. Among Anglo-American philosophers, it is a great fault to speak fast, to react quickly, and to appear articulate in philosophical discussions. People who do this are considered superficial, because presumably they do not see the complexity of the issues in question; the possibility that perhaps they are quicker than their interlocutors, and can see faster and farther than they, is never entertained. This is a problem for most Hispanics, but even for some non-Hispanics.

I remember one time the Department of Philosophy at Buffalo was in the market for a young philosopher and one of the candidates was of Greek origin. As a Mediterranean, he was very quick in his responses. Some faculty immediately concluded he was too glib. Another candidate was hesitant and tentative in responding, and this was taken as a sign of philosophical maturity and depth. In the discussion of the merits of these candidates a faculty member cited the pauses in speech the second candidate made as an indication of thoughtfulness. He said that the pauses, "the spaces put between sentences and words," impressed him. Of course, the person in question is well known for his long, "thoughtful" pauses.

Humor is a serious problem particularly for Hispanics of Caribbean background. The latter especially have a great sense of humor and play in conversation. There is a constant give and take, a bantering manner, and an uninhibited display of humor and laughter. Irony pervades discourse at every level, from the most common of ordinary conversations to the most sophisticated cultural exchanges. Cubans use various terms to refer to this. Some call it *relajito* – the diminutive of a substantive which is a cognate of the English "relaxation" – whereas others call it *choteo*. This attitude extends sometimes even to sad and tragic situations. For us, this behavior is a matter of release, a way of dealing with difficulties out of our control, and of putting things in perspective. It is, in short, a survival mechanism and a source of hope. For, as the saying goes, "Better laugh than cry." Among Cubans and many Latin Americans this is a much appreciated quality, but among Anglo-Saxons it is taken as a major flaw, particularly among Anglo-Saxon philosophers. To laugh is considered to be a lack of proper respect and seriousness. Philosophers are not supposed to laugh. In some circumstances they may be allowed a sardonic smile, *à la* Voltaire, but never a laugh. Laughter is the province of the immature, the mentally handicapped, children, or fools.[40]

The Cuban facility to make fun of the most serious topics, the ability to go from the depths of despair to the heights of mirth in no time at all and without much of a transition is particularly incomprehensible to a culture that requires a complicated process of decompression to go from a tear to a smile. This is, of course, not a problem for the American mainstream alone. Other cultures encounter similar difficulties with Cuban humor. I was recently in Germany speaking about these matters to another Cuban who lives there, and he told me that it would take a regular German several hours to accomplish the transition through which a Cuban goes in a matter of seconds.

I have personally experienced criticism for my humor and laughter. For many years it was customary for a particular faculty member of the Department of Philosophy at Buffalo to phone me after department meetings to point out that my humor, or laughter, had been out of place. This went on until the faculty member in question made a similar criticism of someone else in front of me, and I pointed out to him that his criticism was culturally biased. That stopped him from raising the point with me again, but I doubt it has stopped him from thinking that people who display humor and laughter in philosophical conversations are at fault. As a student told me once, it looks as if the proper countenance for philosophers is a sour one.

Not everyone is so culturally narrow as my colleague. I have frequently found understanding and receptive persons in other cultures. A German friend of mine has frequently told me that, for him, seeing Cubans in conversation in the full game of *choteo* is exhilarating. But then this friend is German, not American, and his field is literature, not philosophy. Anglo-American philosophers take themselves very, very seriously.

About accents, I need not say much. To have a British accent is an enormous asset, particularly in philosophy. Some American philosophers actually adopt one after they visit Britain. Even rather stupid people, when they have a British accent, are placed on a different footing. This country has a love affair with anything British, and the situation with philosophers is even more acute. Part of it has to do with the fact that Britain was a philosophical leader in the Anglo-American philosophical world for three-fourths of the twentieth century. Part of it has to do with the fact that British philosophers have a knowledge of English which is often lacking among Americans. And part of it has to do with the undeniable fact that British philosophers are much better educated by and large than American ones. But, of course, to be British, or to have a British accent, does not imply any of these things. And not to be English, or not to have an English accent, does not entail that one does not know English well or is not well educated.

This attitude creates a problem for those who have neither an American accent nor a British one, for they tend to be regarded as uncouth or stupid. There are exceptions, however. German and French accents are not generally disparaged, and certainly not in the academic community. A French accent is thought of as sophisticated and charming, whereas a German accent is associated with learning and thoroughness. But the situation is different with other accents, a fact Italian, Irish, and Polish immigrants know only too well. For Hispanics, matters are even worse because our accent is not perceived as being European – it is associated with natives from Latin America, Indians, primitive people! For this reason, there is a strong predisposition among American philosophers not to take seriously anything said by Hispanics with an accent.

I know some young Hispanic philosophers who unfortunately have taken an interest in Hispanic philosophy, and I say unfortunately because this has caused them considerable grief and sometimes has even imperilled their careers. Even my limited interest in Hispanic philosophy has caused me some difficulties – not in my department, but in all sorts of other fora – and it has adversely affected the way I am perceived and the way my work is thought about in the profession. One is permitted to do historical work on some obscure person from the German Enlightenment, or even do research on a single anonymous, medieval manuscript from the twelfth century, but one is not permitted to study the work of a Latin American philosopher whose thought may have been revolutionary and influenced the course of events in his country or even in the whole of Latin America. If, to this, we add the typecasting which permeates American philosophy today, we can see how dangerous and alienating it can become for Hispanics to pay attention to Hispanic issues. For, once we are identified as Hispanists, then we can be easily dismissed. This explains also the hostile attitude toward Hispanic thought and issues which some Hispanics themselves have. The interest in Hispanic issues by some Hispanics is perceived as endangering the status achieved by those Hispanics who have put aside anything that has to do with their identity *qua* Hispanics. Because we are Hispanics, any overall emphasis on Hispanic issues tends to typecast us as Hispanists and marginalizes us, undermining our position and achievements. The double standard implied by this state of affairs should be obvious to anyone who has eyes to see. The question is why does it exist?

To repeat, my suggestion is that it has to do to a great extent with the general perception of Hispanics as foreigners, interlopers in America, ethnic immigrants from an alien land. Hispanics who show any interest in Hispanic issues, or Hispanic thought, are perceived as foreigners because they do not fit into the philosophical groups that dominate American philosophy today. They do not belong to any established philosophical family and therefore must belong elsewhere. The fragmentation, the genetic and family organization, and the rivalry between these families in American philosophy, all contribute to the exclusion of Hispanics. The only way Hispanics have of entering the world of American philosophy is to become what American philosophers consider acceptable; Hispanics must prove we belong. For analytic philosophers, this entails an Anglophile attitude. For continental/ pluralist philosophers, it entails a non-Iberian, Europhile attitude. Both entry roads involve substantial modification of the cultural and conceptual background of Hispanics for, after 1492, the conceptual world of Hispanics became estranged from mainstream European thought. Moreover, these roads leave no room for the Hispanic intellectual heritage, and particularly not for Hispanic philosophy. Hispanics who are not willing to surrender their identity, then, find it unpalatable to join the American philosophical community. This in turn explains in part why there are so very few of us in philosophy in this country. Of those of us who do join, most put aside any interest we may have had in issues related to our heritage and condition. It also explains the lack of interest in Hispanic issues among non-Hispanic and Hispanic philosophers in the US.

5 Conclusions

It is clear that Hispanics are not part of the American philosophical establishment to the degree that our numbers in the overall population of the United States would warrant. It is also clear that our issues and concerns are not part of the American philosophical agenda. One important reason, I have claimed, is that we are perceived as foreigners and therefore as marginal to American concerns. Can anything be done about this?

The way some Hispanics have dealt with this problem is by divesting themselves of anything Hispanic, mimicking the American philosophical establishment, and blending as far as possible into one of the philosophical families of the American philosophical community. But this solution appears too costly to those of us who wish to be true to ourselves. For us, the only solution is to continue being who we are and doing what we honestly think we should do as philosophers, in the hope that at some point we will become accepted in the American philosophical community.

In spite of all that I have said and the obvious obstacles in the way of this goal, I am optimistic. We are outside of the American philosophical mainstream today, but tomorrow might be different. If our numbers in the general population continue to increase, and those of us who are philosophers continue on our path, undeterred by the indifference and even hostility of the American philosophical community, I believe the American philosophical establishment will eventually pay attention to us. In the meantime, we must do all we can to keep these issues alive, to make Hispanics and non-Hispanics aware of them, and to maintain a high level of discourse when we address them.

Now, much of what I have said concerning Hispanics in philosophy applies as well to Hispanics in other academic disciplines, although in varying degrees. It applies in most disciplines because the perception of the foreignness of Hispanics is a deep cultural phenomenon that cuts across disciplines. It has to do with some characteristics which are, rightly or wrongly, associated with all Hispanics. Moreover, it is also evident to any academic in the United States who has made a point of observing the American academy, that some of the traits I have associated with the culture of the American philosophical community also apply in other disciplines, for they are traits of the American academy in general rather than of philosophy in particular. Of course, each disciplinary community has developed idiosyncrasies over time, and in some disciplines such idiosyncrasies are perhaps less influential than in others. It is hard to believe, for example, that peculiarities of accent or manner would have great effect in the natural sciences. The humanities, the arts, and the social sciences seem to be more likely to be affected by these. Whence my reference above to varying degrees. Still, they do have some influence and they determine the degree of seriousness with which views are regarded. After all, authority plays a central role in all disciplines, and authority is founded on perceptions.

Even outside the academy, however, what I have said about Hispanics in philosophy seems to apply. The situation of Hispanics in philosophy is but one example of a general situation in which we find ourselves. In one sense, we are part of the country, but in another we are perceived as not belonging in it. And even when we are tolerated, we are never completely accepted.[41]

This brings me back to the general thesis of this book. We do have an identity that unites us and separates us from others. It ties us, Hispanic Americans, to Latin Americans and Iberians, and it separates us from non-Iberian Europe and the American mainstream because that mainstream, except for the African component, is fundamentally non-Iberian European. And yet the stereotypes used by non-Hispanic Americans to view us are false insofar as they are mostly hasty generalizations based on limited observations. Our identification on the basis of common traits is a falsification, because we are not one insofar as we share any set of properties for all times and places. We are one in that we are tied by a complicated and multifaceted web of historical relations.

Conclusion

Much more than what has been said here concerning Hispanic/Latino identity could be said. Indeed, I feel as if the theses I have proposed raise more questions than they answer, but that is as it should be. The aim of this book is not to close the discussion of its topic, but rather to open it, to make others aware of the need to address it and enter into a dialogue about its various dimensions. I do not claim to have the Truth or even any incontestable truths. My purpose has been to raise some questions and give some answers to which I have arrived after some reflection, but which are far from being complete or incontestable. The real work remains to be done by you, the reader. I placed before you these questions and my particular, philosophical point of view. It is now your turn to make something of it, to begin the reflective process that will lead to your own answers. After all, in all important questions, no one's answer is really good for anyone else. Each of us must find his or her own, just as we must find our own way, and live our own lives. All the same, I have suggested some answers and I think it is appropriate that, in closing, I present a brief summary of them in very general terms.

Most important, I have defended the view that there is an identity we Hispanic/Latinos have. We are a people and we can be proud of it, even if this identity is founded on a complex history which includes much suffering. Our history, indeed, is like any human history: a mixture of good and bad. But we must not reject it merely because of the bad in it. If we do, we would be losing the foundation that we need in order to change it, and change is the only way in which we can make the future better, and even transform the past by tying it to a better result. I have very little doubt, then, that we are a people and that this fact cannot be denied in the past, even if it can be neutralized for the future: the future is always open and can be different. We are not trapped in our identity.

But I am also convinced that our identity is not founded on common properties. It is the mistake of all those who have argued for a common identity to Hispanics/Latinos to think that it is. This is the reason that their positions can be easily assailed, for they have failed every time to find something that is shared by all Hispanics/Latinos at all times. As a result, recently there has been a general retreat from the more encompassing position of identity, and claims have been made that such an encompassing notion necessarily excludes various groups. It appears easier to defend positions which see a common identity between Spanish Iberians and Spanish Americans, thus excluding Portuguese Iberians and Portuguese Americans, or vice versa; or a common identity to Latin Americans which excludes Iberians, and vice versa; and so on. These identities have also become difficult to defend, however, for the notions of one Iberia, one Spain, or one Latin America are as problematic as the more encompassing categories which were found to be faulty. So the move toward the more particular has continued. Rather than Iberians, or Latin Americans, or what have you, the effort has gone toward the defense of national identities: Colombian, Bolivian, Portuguese, Brazilian, and so on. But this effort again has been fraught with difficulties, for these political categories often include peoples who are culturally very different and who have harbored rivalries and resentment against other groups encompassed by national categories. This, again, has led to further attempts at particularization, which however have not been more successful than the others.

The fact is that those who have gone in search of identity have gone about it in the wrong way, by engaging in a search for common properties. The reason they have done this is that they have understood identity in essentialistic terms: identity implies the same essence, and essence consists in properties. But not all identity need be understood essentialistically and in terms of properties. In particular, the ethnic identity of groups of people and individual persons themselves is not to be understood in these terms.[1] History is against this view because history involves change, and groups of people and individual persons themselves are historical: they are not static or stationary; they are not immutable. On the contrary, their reality is precisely founded on change. The search for the identity and identification of Hispanics/Latinos, then, should begin with this fact. Not all identity is founded on commonality. Identity can be, and most often is, founded on historical relations that create historical families. If one begins with this assumption, then it becomes clear that some regional, national, and supranational categories are not just possible, but justified. Moreover, it also becomes clear that those categories of identification that are justified, serve to enlighten us about those they encompass in a way that we would miss if we did not use them.

My thesis is that Hispanics/Latinos constitute such a historical family and, therefore, that identifying ourselves as such is not only justified but useful. Moreover, I also propose that, more than any other label, the term "Hispanic" serves to name us. Why? Because it is the only one which appears even remotely justifiable, and it is the only one which can gather within it the historical family constituted by Iberians, Latin Americans, and Hispanic Americans. There are disadvantages to the name, and for some its use may create considerable discomfort, or even pain. But I trust that what I have said in the course of this book has contributed to ameliorate such feelings. In any case, more important than the name is the reality to which I have tried to point.

We are one, then, and we should be called by one name, Hispanics. But this, of course, does not preclude the use of other categorizations. Why should it? That we are mammals does not preclude that we are also humans. So that we are Hispanics should not prevent some of us from being also Mexican, or Argentinian, or Tarahumara, or Chicano, or Iberian, or Mexican and Tarahumara, or Portuguese and African, or whatever. Nor does the fact that we are mammals prevent us from feeling a greater kinship with other humans than with non-human mammals. Likewise, that we are Hispanics should not prevent us from feeling a greater kinship with Mexicans, Argentinians, or Tarahumaras.

Nor should our identity as Hispanics, and the common name used to indicate it, imply homogeneity. Homogeneity is a human invention. Milk is not homogeneous; it is made homogeneous by humans when they submit it to a process. Similarly, no people are homogeneous. Societies are fundamentally heterogeneous. They are rather like human beings themselves, composites of many different parts tied in different ways. Philosophers have been harping on this point for over 2,000 years, yet we tend to forget it. Hispanics, then, are not homogeneous, but neither are Guatemalans, Venezuelans, or any other Hispanic subgroup. Social-group homogeneity is a myth.

If there are no common properties to Hispanics and no homogeneity to them, there cannot either be any successful search for an essence, for there is no essence to search for. All attempts in this direction, in fact, are not only misguided but also dangerous and ought, therefore, to be discouraged. Ethnicism or racism of any kind is pernicious, and it relies on the notion of an essence belonging to the ethnic or racial group. We have suffered enough as a result of ethnicism and racism. Have we not had enough with Hitler and the Ku Klux Klan? Let us not try to put something else in their place. Any kind of ethnicism, let alone racism, can only lead to the privileging of a group over others and thus to discrimination, segregation, and injustice. Those who read this book carefully will find no fuel in it for any kind of exclusivist ethnicism, racism, or nationalism about Hispanics or any other social group. And if some are disappointed because that is what they expected or wanted, they should look elsewhere.

Finally, I hope this book does not engender resentment. My aim is not division, recrimination, or a request for an invitation to dinner to make up for past wrongs. I trust the book is taken as a statement of hope and an argument against any kind of polarization between Hispanics and Anglos, Hispanics and other ethnic and social groups, or even among Hispanics ourselves. Let us recognize our unity in difference and make this the basis not just for tolerance, but for acceptance and the recognition of the value of each other.

Notes

Preface

1 Davis, et al. (1988); "Area and Population of the World" (1997); Vobejda (1998).
2 Butler (1986).
3 Gracia (forthcoming, a).

Chapter 1 What Should We Call Ourselves?

1 The Spanish "Latinos" is the plural of "Latino," the Spanish masculine/ neuter for the English adjective "Latin." "Latinas" is the plural of "Latina," the Spanish feminine for the same adjective.
2 In Spain and some Latin American countries, there is now an effort underway in philosophy to use the term "Ibero-americana" (sometimes written IberoAmericana, Ibero-Americana, or Iberoamericana) to refer to the philosophy of both Iberia and Latin America. Indeed, the first encyclopedia of philosophy to be published in Spanish has the title *Enciclopedia IberoAmericana de Filosofía*. But it should be obvious that the term Ibero-américa (or, alternatively, IberoAmérica, Ibero-América, or Iberoamérica) does not refer to Iberia and America taken together, but rather to that part of America that is somehow Iberian, thus excluding Iberia itself.
3 For other possibilities, see Treviño (1987).
4 For more on this label see Fairchild and Cozens (1981); Marín (1984).
5 *Raza* was proposed and has been used by Hayes-Bautista (1980; 1983), among others. More recently, in Hayes-Bautista and Chapa (1987), however, he favors "Latino."

Notes

6   *Diccionario manual e ilustrado de la lengua española* (1981, p. 829b).
7   Some dictionaries record the use of *hispano* in English for this purpose. See *Webster's Third New International Dictionary* (1966).
8   According to the US Bureau of the Census (1988, p. 51): "A person is of Spanish/Hispanic origin if the person's origin (ancestry) is Mexican, Mexican-American, Chicano, Puerto Rican, Dominican, Ecuadoran, Guatemalan, Honduran, Nicaraguan, Peruvian, Salvadoran; from other Spanish-speaking countries of the Caribbean or Central or South America; or from Spain." Some researchers follow the lead of the Census, e.g. Marín and VanOss Marín (1991), p. 20.
9   Hayes-Bautista and Chapa (1987), p. 64. The use of "Hispanic" for anything related to or derived from the people, speech, or culture of Spain or Spain and Portugal, and as a synonym for "Latin American," is recorded in *Webster's Third New International Dictionary* (1966).
10 But there are exceptions. In 1927, for example, Unamuno suggested a broad sense of *hispano* which encompasses all peoples in the Iberian peninsula and those touched by them elsewhere. See Unamuno (1968), p. 1,081.
11 The confusion is frequently acknowledged, although not always understood.
12 "Generation of '98" refers to a group of Spanish intellectuals that flourished around the turn of the century. They include such figures as Ganivet and Unamuno (see Ramsden 1974). Unamuno (1968) discusses "Hispanicity."
13 Nicol (1961), pp. 53, 61–4, and 161. Unamuno (1968, p. 1,083) anticipated this notion. Heredia (1994) uses it, as does Gracia (1993).
14 Some scholars have recently argued that even literacy itself, the very use of writing, not just the use of names, has functioned as a mechanism of domination in Latin America. See Rama (1984); Mignolo (1993).
15 Among those who favor "Latino" are Hayes-Bautista and Chapa (1987, p. 66) and Pérez Stable (1987). Treviño (1987, p. 69), on the other hand, favors "Hispanic." Apart from the views favored by scholars, it is clear that the Hispanic/Latino population itself also is quite divided as to these labels. See, for example, Fusco (1992) on the reaction of the audience to Latino films.
16 Oboler (1995), p. vii.
17 For others, see ibid., pp. xi–xxi; Nelson and Tienda (1985).
18 The view according to which there are properties that Hispanics share is widespread. In reference to Hispanics in the United States in particular see, for example, Marín and VanOss Marín (1991, pp. 1–2, 5–7, 11–17). Among those who have argued for particular traits are the following: (for collectivism and power distance) Hofstede (1980); (for collectivism)

194

Marín and Triandis (1985); (for simpatía) Triandis, et al. (1984); (for familialism) Moore and Pachón (1976); (for a certain time orientation) Hall (1983); and (for a motley of characteristics) Shorris (1992, p. xvii). For more global approaches, see Mañach (1975); García Calderón (1979, pp. 247–60ff.), and chapter 6, this volume.

19 A political or socio-political understanding in the United States is discussed in Padilla (1985), pp. 75ff.

20 For the emphasis on language as a unifying factor in the United States, see ibid., pp. 151–4. This view is widespread in the press, e.g. "A Minority Worth Cultivating," *Economist* (April 25, 1998), p. 21. For the emphasis outside the US in a philosophical context, see Heredia (1987).

21 I use the term "Amerindian" to refer to what is of pre-Columbian origin. I use "Native American" to refer to what is of pre-Columbian origin in the United States.

22 A cultural criterion of ethnicity in general is proposed by Appiah (1990, p. 498). For this criterion in the Hispanic context, see Heredia (1994, p. 135).

23 Culturalist attempts to define nationality and/or ethnicity have been made by many authors throughout Latin America. In Mexico, Samuel Ramos and Octavio Paz stand out. See Ramos (1963, pp. 125–53) and Paz (1961). For other examples see chapter 6, this volume. For the United States context see Padilla (1985, p. 57). Horowitz (1975, p. 124) criticizes the emphasis on culture in the understanding of ethnicity.

24 In the nineteenth century some of Latin America's more enlightened thinkers had already rejected the notion of race. According to José Martí (1946, p. 2,035), for example, "There are no races. There are only a number of variations in man, in the details of habits and customs, imposed by the climactic and historical conditions under which he lives, which do not change that which is identical and essential." Others questioned the biological bases of race (e.g. Ortíz, 1911). For discussions in the United States see Locke (1992, pp. 10–12) and Outlaw (1996). For other studies on the issue of race, see Appiah and Guttman (1996), Zack (1993), and Harris (1998). The conception of "Hispanic" and other ethnic labels as racial is still quite common. Indeed, until fairly recently the US Census Bureau listed "Hispanic" along with racial categories like "white" and "black." "Mexican" ceased to be listed as a race in the census only in 1940 (Marín and VanOss Marín 1991, p. 20).

25 For South Africa see Minh-Ha (1991, p. 73).

26 Vasconcelos (1957b). In Gracia and Jaksić (1988, pp. 71–100).

27 This argument is proposed for the term "Latino" by Corlett (unpublished ms.) and for ethnicity in general by Corlett (1996, pp. 86–9). The argument is sometimes implicit in some discussions of Hispanic/Latino

Notes

identity. However, for Corlett, the extension of "Latino" *de facto* corresponds to the extension of "Hispanic." Note that sometimes the character of a surname, such as a Spanish surname, is taken to be a necessary or sufficient condition for the use of "Hispanic" or for Hispanic identity. But since surnames are generally dependent on lineage, the arguments I present against lineage apply here as well. For the discussion of surnames as indicators of ethnicity, see Isaacs (1975, p. 50). A related and commonly held view among sociologists is that ethnicity is acquired at birth and involves both physical and socio-cultural elements. See ibid., and Horowitz (1975, p. 113).

28 For a sociological analysis of the role of descent in Hispanic/Latino ethnicity, see Nelson and Tienda (1985). The problems of this approach have been raised in other identity contexts as well, e.g. Ruch (1981, p. 180).

29 This argument has been made by a variety of authors, particularly in the context of those of us who live in the United States (e.g. Hayes-Bautista, 1980, p. 355).

30 See Oboler (1995, pp. 25–7). In 1980 the Spanish American Heritage Association declared that "A Hispanic person is a Caucasian of Spanish ancestry. The Mexican American and Puerto Rican are not Caucasians of Spanish ancestry, and therefore are not Hispanic." Quoted by Hayes-Bautista and Chapa (1987, p. 64).

31 We must keep in mind that although the most egregious cases of discrimination against Hispanics have occurred in the United States, Hispanic immigrant workers have also suffered discrimination in Germany, Switzerland, and other countries in Europe.

32 For other arguments, see Murguia (1991).

33 There are counterparts to this term in Portuguese that refer to descendants of Portuguese immigrants and Portuguese immigrants themselves living in America, and in French, to designate descendants of French immigrants or French immigrants themselves living in America.

34 In fact, the term *criollo* may have been applied originally to children of Africans born in America and only later used self-assertively by descendants of Iberians to distinguish themselves from Iberians. Indeed, in Argentina the terms *criollo* and *criollito* are used to refer to people with dark skin, who look as if they have mixed blood. See Morse (1964, p. 136); also *Diccionario manual* (1981)

35 García Calderón (1979, pp. 154–5).

36 For still other objections to single labels for Hispanics/Latinos in the United States context in particular, see Giménez (1989).

37 Hayes-Bautista and Chapa (1987, p. 61), forgetting the 300 years of Iberian occupation, argue that the only thing Latin American countries

have in common is the presence of United States foreign policy as pronounced in the Monroe Doctrine in 1823. See also Benedetti (1972, p. 357). Not everyone agrees, however; see, for example, Ottocar (1966).

38 For differences in religious practices and affiliation among Hispanics/ Latinos in the United States, see Klor de Alba (1988, pp. 126–8).

39 Schutte (forthcoming).

40 Interestingly enough, Padilla's (1985, pp. 12–13) inference is just the reverse, favoring the use of "Latino" precisely because of the inequality common to Latinos. In Latin America also, analyses along these lines have been made; e.g. Rivano (1965).

41 For related issues, see Belliotti (1995, p. 175) and Corlett (1996, p. 88).

42 For the view that ethnicity is not a natural kind, see Corlett (1996, pp. 83–93).

43 For type mistakes, see Carnap (1959).

44 Oboler (1995, p. xvii). False generic identities are particularly harmful when they are used to formulate and implement social policy. See Cafferty and McCready (1985, p. 253).

45 Particularly at risk are marginalized groups, the poor, the disenfranchised. See Hernández and Torres-Saillant (1992); Giménez (1989, pp. 558–62).

46 Gracia (forthcoming, a).

Chapter 2   What's in a Name? The Relation of Names to Identity and Ethnicity

1 There is no general agreement on the best way to understand similarity and identity. For a different understanding of these notions, see Brennan (1988, p. 6).

2 Gracia (1988a, p. 26).

3 Chisholm (1970). Diachronic identity should not be confused with duration. Duration requires for something to be identical at two or more different times (diachronic identity) and to have been identical throughout the time elapsed between those times. The conditions of duration involve more than the conditions of diachronic identity. See Gracia (1996, pp. 69–79).

4 Mill (1872, p. 21); Russell (1956, pp. 200–1); Wittgenstein (1961, 3.203). The key point to what has come to be called "the theory of direct reference" is the denial that the conceptual content associated with a name secures its referent. See Salmon (1989, p. 445).

5 Searle (1984, pp. 232–3); Quine (1953).

6 Kripke (1981, esp. pp. 48, 109).

7 See note 5; Russell (1948, p. 303).

8 For more on this see Gracia (1988b).

9 Isaacs (1975, p. 46).

10 It is probably not perverse to say that this view, insofar as it rejects "meanings," can be attributed to Quine (1973, p. 35; 1971, pp. 6, 16). For someone else who also appears to hold that the only thing there is is language, or texts, see Derrida (1977).

11 Brewer and Brewer (1971); Marín (1984); Fairchild and Cozens (1981).

12 Isaacs (1975, p. 50).

13 Ethnicity is a fairly new concept. The first recorded usage of the term is in 1953 (*Webster's Third New International Dictionary*, 1961). For the term and its evolving meaning, see Glazer and Moynihan (1975, p. 1ff.).

14 Murguia (1991, p. 12), for example, has proposed the notion of pan-ethnicity and Padilla (1985, pp. 62 et statim) speaks of different levels of ethnic organization.

Chapter 3   What Makes Us Who We Are? The Key to Our Unity in Diversity

1 Other means of doing this involve indexicals such as "this" and "I" and definite descriptions, such as "the last Dodo bird." See Gracia (1988b, ch. 6).

2 Parsons (1975).

3 Mendieta (1997).

4 Stephan (1992, p. 51).

5 Alcoff (1995, p. 261).

6 Wittgenstein (1965, §75, p. 35).

7 The Philippines may have at one time been part of this world, but it is certainly not so at present. The cases of Angola, Mozambique, Goa, and others like these, are borderline.

8 My position, then, is different from that of those who argue for a sense or consciousness of shared history as a necessary condition of ethnicity. See Parsons (1975, p. 60).

9 Wittgenstein (1965, §67, p. 32).

10 Unamuno (1968, p. 1,081).

11 The philosophical foundation of this view goes back to some Wittgensteinians, e.g. Bambrough (1960–1). Sociologists frequently make self-naming, self-definition, and self-awareness necessary conditions of ethnicity. I believe these play a role in ethnicity, but one not necessary. For discussions of these conditions see Isaacs (1975, pp. 34–5); Parsons (1975, p. 56); Horowitz (1975, p. 113); Hayes-Bautista (1983, pp. 275–6).

12 This point has been made with respect to Latin American identity by Schutte (1993, p. 240).

13 Hanke (1974); Las Casas (1992).
14 Mörner (1967, pp. 41–52).
15 See Churchill (1993).
16 There is substantial agreement among scholars on this point. An indication of the difference can be gauged from attitudes toward mixed marriages. Intermarriages between Spaniards and Amerindians were explicitly permitted in Latin America as early as 1501 and, although there was generally Crown opposition to marriages between Spaniards and Africans, these were nonetheless permitted. Moreover, early in the nineteenth century, all legal obstacles to marriage with Amerindians and Africans disappeared. Compare this with the situation in the United States, where mixed marriages were forbidden by law in the State of Virginia as late as 1966 (Mörner, 1967, pp. 25, 38, 65–6, 72–86, 114–15; Morse, 1964, pp. 134–5; Fernández 1992, p. 132). Prohibitions against interracial marriages in the United States have not been only a matter of law, but also of religion. Christian evangelicals have generally justified their opposition to mixed marriages based on the purported biblical separation between the tribes of Israel. In the 1960s this attitude was still being openly defended by some faculty and students in evangelical colleges in the US. Such religious opposition is not generally found in Latin America or Iberia. There is also a philosophical background to Anglo-Saxon racism, which did not infect Latin America until European positivism reached our shores. One does not need to go farther than one of the greatest pillars of Anglo-Saxon philosophy to see it (Hume, 1905, pp. 152–3 footnote). Of course, the legality of intermarriage as well as the degree of intermarriages should not be taken as a sign that there is no racism in Latin America. One must distinguish between social and legal racism, and there is plenty of the former in Latin America.
17 Oboler (1995, p. 26).
18 For the hierarchies and labels used during colonial times see Morse (1964); Mörner (1967, pp. 58–60); Graham (1990).
19 Note that the Spanish American Heritage Association also contrasts Hispanics and *mestizos*.
20 Treviño (1987, p. 71).
21 Padilla (1985); Treviño (1987, p. 71 et statim).
22 For nations as constructed artifacts, see Anderson (1983).
23 Frondizi (1949); Gómez-Martínez (1995); Villegas (1963).
24 In this sense it is concordant with the concerns voiced by postmodernists. See Albó (1995, p. 29); Calderón (1995, pp. 60, 63).

Chapter 4   An Illustration: Hispanic Philosophy

1 Cf. Guy (1985); Solana (1941); Abellán (1979–91).

2 For example, Windelband's (1958) influential study and Jones's (1952–69) extensive multi-volume work do not make a single reference to Latin American philosophers.

3 This is true even in histories of Western philosophy which take into account Iberian developments, e.g. Copleston (1950). It is only recently and sporadically that general dictionaries and encyclopedias of philosophy have included references to Latin American philosophy. For example, the original plans for Craig (1998) did not include any reference to Latin America, even though the previous encyclopedia (Edwards, 1967) did. The situation is nothing short of scandalous. I shall come back to this matter in the context of the American philosophical community in the last chapter of this book. Only general histories of philosophy produced by Latin American philosophers contain materials on Latin American thought, e.g. Vasconcelos (1937).

4 Among histories and studies of Renaissance thought that ignore Latin America are Kristeller (1979; 1961) and Schmitt et al. (1988).

5 Beuchot (1998); Gallegos Rocafull (1974); Furlong (1952); Guy (1989); Méndez Plancarte (1946).

6 For example, Giacon (1946) and Schmitt et al. (1988). Some histories of the period do not, e.g. Kretzman et al. (1982).

7 Concerning Vera Cruz, see Redmond and Beuchot (1987); concerning Briceño, see Hannisch Espíndola (1963, pp. 24–30).

8 Ramos (1962).

9 Romero (1964).

10 In the case of Vitoria, the encounter seems to be a key concern, as is evident in Vitoria (1917), originally published in 1538 and 1539. In fact, there is substantial evidence that colonial Latin American thinkers not only influenced Iberian authors but also European philosophers like Descartes. See Beuchot (1991).

11 On the *transterrados*, see Abellán (1967). The concern of Gaos, Nicol, and other *transterrados* with the relation of Latin American thought to Iberian thought is evident in their writings and can be explained only by the influence that Latin Americans and the Latin American reality had on them. Gaos (1945) and Nicol (1961) make no sense plucked from the Latin American experience.

12 In this I must differ with Nicol (1988) and those who have tried to see some common element to all Hispanic philosophy.

13 *La filosofía en América* (1979); *Ideas en torno de Latinoamérica* (1986); *América Latina* (1992–3); Gracia (1986); Mignolo (1995a; 1995b).

14 For more on Suárez see Scorraille (1912); for Rubio, see Beuchot (1998); Gallegos Rocafull (1974, pp. 262–78); Redmond and Beuchot (1985).
15 Abellán (1967, pp. 103–92); Gaos (1952a); Gómez-Martínez (1995).
16 Abellán (1979–91).
17 Gómez-Martínez (1995); Abellán (1967); Gracia (1998).
18 Hannisch Espíndola (1963, pp. 36–7).
19 Salazar Bondy (1968; 1969); chapter 6, this volume.
20 Pereña (1992). For commerce and economics see Grice-Hutchinson (1952) and Sierra Bravo (1975).
21 Gil Fernández (1984, pp. 15–94).
22 Fuster (1972, p. 72).
23 Bonaventure (1882–1902, p. 422).
24 Ibid. and Gilson (1955, pp. 403–9).
25 The conduct of Renaissance popes like Leo X did not help to assuage the fears of such people. See Chamberlin (1969).
26 John Duns Scotus (1963, pp. 103–6). For skepticism in the Middle Ages see Michalski (1969) and Beuchot (1989, pp. 307–19).
27 For skepticism in the sixteenth century see Popkin (1964).
28 See notes 21 and 22.
29 Pinta Llorente (1953–8); Defourneaux (1973); Quesada (1910, pp. 3–33).
30 Quesada (1910, pp. 3–33).
31 Noreña (1975, pp. 1–35).
32 Gilson (1955, p. 107).
33 Other examples are the *Cursus Conimbricensis* and Juan de Santo Tomás's *Cursus philosophicus*. See Trentman (1982).
34 As late as 1851 the Concordat between Spain and the Holy See states, in article 1: "The Roman, Catholic, and Apostolic religion continues to be the only religion of the Spanish nation" (my translation). See Montalbán et al. (1963, p. 586).
35 Iriarte (1948, p. 236).
36 Hispanic philosophers themselves are relentless in their repetition of this opinion, e.g. Salazar Bondy (1986, p. 234).

Chapter 5   Where Do We Come From? Encounters, Inventions, and Mestizaje

1 Zea (1963, pp. 11–15).
2 Taylor (1984, p. 21).
3 Alcoff (1995, p. 273).
4 The people from Valencia and the Balearic Islands have always objected

Notes

to being called Catalans. They claim to be different peoples. This attitude
is reflected in the title of the major dictionary of the Catalan language:
Diccionari Català–Valencià–Balear, by Alcover and Moll (1968).
5   Cela (1970, p. 123); Mörner (1967, pp. 12–19).
6   Fuentes (1985, p. 27).
7   Sánchez-Albornoz (1956, pp. 7–103) argues, on the contrary, that feudal
institutions never quite took hold in Spain.
8   Mörner (1967, p. 16); Fuentes (1985); Morse (1964, p. 127).
9   Mörner (1967, pp. 9–10).
10 Martínez Estrada (1953, pp. 11, 16, et statim).
11 Coe (1993).
12 Diversity persisted even in the face of strong unifying forces. See Rama
(1982, pp. 124–6).
13 Knight (1990); Rama (1982, pp. 142–6).
14 The attempt by Kusch (1975) to find only two cultures in America, a
superficial culture imposed by Europeans and a deep Amerindian indigenous culture dating from before the encounter, is an oversimplification
of both the Iberian and pre-Columbian realities.
15 Coe (1993, p. 184).
16 On the notion of New World see Elliot (1970, pp. 28 et statim).
17 A pioneer study and still perhaps the best book on this topic is
O'Gorman (1961). See also Todorov (1984); Dussel (1995); Abellán
(1972).
18 Actually this point of view is not new. Augustine (1971, p. 165) identified
the world with our awareness of the world in order to argue against the
skeptics.
19 Aristotle, *Metaphysics* 1010b35.
20 Mörner (1967, p. 16).
21 Ibid., p. 17.
22 Ibid., p. 18.
23 Las Casas (1992).
24 Many other terms were used to describe different kinds of mixtures. For
example, the mixture of a Spaniard and *mestizo* woman was known as
cuarterón, while the mixture of a Spaniard and a *cuarterón* woman was a
quinterón, and so on. But these nomenclatures were not exact, and varied
from place to place. See Mörner (1967, pp. 58–9).
25 Freyre (1986, pp. 418–19); Ortíz (1983).
26 Mörner (1967, pp. 1–2, 95, 136–8, et statim).
27 Ibid., pp. 101–2; Knight (1990, pp. 73ff.).
28 Ortíz (1911; 1952); Helg (1990, pp. 52, 60).
29 Cf. Castro-Gómez (1996, p. 95) and Latin American Subaltern Studies
Group (1995, p. 135).

30 Orrego (1986, p. 1,397). See also Morejón (1982); Ortíz (1983); Lionett (1989).
31 Vasconcelos, cited by Castro-Gómez (1996, p. 83).
32 Oboler (1995, pp. 27–8). The notion of melting pot seems to have originated in Isaac Zangwill's 1909 play *The Melting Pot*. It is now largely discredited. See Thernstrom (1982).
33 Martínez-Echazábal (1998).
34 Cf. Nascimento (1997, p. 114). Sociologists in the United States frequently think of *mestizaje* in terms of fusion, e.g. Acosta-Belén (1988, p. 85).
35 Mörner (1967, p. 5); Horowitz (1975, p. 115).
36 Alcoff (1995, pp. 276–8); Anzaldúa (1987, p. 78); Miller (1992, p. 35).
37 Stephan (1992, p. 58).
38 Ortíz (1983; 1940; 1952; 1991) discusses this and other similar metaphors.
39 The Viceroyalty of New Spain included at one time or another such distant lands as Central America, Mexico, the American south-west, the West Indies, and even the Philippines, although its core was largely coextensive with Mexico. The borders between this colonial entity and Anglo America were fluid until the Adams–Onís treaty in 1819.
40 Díaz del Castillo (1956).
41 Morse (1964, pp. 129–30); Mörner (1967, pp. 22ff.).
42 Fernández (1992, p. 135).
43 Freyre (1946).
44 Mörner (1967, pp. 45–8, 56–68). It appears that hard-core racism found a "scientific" basis in Latin America only after Latin American intellectuals such as José Ingenieros, Carlos Octavio Bunge, and others read Darwin and Spencer and became converted to positivism. See Graham (1990, p. 2).
45 Mörner (1967, pp. 35–9); Morse (1964).
46 Mörner (1967, pp. 62–70).
47 Ibid., p. 1.
48 Rosenblat (1954, pp. 59, 102).
49 Mörner (1967, pp. 32–3).
50 For Peruvian cuisine, see Olivas Weston (1993).
51 Taylor et al. (1998, pp. 158–69).
52 Zea (1978, pp. 167ff.).
53 Schutte (1993, p. 122).
54 Vega (1959, pp. 566–7).
55 This sense of *mestizaje* appears already in Martí (1963).
56 Mörner (1967, pp. 140–2).
57 Bolívar (1951, vol. 1, p. 181). Bolívar himself may have had Amerindian blood: see Mörner (1967, p. 87).

58 For various attitudes towards Blacks in Brazil see Guerreiro Ramos (1957).
59 Helg (1990, p. 43).
60 Ibid., p. 56.
61 Oboler (1995, pp. 158–9).
62 Acosta-Belén (1988, pp. 81–106).
63 McWilliams (1990, pp. 43–53).
64 For examples see Shorris (1992).
65 Glazer (1996).

Chapter 6   The Search for Identity: Latin America and Its Philosophy

1 Stavans (1995, pp. 147–65) presents a general, non-technical, and non-philosophical history of these discussions. Among other important texts are Acosta-Belén (1986); Acuña (1971), and Rodríguez (1981).
2 In political thought it surfaces in Bolívar (1991) and Martí (1977, pp. 84–94); in a socio-cultural context it is evident in Rama (1982); and in literature we find it in García Márquez (1989) and Cortázar (1965).
3 The bibliography on this topic is very extensive. In addition to the classic texts to which I refer later, the following should be mentioned: Hernández Luna (1956); Villegas (1960); Larroyo (1958); Gómez Robledo (1958); Romanell (1954); Ramos (1951, pp. 103–14; 1949, pp. 175–85); O'Gorman (1951); Villoro (1950); Salmerón (1980); Roig (1993); Miró Quesada (1986); Martí (1984); Gracia and Jaksić (1984); Schutte (1993); Medina (1992). Also *La filosofía en América* (vol. 1, pp. 167–253); the volumes for 1950 of *Cuadernos Americanos* and *Filosofía y Letras*; and the bibliographies in the *Handbook of Latin American Studies 1935–present*. The classic texts have been gathered in Gracia and Jaksić (1988).
4 Frondizi (1949, p. 355).
5 Ortega y Gasset (1964a, p. 115). This point of view is alive and well among historians of philosophy who favor a sociological approach. See Kusch (forthcoming) and Gracia (forthcoming, c; 1992b, pp. 226–34).
6 Cf. Ramos (1943, p. 149).
7 Gracia (1992b, pp. 158–68, 226–8).
8 For a brief survey of Latin American philosophy in the twentieth century see Gracia (1988–9).
9 Alberdi (1895–1901, p. 613).
10 Alberdi (1963, pp. 53–5).
11 Ibid., p. 69.
12 Most Latin American writers to this day refer to the region as "America." North America is used to refer to the United States. Thus frequently they

speak of "American philosophy" to refer to what is called "Latin American philosophy" in the United States.

13 Alberdi (1963, pp. 67, 68--9, 73–5) spelled out some of his fundamental ideas on order, progress, and industry, which became commonplaces in Latin American positivist discourse.

14 Stabb (1967); Arguedas (1959); Bunge (1903); García Calderón (1979).

15 See Crawford (1961); Arciniegas (1967); Jorrín and Martz (1970); Davis (1972); Gracia (1975).

16 Rodó (1957a); see also Jaksić (1996).

17 Ibid., pp. 202, 242.

18 Rodó was far from being egalitarian malgré Fernández Retamar (1974).

19 Vasconcelos (1957b, p. 920).

20 Ibid., pp. 926–7.

21 Ibid., p. 910.

22 Ibid., pp. 917–42.

23 Ibid., pp. 930, 931, 935.

24 Ramos (1963, p. 143).

25 Ibid., p. 145.

26 Ibid., p. 146.

27 Ibid., p. 148.

28 Ibid., p. 151.

29 Ibid., p. 152.

30 Ramos's influence extends beyond philosophy. Among the literary writers who were influenced by him is Octavio Paz.

31 Zea (1948, pp. 160–1), for instance, understands *lo mexicano* as one of the bases for a Latin American philosophy.

32 Ramos (1963, pp. 69–87).

33 Ortega y Gasset (1957, p. 85).

34 Schwartzmann (1950, vol. 1, p. 111).

35 Ibid., pp. 111–12.

36 Ibid., p. 104.

37 Ibid.

38 Gaos (1952b, pp. 53–4, 88).

39 Zea (1948, p. 166).

40 Ibid., p. 201.

41 Villegas (1963); Domínguez Caballero (1968); Francovich (1956; 1968).

42 Frondizi (1949).

43 Vasconcelos (n.d., pp. 109–10).

44 Nicol (1961, pp. 53, 61–4, 161).

45 Ibid., p. 54.

46 Ibid., pp. 67–8, 94.

47 Mayz Vallenilla (1969, pp. 69, 90).

48 Mayz Vallenilla (1976, p. 6).
49 Ibid., p. 15.
50 Salazar Bondy (1968, "Una interpretación").
51 Rivano (1971).
52 Salmerón (1952).
53 Salmerón (1969, p. 29).
54 Ibid.
55 Miró Quesada (1976, section 3).
56 Another example is Sambarino (1980).
57 Roig (1986, pp. 255–7).
58 Castro-Gómez (1996).
59 Martí (1984, p. 51).
60 Gracia (1992a).
61 Schutte (1993, p. 239).
62 Ibid., pp. 240–1.

Chapter 7   Foreigners in Our Own Land: Hispanics in American Philosophy

1 *Proceedings and Addresses of the American Philosophical Association* (1993, pp. 45–6).
2 US Bureau of the Census (1996, chart 13).
3 National Research Council (1987).
4 *Proceedings and Addresses of the American Philosophical Association* (1987, pp. 359–60).
5 "Philosophy in America in 1994" (1996, pp. 135–7).
6 Ibid., p. 149.
7 Bunge is now retired but taught at McGill for many years. The others teach in the following institutions: Angelelli (Texas at Austin), Gómez-Lobo (Georgetown), Sosa (Brown), Schutte (Florida at Gainesville), and Gracia (State University of New York at Buffalo).
8 Héctor-Neri Castañeda (1924–91) was an important member of the established group until recently. He was born in Guatemala. Among the younger group are Jorge García (Rutgers), Reinaldo Elugardo (Oklahoma), Linda López McAllister (South Florida), and Linda Martín Alcoff (Syracuse).
9 Here are some examples of African Americans: Leonard Harris (Purdue), Howard McGary (Rutgers), and Lucius Outlaw (Haverford). Among established women philosophers known for their work in feminist issues are Kathryn P. Addelson (Smith), Louise Antony (North Carolina at Chapel Hill), Susan Bordo (Kentucky), Lorraine Code (York, Ontario), Nancy Frankenbury (Dartmouth), Alison Jaggar (Colorado at Boulder),

Carolyn Korsmeyer (Buffalo), Elizabeth Spellman (Smith), and Nancy Tuana (Oregon).

10 Bunge, for example, has expressed impatience with those who work on the history of Hispanic philosophy and is on record as noting that there is not much philosophy even in Argentina, which is certainly one of the most philosophically sophisticated countries in Latin America. See Bunge (1995, p. 60).

11 *Proceedings and Addresses of the American Philosophical Association* 1996, p. 153.

12 Donoso (1976; 1992, p. 238).

13 Jaffe et al. (1980, pp. 51–62). This source is dated, but its data are particularly pertinent for explaining the number of Hispanic philosophers today, for they concern primary- and secondary-school students at the time of the survey. See also Davis et al. (1988, pp. 42–9).

14 Jaffe et al. (1980, pp. 29–39); Davis et al. (1988, pp. 40–2).

15 Jaffe et al. (1980, pp. 29–39).

16 Ibid., pp. 38–9.

17 Certainly philosophers play no great role in public life in the United States, whereas they do in Iberian and Latin American countries. See Gracia (forthcoming, b).

18 "Area and Population of the World" (1997, p. 838).

19 *International Directory of Philosophers and Philosophy* (1996).

20 Consider, for example, that this source neglects to list important universities in many countries, such as the Universidad de San Marcos in Peru.

21 The figures on the United States population are taken from Chart 4, "Components of Population Change, 1980 to 1995, and Projections, 1996 to 2050," US Bureau of the Census (1996, p. 9).

22 They also appear to have lower grade-point averages than European Americans. See *Black, Hispanic, and White Doctoral Students: Before, During, and After Enrolling in Graduate School* (1990, p. 2).

23 See *Proceedings and Addresses of the American Philosophical Association* 1996, pp. 21–75.

24 Bernstein (1987).

25 Black (1963, p. v).

26 Bernstein (1987); Mandt (1990, pp. 77–101).

27 I have provided a more in-depth and extensive analysis of the current situation of Western philosophy in the Introduction to Gracia (1992b, pp. 1–37).

28 Quine (1970; 1987). I respond to Quine in Gracia (1995, pp. 189–214).

29 Quine (1969; 1953).

30 Heidegger (1962). I respond to Heidegger in Gracia (1995, pp. 189–214).

31 Foucault (1980; 1990).

32 Bernstein (1987).
33 Gracia (1992, chs. 1 and 2).
34 See Hare (1988).
35 Taylor (1984). I argue against historicism in Gracia (1992, pp. 111–14).
36 For some criticisms, see Hintikka (1997, pp. 169–70).
37 On the technique of dismissal see Gracia (1992, pp. 24–5, 32).
38 For the general perception of Hispanics as foreign see Oboler (1995, pp. 18–19) and Berkhofer (1978).
39 Kozol (1995, p. 41, passim).
40 Chesterfield (1992, pp. 72–3).
41 I discuss the role of Affirmative Action in this context in Gracia (forthcoming, a).

Conclusion

1 Groups are collections of individuals and, therefore, individual themselves, and individuality cannot be understood in essentialist terms. For a defense of this point of view see Gracia (1988b).

Bibliography

Abalos, David, T. (1986). *Latinos in the United States: The Sacred and the Political*, University of Notre Dame Press.

Abellán, José Luis (1972). *La idea de América: origen y evolución*, ISTMO.

—— (1967). *Filosofía española en América (1936–1966)*, Ediciones Guadarrama.

—— (1979–91). *Historia crítica del pensamiento español*, 7 vols., Espasa-Calpe.

Acosta-Belén, Edna, ed. (1986). *The Puerto Rican Woman: Perspectives on Culture, History, and Society*, 2nd edn., Praeger.

—— (1988). "From Settlers to Newcomers: The Hispanic Legacy in the United States," in E. Acosta-Belén and B. R. Sjostrom, eds., *The Hispanic Experience in the United States: Contemporary Issues and Perspectives*, Praeger, pp. 81–106.

Acosta-Belén, Edna and Sjostrom, Barbara, eds. (1988). *The Hispanic Experience in the United States: Contemporary Issues and Perspectives*, Praeger.

Acuña, Rodolfo (1971). *A Mexican American Chronicle*, American Book Co.

Adorno, Rolena (1993). "Reconsidering Colonial Discourse for Sixteenth- and Seventeenth-Century Spanish America," *Latin American Research Review* 28: 135–45.

Alberdi, Juan Bautista (1963). *Bases y puntos de partida para la organización de la confederación argentina*, Librería y Editorial Castellvi.

—— (1895–1901). "Ideas para presidir la confección del curso de filosofía contemporánea," in *Escritos póstumos de Juan Bautista Alberdi*, vol. 15, Imprenta Europea, Moreno y Defensa.

Albó, Xavier (1995). "Our Identity Starting from Pluralism in the Base," in J. Beverly, M. Aronna, and J. Oviedo, eds., *The Postmodernism Debate in Latin America*, Duke University Press, pp. 18–33.

Bibliography

Alcoff, Linda Martín (1995). "Mestizo Identity," in Naomi Zack, ed., *American Mixed Race: The Culture of Microdiversity*, Rowan & Littlefield, pp. 257–78.

Alcover, Antoni and Moll, Francesc de B. (1968). *Diccionari Català–Valencià–Balear*, 2nd edn., 10 vols., Editorial Moll.

América Latina: Historia y destino (Homenaje a Leopoldo Zea) (1992–3). 3 vols., Universidad Nacional Autónoma de México.

Anderson, Benedict (1983). *Imagined Communities: Reflections on the Origin and Spread of Nationalism*, Verso.

Anzaldúa, Gloria (1987). *Borderlands/La Frontera*, Spinsters/Aunt Lute.

Appiah, Anthony K. (1990). "But Would That Still Be Me? Notes on Gender, 'Race,' Ethnicity, as Sources of 'Identity,'" *Journal of Philosophy* 87: 493–9.

Appiah, Anthony K. and Guttman, Amy (1996). *Color Conscious: The Political Morality of Race*, Princeton University Press.

Arciniegas, German (1967). *Latin America: A Cultural History*, trans. Joan McLean, Alfred A. Knopf.

"Area and Population of the World" (1997). In *The World Almanac and Book of Facts*, World Almanac Books, p. 838.

Arguedas, Alcides (1959). *Pueblo enfermo: Contribución a la psicología de los pueblos hispano-americanos*, in Luis Alberto Sánchez, ed., *Obras completas*, vol. 1, Aguilar, pp. 395–617.

Aristotle (1941). *The Basic Works of Aristotle*, ed. R. McKeon, Random House.

Arrington, Robert L., ed. (1999). *A Companion to the Philosophers*, Blackwell Publishers.

Augustine (1971). *Contra academicos*, ed. V. Capanaga et al., in *Obras completas de San Agustín*, vol. 3, Biblioteca de Autores Cristianos.

Bambrough, R. (1960–1). "Universals and Family Resemblances," *Proceedings of the Aristotelian Society* 61: 207–22.

Belliotti, Raymond A. (1995). *Seeking Identity: Individualism versus Community in an Ethnic Context*, University Press of Kansas.

Benedetti, Mario (1972). "Temas y problemas," in C. Fernández Moreno, ed., *América Latina en su literatura*, Siglo XXI, pp. 354–71

Benedict, Ruth (1934). *Patterns of Culture*, Houghton Mifflin.

Berkhofer, Robert (1978). *The White Man's Indian: Images of the American Indian from Columbus to the Present*, Knopf.

Bernal, Martha E. and Knight, George P., eds. (1993). *Ethnic Identity: Formation and Transmission among Hispanics and Other Minorities*, SUNY Press.

Bernstein, Richard (1987). "Philosophical Rift: A Tale of Two Approaches," *New York Times* (December 29), pp. A1, A15.

Beuchot, Mauricio (1985). *La lógica mexicana del Siglo de Oro*, Universidad Nacional Autónoma de México.

—— (1989). "Escepticismo en la edad media: El caso de Nicolás de Autrecourt," *Revista Latinoamericana de Filosofía* 15, 3: 307–19.

Bibliography

——— (1991). "Aportaciones de pensadores novohispanos a la filosofía universal," in *Estudios de historia y de filosofía en el México colonial*, Universidad Nacional Autónoma de México, pp. 43–51.

——— (1998). *The History of Philosophy in Colonial Mexico*, Catholic University of America Press.

Beuchot, Mauricio and Redmond, Walter (1987). *Pensamiento y realidad en Alonso de la Vera Cruz*, Universidad Nacional Autónoma de México.

Beverly, J., Aronna, M., and Oviedo, J., eds. (1995). *The Postmodernism Debate in Latin America*, Duke University Press.

Black, Max (1963). *Philosophical Analysis: A Collection of Essays*, Prentice-Hall.

"Black, Hispanic, and White Doctoral Students: Before, During, and After Enrolling in Graduate School" (1990). Educational Testing Service.

Bodunrin, Peter O. (1991). "The Question of African Philosophy," in Tsenay Serequeberhan, ed., *African Philosophy: The Essential Readings*, Paragon House, pp. 63–86.

Bolívar, Simón (1951). *Selected Writings of Bolívar*, 2 vols., ed. Vicente Lecuna and Harold A. Bierck, Jr., Colonial Press.

——— (1991). *Para nosotros la patria es América*, Biblioteca Ayacucho.

Bonaventure (1882–1902). *Collationes in Hexaemeron 19*, in *Opera omnia*, vol. 5, Collegium S. Bonaventurae.

Brennan, Andrew (1988). *Conditions of Identity: A Study of Identity and Survival*, Clarendon Press.

Brewer, R. E. and Brewer, M. B. (1971). "Expressed Evaluation Toward a Social Object as a Function of Label," *Journal of Sociological Psychology* 84: 257–60.

Bunge, Carlos Octavio (1903). *Nuestra América*, Henrich.

Bunge, Mario (1995). "Testimonio de Mario Bunge," in Ana Baron, Mario del Carril, and Albino Gómez, eds., *¿Porqué se fueron? Testimonios de argentinos en el exterior*, EMECE, pp. 49–80.

Butler, R. E. (1986). *On Creating a Hispanic America: A Nation within a Nation?*, Council for Inter-American Security.

Cafferty, Pastora San Juan and McCready, William C., eds. (1985). *Hispanics in the United States: A New Social Agenda*, Transaction Books.

Calderón, F. (1995). "Latin American Identity and Mixed Temporalities; or, How to Be Postmodern and Indian at the Same Time," in J. Beverly, J. Oviedo, and M. Aronna, eds., *The Postmodernism Debate in Latin America*, Duke University Press, pp. 55–64.

Carnap, Rudolph (1959). "The Elimination of Metaphysics Through Logical Analysis of Language," trans. Arthur Pap, in A. J. Ayer, ed., *Logical Positivism*, Free Press, pp. 60–81.

Castro-Gómez, Santiago (1996). *Crítica de la razón latinoamericana*, Puvill Libros.

Bibliography

Cela, Camilo José (1970). "Spain: Its People, Language, and Culture," in E. Jones and F. Dean, eds., *The Americas and Self-Identification*, Texas A & M University Press, pp. 118–24.

Chamberlin, E. R (1969). *The Bad Popes*, Dorset Press.

Chesterfield, Lord (1992). *Letters*, Oxford University Press.

Chisholm, Roderick (1970). "Identity through Time," in H. E. Kiefer and M. K. Munitz, eds., *Language, Belief, and Metaphysics*, SUNY Press, pp. 163–82.

Churchill, Ward (1993). *Struggle for the Land: Indigenous Resistance to Genocide, Ecocide, and Expropriation in Contemporary North America*, Common Courage Press.

Coe, Michael D. (1993). *The Maya*, Thames and Hudson.

Copleston, Frederick (1950). *A History of Philosophy*, Image Books.

Corlett, J. Angelo (forthcoming). "Latino Identity," *Public Affairs Quarterly*.

—— (1996). "Parallels of Ethnicity and Gender," in Naomi Zack, ed., *Race/ Sex: Their Sameness, Difference and Interplay*, Routledge, pp. 83–93.

Cortázar, Julio (1965). *Rayuela*, Editorial Sudamericana.

Craig, Edward (1998). *Routledge Encyclopedia of Philosophy*, 10 vols., Routledge.

Crawford, William R. (1961). *A Century of Latin American Thought*, Harvard University Press.

Cuadernos Americanos (1950) Mexico.

Cursus Conimbricensis (1600 ff.). Universidade de Coimbra, Collegium Conimbricense Societatis Jesu.

Dane, Leila, F. (1997). "Ethnic Identity and Conflict Transformation," *Peace Review* 9, 4: 503–7.

Davis, C. et al. (1988). "US Hispanics: Changing the Face of America," in E. Acosta-Belén and B. R. Sojstrom, eds., *The Hispanic Experience in the United States: Contemporary Issues and Perspectives*, Praeger, pp. 3–78.

Davis, Harold E. (1961). *Latin American Social Thought*, Washington University Press.

—— (1972). *Latin American Thought: A Historical Introduction*, Louisiana State University Press.

Defourneaux, M. (1973). *Inquisición y censura de libros en la España del siglo XVIII*, Taurus.

Derrida, Jacques (1977). "Signature Event Context," *Glyph* 1: 172–97.

Díaz del Castillo, Bernal (1956). *The Discovery and Conquest of Mexico*, trans. A. P. Mandslay, Farrar, Strauss and Cudahy.

Diccionario manual e ilustrado de la lengua española (1981). Espasa-Calpe.

Domínguez Caballero, Diego (1968). "Motivo y sentido de una investigación de lo panameño," in Leopoldo Zea, ed., *Antología de la filosofía americana contemporánea*, B. Costa Amic, pp. 157–69.

Donoso, Antón (1976). "The Society for Iberian and Latin American Thought

Bibliography

(SILAT): An Interdisciplinary Project," *Los Ensayistas: Boletín Informativo* 1–2: 38–42.

—— (1992). "Latin American Applied Philosophy," *Latin American Research Review* 27, 2: 237–57.

Dussel, Enrique (1995). *The Invention of America: Eclipse of "the Other" and the Myth of Modernity*, trans. Michael D. Barber, Continuum.

Edwards, Paul (1967). *The Encyclopedia of Philosophy*, 8 vols., Collier Macmillan.

Elliot, J. H. (1970). *The Old World and the New, 1492–1650*, Cambridge University Press.

English, Parker and Kalumba, Kibujjo M. (1996). *African Philosophy: A Classical Approach*, Prentice-Hall.

Fairchild, H. H. and Cozens, J. A. (1981). "Chicano, Hispanic or Mexican American: What's in a Name?" *Hispanic Journal of Behavioral Sciences* 3: 191–8.

Fernández, Carlos A. (1992). "La Raza and the Melting Pot: A Comparative Look at Multiethnicity," in Maria P. P. Root, ed., *Racially Mixed People in America*, SAGE, pp. 126–43.

Fernández Retamar, Roberto (1974). *Calibán: Apuntes sobre la cultura en nuestra América*, 2nd edn., Editorial Diógenes.

La filosofía en América: Trabajos presentados en el IX Congreso Interamericano de Filosofía (1979), 2 vols., Sociedad Venezolana de Filosofía.

Filosofía y Letras (1950).

Foucault, Michel (1980). "Prison Talk," in Colin Gordon, ed., *Power/Knowledge*, Pantheon Books, pp. 37–54.

—— (1990). "Nietzsche, Freud, Marx," in G. L. Orminston and A. D. Schrift, eds., *Transforming the Hermeneutic Circle: From Nietzsche to Nancy*, SUNY Press, pp. 59–68.

Fox, Geoffrey (1996). *Hispanic Nation: Culture, Politics, and the Constructing of Identity*, Carol Publishing.

Francovich, Guillermo (1956). *El pensamiento boliviano en el siglo XX*, Fondo de Cultura Económica.

—— (1968). "Pachamama," in Leopoldo Zea, ed., *Antología de la filosofía americana contemporánea*, B. Costa Amic, pp. 79–87.

Freyre, Gilberto (1946). *The Masters and the Slaves*, trans. S. Putnam, Knopf.

—— (1986). *The Mansions and the Shanties*, trans. Harriet de Onís, University of California Press.

Frondizi, Risieri (1949). "Is There an Ibero-American Philosophy?" *Philosophy and Phenomenological Research* 9: 345–55.

Fuentes, Carlos (1985). *Latin America at War with the Past*, CBC Enterprises.

Furlong, Guillermo (1952). *Nacimiento y desarrollo de la filosofía en el Río de La Plata, 1536–1810*, Guillermo Kraft.

Fusco, Coco (1992). "The Latino 'Boom' in American Film," *Centro de Estudios Puertorriqueños Bulletin*, El Centro, pp. 49–56.

Fuster, J. (1972). *Rebeldes y heterodoxos*, Edicions Ariel.

Gallegos Rocafull, José M. (1974). *El pensamiento mexicano en los siglos XVI y XVII*, 2nd edn., Universidad Nacional Autónoma de México.

Gaos, José (1945). *Historia del pensamiento de lengua española en la edad contemporánea (1744–1944)*, Séneca.

—— (1952a). *En torno a la filosofía mexicana*, Porrúa y Obregón.

—— (1952b). *Sobre Ortega y Gasset*, Imprenta Universitaria de Mexico.

García Calderón, Francisco (1979). *Las democracias latinas de América: La creación de un continente*, Biblioteca Ayacucho, first published in French in 1912.

García Márquez, Gabriel (1989). *El general en su laberinto: Novela*, Editorial Diana.

Garza, Rodolfo O. de la et al. (1998). "Family Ties and Ethnic Lobbies: Latino Relations with Latin America," Policy Brief, Tomás Rivera Policy Institute.

Giacon, Carlo (1946). *La seconda scolastica*, 2 vols., Fratelli Bocca.

Gil Fernández, Luis (1984). *Estudios de humanismo y tradición clásica*, Editorial Complutense.

Gilson, Etienne (1955). *History of Christian Philosophy in the Middle Ages*, Random House.

Giménez, Martha (1989). " 'Latino?/Hispanic' – Who Needs a Name? The Case Against a Standardized Terminology," *International Journal of Health Services* 19, 3: 557–71.

Glazer, Nathan (1996). "The Hard Questions: Race for the Cure," *New Republic* (October 7): 29.

Glazer, Nathan and Moynihan, Daniel P. (1963). *Beyond the Melting Pot*, Harvard University Press.

—— eds. (1975). *Ethnicity: Theory and Experience*, Harvard University Press.

Gobineau, Arthur, comte de (1967). *The Inequality of Human Races*, trans. Adrian Collins, H. Fertig; originally published in 1853.

Gómez-Martínez, José Luis (1995). *Pensamiento de la liberación: Proyección de Ortega en Iberoamérica*, Ediciones EGE.

Gómez Robledo, Antonio (1958). *Ideas y experiencia de América*, Fondo de Cultura Económica.

González, Justo L. (1992). "Hispanics in the United States," *Listening: Journal of Religion and Culture* 27, 1: 7–16.

Gracia, Jorge J. E. (1975). "Importance of the History of Ideas in Latin America: Zea's Positivism in Mexico," *Journal of the History of Ideas* 36: 177–84.

—— ed. (1986). *Latin American Philosophy in the Twentieth Century*, Prometheus Books.

Bibliography

—— (1988a). *Introduction to the Problem of Individuation in the Early Middle Ages*, 2nd revd. edn., Philosophia Verlag.

—— (1988b). *Individuality: An Essay on the Foundations of Metaphysics*, SUNY Press.

—— ed. (1988c). *Directory of Latin-American Philosophers*, Council of International Studies and Programs of SUNY at Buffalo.

—— (1988–9). "Latin American Philosophy Today," *Philosophical Forum* 20: 4–32.

—— (1992a). "Zea y la liberación latinoamericana," in various authors, *América Latina: Historia y destino (Homenaje a Leopoldo Zea)*, Universidad Nacional Autónoma de México, vol. 2, pp. 95–105.

—— (1992b). *Philosophy and Its History: Issues in Philosophical Historiography*, SUNY Press.

—— (1993). "Hispanic Philosophy: Its Beginning and Golden Age," *Review of Metaphysics* 46, 3: 475–502. Reprinted in K. White, ed. (1997) *Hispanic Philosophy in the Age of Discovery*, Catholic University Press of America, pp. 3–27.

—— (1995). *A Theory of Textuality: The Logic and Epistemology*, SUNY Press.

—— (1996). *Texts: Ontological Status, Identity, Author, Audience*, SUNY Press.

—— (1998). *Filosofía hispánica: Concepto, origen y foco historiográfico*, Universidad de Navarra.

—— (1999). "The Nature of Ethnicity with Special Reference to Hispanic/ Latino Identity," *Public Affairs Quarterly*, 13, 1: 25–42.

—— (forthcoming, a). "Affirmative Action for Hispanics/Latinos? Yes and No," in Jorge J. E. Gracia and Pablo De Greiff, eds., *Ethnic Identity, Race, and Group Rights: Hispanics/Latinos in the US*, Routledge.

—— (forthcoming, b). "Philosophy in American Public Life: *De facto* and *De jure*," *Proceedings and Addresses of the American Philosophical Association*.

—— (forthcoming, c). "Sociological Accounts in the History of Philosophy," in Martin Kusch, ed., *The Sociology of Philosophical Knowledge*, Kluwer.

Gracia, Jorge J. E. and Jaksić, Iván (1984). "The Problem of Philosophical Identity in Latin America: History and Approaches," *Inter-American Review of Bibliography* 34: 53–71.

—— eds. (1988). *Filosofía e identidad cultural en América Latina*, Monte Avila.

Gracia, Jorge J. E. et al., eds. (1984). *Philosophical Analysis in Latin America*, Reidel.

Graham, Richard, ed. (1990). *The Idea of Race in Latin America, 1870–1940*, University of Texas Press.

Grice-Hutchinson, M. (1952). *The School of Salamanca: Readings in Spanish Monetary Theory, 1544–1605*, Clarendon Press.

Guerreiro Ramos, A. (1957). *Introdução crítica à sociologia brasileira*, Editorial Andes.

Guy, Alain (1985). *Histoire de la philosophie espagnole*, 12th edn., Université de Toulouse-La Mirail.

—— (1989). *Panorama de la philosophie Ibero-Américaine du XVIe siècle a nos jours*, Edicions Patiño.

Haddox, John H. (1970). "Latin America: One and/or Many: A Philosophical Exploration," in E. Jones and F. Dean, eds., *The Americans and Self-Identification*, Texas A & M University Press, pp. 62–75.

Hall, E. T. (1983). *The Dance of Life*, Anchor Books.

Handbook of Latin American Studies (1935–present). University of Florida Press.

Hanke, Lewis (1974). *All Mankind is One: A Study of the Disputation Between Bartolomé de Las Casas and Juan Ginés de Sepúlveda in 1550 on the Intellectual and Religious Capacity of the American Indians*, Northern Illinois University Press.

Hannisch Espíndola, Walter (1963). *En torno a la filosofía en Chile, 1594–1810*, Universidad Católica de Chile.

Hare, Peter H., ed. (1988). *Doing Philosophy Historically*, Prometheus Books.

Harris, Leonard, ed. (1998). *Racism: Key Concepts in Critical Theory*, Humanities Press.

Hayes-Bautista, David E. (1980). "Identifying 'Hispanic' Populations: The Influence of Research Methodology upon Public Policy," *American Journal of Public Health* 70: 353–6.

—— (1983). "On Comparing Studies of Different Raza Populations," *American Journal of Public Health* 73: 274–6.

Hayes-Bautista, David E. and Chapa, Jorge (1987). "Latino Terminology: Conceptual Bases for Standardized Terminology," *American Journal of Public Health* 77: 61–8.

Heidegger, Martin (1962). *Being and Time*, trans. J. Macquarie and E. Robinson, Harper Books.

Helg, Aline (1990). "Race in Argentina and Cuba, 1880–1930: Theory, Policies, and Popular Reaction," in Richard Graham, ed., *The Idea of Race in Latin America, 1870–1940*, University of Texas Press, pp. 36–69.

Heredia, Antonio (1987). "Espacio, tiempo y lenguaje de la filosofía hispánica," in Eudaldo Forment, ed., *Filosofía de Hispanoamérica: Aproximación al panorama actual*, PPU, pp. 43–59.

—— (1994). "Hispanismo filosófico: Problemas de su constitución," in José L. Abellán, ed., *Identidades culturales en el cambio de siglo*, Trotta, pp. 133–42.

Hernández Luna, Juan (1956). *Samuel Ramos (su filosofar sobre México)*, Universidad Nacional Autónoma de México.

Hernández, Ramona and Torres-Saillant, Silvio (1992). "Marginality and Schooling: Editor's Foreword," *Punto 7 Review: A Journal of Marginal Discourse* 2: 1–7.

Bibliography

Hintikka, Jaako (1997). "Letter to the Editor," *Proceedings and Addresses of the American Philosophical Association* 70, 5: 169–70.

Historia de la Iglesia Católica (1953). Biblioteca de Autores Cristianos.

Hofstede, G. (1980). *Culture's Consequences: International Differences in Work-Related Values*, SAGE.

Horowitz, Donald L. (1975). "Ethnic Identity," in N. Glazer and D. P. Moynihan, eds., *Ethnicity: Theory and Experience*, Harvard University Press, pp. 111–40.

Hountondji, Paulin J. (1991). "African Philosophy: Myth and Reality," in Tsenay Serequeberhan, ed., *African Philosophy: The Essential Readings*, Paragon House, pp. 111–31.

Hume, David (1905). "Of Natural Characters," in *Hume's Essays*, Routledge, pp. 144–58.

Ideas en torno de Latinoamérica (1986). 2 vols., Universidad Nacional Autónoma de México.

International Directory of Philosophers and Philosophy (1996). Philosophy Documentation Center, University of Bowling Green.

Iriarte, J. (1948). "La proyección sobre Europa de una gran metafísica, o Suárez en la filosofía en los días del Barroco," *Razón y Fe, número extraordinario*: 229–63.

Isaacs, Harold R. (1975). "Basic Group Identity," in Nathan Glazer and Daniel P. Moynihan, eds., *Ethnicity: Theory and Experience*, Harvard University Press, pp. 29–52.

Jaffe, A. J. et al. (1980). *The Changing Demography of Spanish America*, Academic Press

Jaksić, Iván (1996). "The Machine and the Spirit: Anti-Technological Humanism in Twentieth-Century Latin America," *Revista de Estudios Hispánicos* 30: 179–201.

John Duns Scotus (1963). *Philosophical Writings*, ed. Allan Wolter, Nelson.

Jones, W. T. (1952–69). *A History of Western Philosophy*, Harcourt.

Jorrín, Miguel and Martz, John D. (1970). *Latin American Political Thought and Ideology*, University of North Carolina Press.

Juan de Santo Tomás (1930). *Cursus philosophicus*, 3 vols., ed. B. Reiser, Marietti.

Klor de Alba, Jorge (1988). "Telling Hispanics Apart: Latino Socio-cultural Diversity," in E. Acosta-Belén and B. R. Sojstrom, eds., *The Hispanic Experience in the United States: Contemporary Issues and Perspectives*, Praeger, pp. 107–36.

Knight, Alan (1990). "Racism, Revolution, and Indigenismo: Mexico, 1910–1940," in Richard Graham, ed., *The Idea of Race in Latin America, 1870–1940*, University of Texas Press, pp. 71–113.

Bibliography

Kozol, Jonathan (1995). *Amazing Grace: The Lives of Children and the Conscience of a Nation*, Harper Perennial.

Kretzman, Norman et al., eds. (1982). *The Cambridge History of Later Medieval Philosophy*, Cambridge University Press.

Kripke, Saul (1981). *Naming and Necessity*, Harvard University Press.

Kristeller, Paul Oskar (1961). *Renaissance Thought: The Classic, Scholastic, and Humanistic Strains*, Harper and Brothers.

—— (1979). *Renaissance Thought and Its Sources*, Columbia University Press

Kusch, Martin, ed. (forthcoming). *The Sociology of Philosophical Knowledge*, Kluwer.

Kusch, Rodolfo (1975). *América profunda*, Editorial Bonum.

Ladd, John (1997). "Philosophical Reflections on Race and Racism," *American Behavioral Scientist* 41, 2: 212–22.

Larroyo, Francisco (1958). *La filosofía americana: su razón y su sin razón de ser*, Universidad Nacional Autónoma de México.

Las Casas, Bartolomé de (1992). *In Defense of the Indians*, trans. and ed. C. M. Stafford Poole, Northern Illinois University Press.

Latin American Subaltern Studies Group (1995). "Founding Statement," in J. Beverly, M. Aronna, and J. Oviedo, eds., *The Postmodernism Debate in Latin America*, Duke University Press, pp. 135–46.

Lionett, Françoise (1989). *Autobiographical Voices: Race, Gender, Self-Portraiture*, Cornell University Press.

Locke, Alain LeRoy (1992). *Race Contacts and Interracial Relations: Lectures on the Theory and Practice of Race*, ed. Jeffrey C. Stewart, Howard University Press.

Lowry, I. S. (1984). "The Science and Politics of Ethnic Enumeration," in W. A. Van Horne, ed., *Ethnicity and Public Policy*, University of Wisconsin Press.

McWilliams, Carey (1990). *North from Mexico: The Spanish-Speaking People of the United States*, Greenwood Press.

Mañach, Jorge (1975). *Frontiers in the Americas: A Global Perspective*, trans. Philip H. Phenix, Teachers College–Columbia University.

Mandt, A. J. (1990). "The Inevitability of Pluralism: Philosophical Practice and Philosophical Excellence," in Avner Cohen and Marcelo Dascal, eds., *The Institution of Philosophy: A Discipline in Crisis*, Open Court, pp. 77–101.

Marín, G. (1984). "Stereotyping Hispanics: The Differential Effect of Research Method, Label and Degree of Contact," *International Journal of International Relations* 8: 17–27.

Marín, G. and Triandis, H. C. (1985). "Allocentrism as an Important Characteristic of the Behavior of Latin Americans and Hispanics," in R. Díaz-Guerrero, ed., *Cross-cultural and National Studies in Social Psychology*, Elsevier Science Publishers, pp. 85–104.

Marín, G. and VanOss Marín, B. (1991). *Research with Hispanic Populations*, SAGE.

Bibliography

Martí, José (1946). "La verdad sobre los Estados Unidos," in *Obras completas*, vol. 1, Editorial Lex, pp. 2,035–8.

—— (1963). "Nuestra América," in *Obras completas*, vol. 6, Editorial Nacional de Cuba, pp. 15–23.

—— (1977). *Our America: Writings on Latin America and the Struggle for Cuban Independence*, ed. Philip S. Foner, trans. Elinor Randall et al., Monthly Review Press.

Martí, Oscar (1984). "Is There a Latin American Philosophy?" *Metaphilosophy* 14: 46–52.

Martínez-Echazábal, Lourdes (1998). "Mestizaje and the Discourse of National/Cultural Identity in Latin America, 1845–1959," *Latin American Perspectives* 25: 21–42.

Martínez Estrada, Ezequiel (1953). *Radiografía de la pampa*, Losada.

Mayz Vallenilla, Ernesto (1969). *El problema de América*, 2nd edn., Universidad Central de Venezuela.

—— (1976). *Latinoamérica en la encrucijada de la técnica*, Universidad Simón Bolívar.

Medina, Vicente (1992). "The Possibility of an Indigenous Philosophy: A Latin American Perspective," *American Philosophical Quarterly* 29, 4: 373–80.

Méndez Plancarte, Gabriel (1946). *Humanismo mexicano del siglo XVI*, Universidad Nacional Autónoma de México.

Mendieta, Eduardo (1997). "Identity and Liberation," *Peace Review* 9, 4: 494–502.

"Mexico" (1993). *The New Encyclopaedia Britannica*, vol. 8, Encyclopaedia Britannica, pp. 79–81.

Michalski, K. (1969) *La philosophie au XIVe siècle: Six ètudes*, Minerva.

Mignolo, Walter (1993). "Colonial and Postcolonial Discourse: Cultural Critique or Academic Colonialism?" *Latin American Research Review* 28: 120–34.

—— (1995a). "Occidentalización, Imperialismo, Globalización: Herencias coloniales y teorías postcoloniales," *Revista Iberoamericana* 170–1: 27–40.

—— (1995b). "On Describing Ourselves Describing Ourselves: Comparatism, Differences, and Pluritopic Hermeneutics," in *The Darker Side of the Renaissance: Literacy, Territoriality and Colonization*, University of Michigan Press, pp. 1–25.

Mill, John Stuart (1872). *A System of Logic*, Longmans.

Miller, Robin, L. (1992). "The Human Ecology of Multiracial Identity," in Marla P. P. Root, ed., *Racially Mixed People in America*, SAGE, pp. 24–36.

Minh-Ha, Trinh T. (1991). *When the Moon Waxes Red*, Routledge.

"A Minority Worth Cultivating" (1998). *Economist* (April 25), p. 21.

Miró Quesada, Francisco (1976). *El problema de la filosofía latinoamericana*, Fondo de Cultura Económica.

—— (1986). "La filosofía de lo americano: treinta años después," in various authors, *Ideas en torno a Latinoamérica*, vol. 2, pp. 1,024–34.

Montalbán, Francisco J. et al. (1963). *Historia de la Iglesia Católica en sus cuatro edades: Antigua, media, nueva, moderna*, Biblioteca de Autores Cristianos.

Moore, Joan and Pachón, Harry (1976). *Mexican-Americans*, 2nd edn., Prentice-Hall.

—— (1985). *Hispanics in the United States*, Prentice-Hall.

Morales Padrón, F. (1955). *Fisonomía de la conquista indiana*, Escuela de Estudios Hispanoamericanos de Sevilla.

Morejón, Nancy (1982). *Nación y mestizaje en Nicolás Guillén*, Unión Nacional de Escritores y Artistas de Cuba.

Mörner, Magnus (1967). *Race Mixture in the History of Latin America*, Little, Brown.

Morse, Richard (1964). "The Heritage of Latin America," in L. Hartz, ed., *The Founding of New Societies*, Harcourt, Brace and World, pp. 123–77.

Murguia, Edward (1991). "On Latino/Hispanic Ethnic Identity," *Latino Studies Journal* 2: 8–18.

Nascimento, Amós (1997). "Identities in Conflict? Latin (African) American," *Peace Review* 9, 4: 489–95.

National Research Council (1987). *Summary Report: Doctorate Recipients from the United States Universities, Appendix C*, National Academy Press, pp. 66–71.

Nelson, C. and Tienda, Marta (1985). "The Structuring of Hispanic Identity: Historical and Contemporary Perspectives," *Ethnic and Racial Studies* 8, 1: 49–74.

Nicol, Eduardo (1961). *El problema de la filosofía hispánica*, Editorial Técnos.

—— (1988). "Meditación del propio ser: La hispanidad," in Jorge J. E. Gracia and Iván Jaksić, eds., *Filosofía e identidad cultural en América Latina*, Monte Avila, pp. 231–63.

Noreña, Carlos (1975). *Studies in Spanish Renaissance Thought*, M. Nijhoff.

Oboler, Suzanne (1995). *Ethnic Labels, Latino Lives: Identity and the Politics of (Re)Presentation in the United States*, University of Minnesota Press.

O'Gorman, Edmundo (1951). *La idea del descubrimiento de América*, Universidad Nacional Autónoma de México.

—— (1961). *The Invention of America: An Inquiry into the Historical Nature of the New World and the Meaning of Its History*, Indiana University Press, originally published 1958.

Olivas Weston, Rosario, ed. (1993). *Cultura, identidad y cocina en el Perú*, Universidad San Martín de Porres.

Onyewuenyi, Innocent (1991). "Is There an African Philosophy?" in Tsenay Serequeberhan, ed., *African Philosophy: The Essential Readings*, Paragon House, pp. 26–46.

Orrego, Antenor (1986). "La configuración histórica de la circunstancia americana," in various authors, *Ideas en torno de Latinoamérica*, vol. 2, Universidad Nacional Autónoma de México, pp. 1,380–1407.

Ortega y Gasset, José (1957). *Meditación de la técnica*, 3rd edn., Revista de Occidente.

—— (1964a). *El hombre y la gente*, in *Obras completas*, vol. 7, Revista de Occidente, pp. 69–271.

—— (1964b). *Obras completas*, 11 vols., Revista de Occidente.

Ortíz, Fernando (1911). *La reconquista de América*, Ollendorf.

—— (1940). "Los factores humanos de la cubanidad," *Revista Bimestre Cubana* 11, 2: 161–86.

—— (1952). "La transculturación blanca de los tambores negros," *Archivos Venezolanos de Folklore* 1, 2: 235–56.

—— (1983). *Contrapunto cubano del tabaco y el azúcar*, Ciencias Sociales; English trans by Harriet de Onis (1947). *Cuban Counterpoint: Tobacco and Sugar*, A. A. Knopf.

—— (1991). *Estudios etnosociológicos*, Ciencias Sociales.

Ottocar, Rosarios (1966). *América Latina: Veinte repúblicas, una nación*, Editores Emecé.

Outlaw, Lucius (1996). *On Race and Philosophy*, Routledge.

Padilla, Amado M., ed. (1995). *Hispanic Psychology: Critical Issues in Theory and Research*, SAGE.

Padilla, Félix (1985). *Latino Ethnic Consciousness: The Case of Mexican Americans and Puerto Ricans in Chicago*, University of Notre Dame Press.

Pappas, Gregory (1998). "The Latino Character of American Pragmatism," *Transactions of the Charles S. Peirce Society* 34, 1: 93–112.

París Pombo, M. D. (1990). *Crisis e identidades colectivas en América Latina*, Plaza y Valdés.

Parsons, Talcott (1975). "Some Theoretical Considerations on the Nature and Trends of Change of Ethnicity," in N. Glazer and D. P. Moynihan, eds., *Ethnicity: Theory and Experience*, Harvard University Press, pp. 53–83.

Paz, Octavio (1961). *El laberinto de la soledad*, Cuadernos Americanos; trans. Lysander Kemp (1961). *The Labyrinth of Solitude: Life and Thought in Mexico*, Grove Press.

Pereña, Luciano (1992). *The Rights and Obligations of Indians and Spaniards in the New World*, Universidad Pontificia de Salamanca and Catholic University of America Press.

Pérez Stable, E. J. (1987). "Issues in Latino Health Care," *Western Journal of Medicine* 146: 213–18.

"Philosophy in America in 1994" (1996). *Proceedings and Addresses of the American Philosophical Association* 70, 2: 131–53.

Pinta Llorente, M. de la (1953–8). *La Inquisición española y los problemas de la cultura y de la intolerancia*, Ediciones Cultura Hispánica.

Popkin, Richard (1964). *The History of Scepticism from Erasmus to Descartes*, Van Gorcum.

Proceedings and Addresses of the American Philosophical Association 61, 2 (1987); 65, 5 (1992); 66, 5 (1993); 70, 1 and 2 (1996).

Quesada, Vicente G. (1910). *La vida intelectual en la América española durante los siglos XVI, XVII y XVIII*, Arnoldo Moen y Hermano.

Quijano, Aníbal (1995). "Modernity, Identity, and Utopia in Latin America," in J. Beverly, M. Aronna, and J. Oviedo, eds., *The Postmodernist Debate in Latin America*, Duke University Press, pp. 201–16.

Quine, W. V. O (1953). *From a Logical Point of View*, Harvard University Press, pp. 1–19.

—— (1969). "Ontological Relativity," in *Relativity and Other Essays*, Columbia University Press, pp. 69–90.

—— (1970). "On the Reasons for the Indeterminacy of Translation," *Journal of Philosophy* 67, 178–83.

—— (1971). "On What There Is," in Charles Landesman, ed., *The Problem of Universals*, Basic Books, pp. 215–27.

—— (1973). *The Roots of Reference*, Open Court.

—— (1987). "Indeterminacy of Translation Again," *Journal of Philosophy* 84, 5–10.

Rama, Angel (1982). *Transculturación narrativa en América Latina*, Siglo XXI.

—— (1984). *La ciudad letrada*, 1st edn., Ediciones del Norte.

Ramos, Samuel (1943). *Historia de la filosofía mexicana*, Imprenta Universitaria.

—— (1949). "La cultura y el hombre en México," *Filosofía y Letras* 36: 175–85.

—— (1951). "En torno a las ideas sobre el mexicano," *Cuadernos Americanos* 10: 103–14.

—— (1962). *Hacia un nuevo humanismo: Programa de una antropología filosófica*, Fondo de Cultura Económica, originally published 1940.

—— (1963). *El perfil del hombre y la cultura en México*, Universidad Nacional Autónoma de México; trans. P. G. Earle, intro. by T. B. Irwing (1962). *Profile of Man and Culture in Mexico*, University of Texas Press.

Ramsden, H. (1974). *The 1898 Movement in Spain*, Manchester University Press.

Redmond, Walter and Beuchot, Mauricio (1985). *La lógica mexicana en el Siglo de Oro*, Universidad Nacional Autónoma de México.

—— (1987). *Pensamiento y realidad en Alonso de la Vera Cruz*, Universidad Nacional Autónoma de México.

Ribeiro, Darcy (1971). *The Americas and Civilization*, Dutton.

Rivano, Juan (1965). *El punto de vista de la miseria*, Universidad de Chile.

—— (1971). "Proposiciones sobre la totalización tecnológica," *En el Límite* 1: 46–64.

Bibliography

Rodó, José Enrique (1957a). *Ariel*, in *Obras completas*, Editorial Aguilar, pp. 226–37, trans. F. J. Stimson (1922). *Ariel*, Riverside Press.

——— (1957b). *Obras completas*, Editorial Aguilar.

Rodríguez, Richard (1981). *Hunger of Memory: The Education of Richard Rodriguez. An Autobiography*, D. R. Godine.

Roig, Arturo Andrés (1986). "The Actual Function of Philosophy in Latin America," in Jorge J. E. Gracia, ed., *Latin American Philosophy in the Twentieth Century*, Prometheus Books, pp. 247–59.

——— (1993). *Rostro y filosofía de América Latina*, EDIUNC.

Romanell, Patrick (1954). *La forma de la mentalidad mexicana: Panorama actual de la filosofía en México*, El Colegio de México.

Romero, Francisco (1964). *Theory of Man*, trans. William Cooper, University of California Press.

Root, Marla P. P., ed. (1992). *Racially Mixed People in America*, SAGE.

Rosenblat, Angel (1954). *La población indígena y el mestizaje en América*, 2 vols., Editorial Nova.

Ruch, E. A. (1981). "African Philosophy: The Origins of the Problem," in E. A. Ruch and K. C. Anyanwu, eds., *African Philosophy: An Introduction to the Main Philosophical Trends in Contemporary Africa*, Catholic Book Agency, pp. 180–98

Russell, Bertrand (1948). *Human Knowledge: Its Scope and Limits*, Simon and Schuster.

——— (1956). *Logic and Knowledge, Essays 1901–1950*, ed. R. C. Marsh, Allan and Unwin.

Salazar Bondy, Augusto (1968). *¿Existe una filosofía de nuestra América?* Siglo XXI.

——— (1969). *Sentido y problema del pensamiento hispano-americano*, with English trans. by Donald L. Schmidt, University of Kansas Center for Latin American Studies, pp. 28–34.

——— (1986). "The Meaning and Problem of Hispanic American Thought," in Jorge J. E. Gracia, ed., *Latin American Philosophy in the Twentieth Century*, Prometheus Books, pp. 233–44.

Salmerón, Fernando (1952). "Una imagen del mexicano," *Filosofía y Letras* 41–2; reprinted (1980) in *Cuestiones educativas y páginas sobre México*, Universidad Veracruzana, pp. 197–209.

——— (1958). "Los problemas de la cultura mexicana desde el punto de vista de la filosofía," *La Palabra y el Hombre* 6 ; reprinted (1980) in *Cuestiones educativas y páginas sobre México*, Universidad Veracruzana, pp. 135–7.

——— (1969). "Notas al margen del sentido y problema del pensamiento hispanoamericano," in Augusto Salazar Bondy, ed., *Sentido y problema del pensamiento filosófico hispanoamericano*, University of Kansas Center for Latin American Studies.

—— (1980). "Los filósofos mexicanos del siglo XX," in *Cuestiones educativas y páginas sobre México*, 2nd edn., Universidad Veracruzana, pp. 138–81.

Salmon, Nathan (1989). "Names and Descriptions," in D. Gabbay and F. Guenthner, eds., *Handbook of Philosophical Logic. Vol. IV: Topics in the Philosophy of Language*, Reidel, pp. 409–61.

Sambarino, Mario (1980). *Indentidad, tradición, autenticidad: Tres problemas de América Latina*, Centro de Estudios Latinoamericanos Rómulo Gallegos.

Sánchez-Albornoz, C. (1956). *España, un enigma histórico*, 2 vols., Editorial Sudamericana.

Sarmiento, Domingo Faustino (1998). *Facundo: Civilization and Barbarism*, Penguin Books.

Schmitt, Charles B. et al., eds. (1988). *The Cambridge History of Renaissance Philosophy*, Cambridge University Press.

Schutte, Ofelia (1987). "Toward an Understanding of Latin-American Philosophy: Reflections on the Foundations of Cultural Identity," *Philosophy Today* 31, 21–34.

—— (1993). *Cultural Identity and Social Liberation in Latin American Thought*, SUNY Press.

—— (forthcoming). "Negotiating Latina Identities," in Jorge J. E. Gracia and Pablo De Greiff, eds., *Ethnic Identity, Race, and Group Rights: Hispanics in the US*, Routledge.

Schwartzmann, Félix (1950, 1953). *El sentimiento de lo humano en América*, 2 vols., Univérsidad de Chile.

Scorraille, Raoul (1912). *François Suárez de la Compagnie de Jésus*, 2 vols., P. Lethielleux.

Searle, John R. (1984). *Intentionality: An Essay in the Philosophy of Mind*, Cambridge University Press.

Sedillo López, Antoinette (1995). *Historical Themes and Identity: Mestizaje and Labels.* "Latinos in the United States: History, Law and Perspective Series," vol 1, Garland Publishing.

Seed, Patricia (1993). "More Colonial and Postcolonial Discourses," *Latin American Research Review* 28: 146–52.

Shorris, Earl (1992). *Latinos: A Biography of the People*, W. W. Norton.

Sierra Bravo, R. (1975). *El pensamiento social y económico de la escolástica desde sus orígenes al comienzo del catolicismo social*, 2 vols., Consejo Superior de Investigaciones Científicas.

Solana, Marcial (1941). *Historia de la filosofía española: Epoca del Renacimiento (siglo XVI)*, 3 vols., Real Academia de Ciencias Exactas, Físicas y Naturales.

Stabb, Martin (1967). *In Quest of Identity: Patterns in the Spanish-American Essay of Ideas, 1890–1960*, University of North Carolina Press.

Bibliography

Stavans, Ilan (1995). *The Hispanic Condition: Reflections on Culture and Identity in America*, HarperCollins.

Stephan, Cookie White (1992). "Mixed-Heritage Individuals: Ethnic Identity and Trait Characteristics," in Marla P. P. Root, ed., *Racially Mixed People in America*, SAGE, pp. 50–63.

Szalay, Lorand B. and Díaz-Guerrero, Rogelio (1985). "Similarities and Differences between Subjective Cultures: A Comparison of Latin, Hispanic, and Anglo Americans," in Rogelio Díaz-Guerrero, ed., *Cross-cultural and National Studies in Social Psychology*, North-Holland, pp. 105–32.

Taylor, Charles (1984). "Philosophy and Its History," in Richard Rorty et al., eds., *Philosophy in History: Essays in the Historiography of Philosophy*, Cambridge University Press, pp. 17–30.

Taylor, Dicey et al. (1998). "Epilogue: The Beaded Zemí in the Pigorini Museum," in Fatima Bercht et al., *Taíno: Pre-Columbian Art and Culture in the Caribbean*, El Museo del Barrio, pp. 158–69.

Thernstrom, Stephan (1982). "Ethnic Groups in American History," in *Ethnic Relations in America*, Prentice-Hall, pp. 3–27.

Tienda, M. and Ortíz, V. (1986). "'Hispanicity' and the 1980 Census," *Social Sciences Quarterly* 67, 3–20.

Todorov, Tzvelan (1984). *The Conquest of America: The Quest of the Other*, trans. Richard Howard, Harper and Row.

Trentman, John (1982). "Scholasticism in the Seventeenth Century," in Norman Kretzman et al., eds., *The Cambridge History of Later Medieval Philosophy*, Cambridge University Press, pp. 835–7.

Treviño, Fernando (1987). "Standardized Terminology for Hispanic Populations," *American Journal of Public Health* 77: 69–72.

Triandis, H. C. et al. (1984). "Simpatía as a Cultural Script of Hispanics," *Journal of Personality and Social Psychology* 47: 1,363–75.

Unamuno, Miguel de (1968). "Hispanidad," in *Obras completas*, vol. 4, Excelsior, pp. 1,081–4.

USA Today, August 8, 1997.

US Bureau of the Census (1988). *Development of the Race and Ethnic Items for the 1990 Census*, Population Association of America.

—— (1996). *Statistical Abstracts of the United Sattes, 1996*, 116th edn., US Government Printing Office.

Vasconcelos, José (1937). *Historia del pensamiento filosófico*, Imprenta Universitaria.

—— (1957a). *Obras completas*, 4 vols., Libreros Mexicanos.

—— (1957b). *La raza cósmica*, in *Obras completas*, vol. 2, Libreros Mexicanos, pp. 903–42.

(n.d.). *Indología: una interpretación de la cultura iberoamericana*, Agencia Mundial de Librería.

Bibliography

Vega, Bernardo (1984). *Memoirs of Bernardo Vega: A Contribution to the History of the Puerto Rican Community in New York*, ed. César Andreu Iglesias, trans. Juan Flores, Monthly Review Press.

Vega, Inca Garcilaso de la (1959). *Comentarios Reales de los Incas*, EMECE.

Vidal, Hernán (1993). "The Concept of Colonial and Postcolonial Discourse: A Perspective from Literary Criticism," *Latin American Research Review* 28: 113–19.

Villegas, Abelardo (1960). *La filosofía de lo mexicano*, Fondo de Cultura Económica.

—— (1963). *Panorama de la filosofía iberoamericana actual*, Editorial Universitaria de Buenos Aires.

Villoro, Luis (1950). *Los grandes momentos del indigenismo en México*, El Colegio de México.

Vincent, Joan (1974). "The Structuring of Ethnicity," *Human Organization* 33, 4: 375–9.

Vitoria, Francisco de (1917). *De indis et De iure belli relectiones*, ed. Ernest Nip, Carnegie Institution of Washington.

Vobejda, Barbara (1998). "Hispanic Children Are Leading Edge of the US Demographic Wave," *Washington Post*, reprinted in *Buffalo News*, July 15, A-6.

Webster's Third New International Dictionary (1966). Encyclopaedia Britannica.

—— (1961). G. & C. Merriman.

Weyr, Thomas (1988). *Hispanic USA: Breaking the Melting Pot*, Harper and Row.

Windelband, Wilhelm (1958). *A History of Philosophy*, 2 vols., Harper and Brothers.

Wiredu, Kwasi (1991). "On Defining African Philosophy," in Tsenay Serequebarhan, ed., *African Philosophy: The Essential Readings*, Paragon House, pp. 87–110.

Wittgenstein, Ludwig (1961). *Tractatus Logico-Philosophicus*, trans. D. F. Pears and B. F. McGuiness, Routledge and Kegan Paul.

—— (1965). *Philosophical Investigations*, trans. G. E. M. Anscombe, Macmillan.

Zack, Naomi (1993). *Race and Mixed Race*, Temple University Press.

—— ed. (1995). *America Mixed Race: The Culture of Microdiversity*, Rowman & Littlefield.

—— ed. (1996). *Race/Sex*, Routledge.

Zea, Leopoldo (1948). *Ensayos sobre filosofía en la historia*, Stylo.

—— (1963). *The Latin American Mind*, trans. James H. Abbott and Lowel Dunham, University of Oklahoma Press.

—— (1968a). *El positivismo en México: Nacimiento, apogeo, y decadencia*, Fondo de Cultura Económica.

—— ed. (1968b). *Antología de la filosofía americana contemporánea*, B. Costa Amic.

—— (1978). *Filosofía de la historia americana,* Fondo de Cultura Económica.

—— (1983). *América como conciencia,* 2nd edn., Universidad Nacional Autónoma de México.

—— (1996). *La filosofía americana como filosofía sin más,* 16th edn., Siglo XXI.

Index of Names

Index of Names

Index of Names

Index of Subjects

affirmative action, x–xii
Africans, 105–7; and diversity, 105–7;
and homogeneity, 105; unity of, 106
America, concept of, 104; discovery of,
89, 101; encounter(s) with, 78, 89;
invention of, 102–4; the name, xvi;
pre-encounter, 97–100; *see also*
encounter(s)
American Philosophical Association,
168, 175; Eastern Division of, 168–9
American philosophy, 167–80; and
accents, 184–5; and the curriculum,
161–2; and dynasties, 179; and
editorial policy and practice, 173–4;
and Hispanic philosophy, 185–6; and
Hispanics, 159–67, 180–8; and
philosophical families, 172–3, 181,
182; and system of refereeing,
172–3; and typecasting, 178
analytic philosophers, 169–80

caballero, 95–6
Common Bundle View of Hispanic
identity, 58–9
concept(s), 39; of Hispanics, 51–2; and
names, 39
continental philosophers, 169–80
criollo(s), 18, 64, 118
culturalist view, of Latin American
philosophy, 132–5, 136–9, 147, 150,
151

curriculum, in American philosophy,
161–2; and Hispanic philosophy,
161–2

demographics, of Hispanics/Latinos,
vii–ix
descriptions, 34; definite, 34; and
names, 37–9
difference, vs identity and similarity,
30
diversity, in African slaves, 105–7; in
Hispanic Americans, 123–9; in pre-
encounter America, 97–100; in pre-
encounter Iberia, 90–6

encomienda, 113
encounter(s), 100–5; with America,
78, 89; and Hispanic philosophy, 79
ethnic essences, 7, 36, *see also* ethnicity
ethnic groups, and conflicts, 127–8
ethnic identity, and ethnic nationalism,
126; and Hispanic Americans, 126
ethnic names, 25, 39–42, 44; vs
identity, 44–7; use of and value,
45–7
ethnicity, 39–42; conditions of, 40–2;
global, 42; and names, 39–42;
national, 42; regional, 42; and self-
naming, 24